Weapon

Weapon of the Strong

Conversations on US State Terrorism

Interviews by
Cihan Aksan and Jon Bailes

PlutoPress
www.plutobooks.com

First published 2013 by Pluto Press
345 Archway Road, London N6 5AA

www.plutobooks.com

Distributed in the United States of America exclusively by
Palgrave Macmillan, a division of St. Martin's Press LLC,
175 Fifth Avenue, New York, NY 10010

British Library Cataloguing in Publication Data
A catalogue record for this book is available from the British Library

ISBN   978 0 7453 3242 0   Hardback
ISBN   978 0 7453 3241 3   Paperback
ISBN   978 1 8496 4794 6   PDF eBook
ISBN   978 1 8496 4796 0   Kindle eBook
ISBN   978 1 8496 4795 3   EPUB eBook

Library of Congress Cataloging in Publication Data applied for

This book is printed on paper suitable for recycling and made from fully managed
and sustained forest sources. Logging, pulping, and manufacturing processes are
expected to conform to the environmental standards of the country of origin.

10   9   8   7   6   5   4   3   2   1

Designed and produced for Pluto Press by Chase Publishing Services Ltd
Typeset from disk by Stanford DTP Services, Northampton, England
Simultaneously printed digitally by CPI Antony Rowe, Chippenham, UK and
Edwards Bros in the United States of America

For Yüksel Hasan

Contents

Acknowledgements

First and foremost, we are indebted to all our interviewees. We thank them for giving their time, effort, and enthusiasm to this book. Indeed, there would be no book without them. Special thanks to Gilbert Achcar, who met with us in London when the book was simply an idea, and gave us valuable advice and encouragement to pursue it.

Thanks also to our editors at Pluto Press. Roger van Zwanenberg was instrumental in the early stages of the book and David Shulman was always helpful and patient throughout the whole process. We are also grateful to Anthony Winder for his careful copy-editing.

Since we started our online journal, *State of Nature*, in 2005, we have had the privilege of working with many academics, journalists, and activists from all over the world. They have enriched our ideas immeasurably and made us part of a wider community. We thank them all.

We have also benefited greatly from our interaction with many great minds at our respective universities, including Professors Stephen Houlgate and Richard J. Aldrich at the University of Warwick, and Dr Kevin Inston at University College London.

1

Introduction

The idea that terrorism is a 'weapon of the weak' has become a truism. We are constantly told that it is sub-state *desperadoes* with limited power and resources who resort to such indiscriminate and horrific violence, whilst states are left to defend the innocent. So if you happen to have political legitimacy, command a large and well-equipped military, and influence international affairs, you cannot be called a terrorist. However, to immediately associate a word such as 'terrorism' with one particular aspect of its possible meaning is to accept an ideology imbedded with certain political interests. Furthermore, the more dominant that meaning becomes, the more we lose any notion that there is an alternative; the whole concept becomes 'one-dimensional' and 'has no other content than that designated by the word in the publicized and standardized usage'.[1] Thus, the question, 'Who is a terrorist?' already implies an answer, specifically one that excludes consideration of the 'strong'.

Undoubtedly, terrorism *can* be a tactic of the 'weak'. But this is not its predominant form, let alone its very definition. For instance, the US State Department estimates that the number of deaths caused by 'transnational terrorism' globally between 1975 and 2003 was 13,971. Meanwhile, the US National Consortium for the Study of Terrorism and Responses to Terrorism (START) claims in its Global Terrorism Database that there were 3,292 fatalities from both domestic and international terrorist incidents in the United States from 1970 to 2007. Most of these, we hardly need reminding, were the result of the attacks of 11 September 2001.[2] On the other hand, to take one extreme (but far from unique) example, from 1975 to 1999 Indonesia's US-backed repression in East Timor killed an estimated 200,000 people, one quarter of the population.[3] In sum, that the 'strong' can terrorise populations on a far greater scale than 'weaker' sub-state terrorist groups is hardly debatable. And yet we would never guess this from the way terrorism is discussed in the public sphere.

In this book we attempt to address the imbalance between representations of different forms of terrorism. In academic terms, this means that we take a firm stand against mainstream terrorism studies, which focus almost exclusively on the targeting of liberal democratic states by sub-state groups or 'rogue states'. With a more critical approach to terrorism studies, we aim to challenge prevailing ideas by demonstrating that it is in fact the United States,[4] the self-proclaimed 'leader of the free world', which is the most consistent perpetrator and supporter of terrorism in post-Second World War history. Obviously, such an assertion raises many questions: What do we mean by terrorism, and what counts as a terrorist act? How responsible has the United States been for various terrorist acts? What are the legal and moral implications? Does the United States have good reason to carry out or support terrorism? And how do the American people understand these actions? We answer such questions through a series of interviews with leading scholars from a range of fields, including politics, law, philosophy, economics, and social theory.

*   *   *

There is nothing immediately counterintuitive in the idea that a state agent can commit terrorism. Yet, in the dominant discourse, such thinking tends to be bracketed out from the start. Take, for instance, the *US Code*, which defines terrorism as 'premeditated politically motivated violence perpetrated against non-combatant targets by subnational groups or clandestine agents'.[5] This definition is used by the State Department and the CIA, and is the definition upon which they rely in their official pronouncements on terrorism.[6] Crucially, the *US Code* restricts terrorism to 'sub-national groups' and 'clandestine agents', which appears to exclude state terrorism. True, 'clandestine agents' could carry out terrorist acts on behalf of states, but this still rules out many cases in which states commit such acts overtly or at least in tandem with clandestine activity. Under the *US Code*, states and their authorised agents that commit crimes analogous to those of sub-state terrorist groups are not classified as terrorists.[7]

Meanwhile, the FBI uses the definition in the *Code of Federal Regulations* which claims that terrorism is 'the unlawful use of force and violence against persons or property to intimidate or coerce a government, the civilian population, or any segment thereof, in furtherance of political or social objectives'.[8] This definition does not appear to have any clause explicitly excluding state terrorism, but the use of the word 'unlawful' carries certain implications. This is because (a) it suggests that state agents do not commit state terrorism in the lawful exercise of their official duties;[9] and (b) if state authorities introduce 'temporary' or 'emergency' legislation for 'security' reasons, or even build the whole apparatus of terrorising into the legal system, then their actions receive the backing of the law.[10] The *US Army Field Manuals* follow similar lines, stating that 'terrorism is the calculated use of unlawful violence or threat of unlawful violence to inculcate fear ... intended to coerce or intimidate governments or societies'. They also claim that it is 'enemies who cannot compete with Army forces conventionally [who] often turn to terrorist tactics'.[11] The possibility that a non-enemy or state force could commit terrorism is never considered.

One question that might be asked is why should we focus on terrorism in the first place? Why not, say, genocide or war crimes? An obvious reason is that the word 'terrorism' has exceptional rhetorical significance, particularly in the United States. Ever since President Reagan declared war on international terrorism in the early 1980s, it has become central to the self-image of the American nation, allowing it to define itself against its enemies. The reinforcement of the message that it is always *they*, the enemy, that are the terrorists has resulted in a highly warped dominant idea of terrorism, and while terms such as 'genocide' and 'war crimes' are undoubtedly also appropriated in this way, they are nowhere near as ubiquitous or versatile. Clearly, when terrorism can be mentioned alongside acts of protest and civil disobedience such as the Occupy movement, for some people it has become synonymous with any resistance to the status quo.

The much lauded terrorism 'expert', Walter Laqueur, claims that 'people reasonably familiar with the terrorist phenomenon will agree 90 per cent of the time about what terrorism is, just as they will agree upon democracy and nationalism or other concepts. In fact, terrorism is an unmistakable phenomenon'.[12] But this 'we-know-it-when-we-see-it' attitude only reinforces the double standards. It is precisely when theory is kept to a minimum (which Laqueur also advocates) that terrorism becomes what *they* do to *us*, and never what *we* do to *them*. The less we contest terms, the more people are likely to assimilate a dominant usage, and the connotations of the term 'terrorism' in particular mean it should be proactively reclaimed for more considered discussion.

Terrorism is also especially significant because it is an act defined by its political purpose. In other words, it is not only killing and maiming that constitutes terrorism, but the fact that such actions are irrevocably linked to a wider strategy. This book sets out to demonstrate a general trend in US foreign policy, arguing that terrorism describes the common thread running through a wide range of coercive and destructive measures employed under varying circumstances. Of course, such an argument requires a certain clarity about the meaning of terrorism as we understand it. We do not feel it necessary to be overly precise, but, in brief, we consider the following parameters to be central to the concept: (a) the intentional use of violence or credible threat of violence; (b) directed at civilians; (c) with the purpose of inducing widespread fear among an audience beyond the immediate victim(s); (d) to achieve political ends. With these parameters, we can at least establish which state actions can be viewed as terrorism.

Let us begin with war. Although war is not terrorism per se (since it does not *necessarily* involve targeting civilians in order to induce widespread fear), terrorism can be used in war, and can even be an overt military objective. Take the doctrine of 'shock and awe' through 'rapid dominance', which was famously used by the US military in Iraq in 2003. The authors of the doctrine explain that 'the goal of Rapid Dominance [is] to destroy or so confound the will to resist that an adversary will have no alternative except to accept our strategic aims and military objectives'.[13] This means that 'psychological and intangible, as well as physical and concrete, effects beyond the destruction of enemy forces and supporting military infrastructure will have to be achieved'.[14] So the 'adversary' is not only the military or political leadership of the target nation, but also the civilian population, which is forced through a terrifying show of mass destruction to accept political change. Moreover, the 'threats' considered significant enough to call for 'rapid dominance' are not only military aggression and WMDs, but 'actions that ... endanger ... access to free markets',[15] which effectively makes every single nation that undertakes economic restructuring counter to US interests an 'adversary'.

One mitigating factor for 'rapid dominance' could be its insistence that civilian casualties are not desirable, but this claim relies on some spurious twists of logic. The document frequently alludes to the importance of minimising 'collateral damage' (albeit if only 'to avoid the political pitfalls') and the need for 'increased targeting precision' in attacks. And yet while this 'collateral damage' is described as 'unintended', it is simultaneously deemed 'inevitable',[16] creating an obvious paradox which culminates in the audacious claim that it is

> a responsible state's worst nightmare to have successfully struck a chemical, biological, or nuclear production facility with precision only to learn the next day that hundreds of civilians have been killed due to the inadvertent release of chemical, biological, or nuclear materials.[17]

The truth is that however precise the attack, if the target struck is known to contain civilians or likely to result in mass civilian casualties, then terror is intended. As critical terrorism theorist Ruth Blakeley argues, 'where [intimidation] was not the primary intention, but a welcome secondary effect of some other malign act, this still constitutes state terrorism'.[18] Ultimately, 'rapid dominance' was designed to attack civilians and civilian infrastructure. How else is one to interpret the assertion that it 'seeks to impose (in extreme cases) ... the non-nuclear equivalent of the impact that the atomic weapons dropped on Hiroshima and Nagasaki had on the Japanese'?[19]

Also, merely stating a desire to minimise civilian casualties does not mean it is carried through in practice. Even the most conservative estimates of civilian casualties during the invasion of Iraq run into the thousands. Afterwards, the death toll continued to rise in the occupation, with the sieges and assaults on Fallujah in particular demonstrating how cheap civilian lives can be. Journalist and eyewitness Dahr Jamail has described some of the tactics employed by US forces there, such as the 'use of illegal weapons (white phosphorous, cluster bombs, depleted uranium munitions), deliberate targeting of medical personnel, ambulances, hospitals and clinics, [and] deliberate targeting of civilians', leading to the deaths of between 4,000 and 6,000 civilians and the destruction of approximately 70 per cent of all buildings.[20] More recently, in response to negative publicity (those 'political pitfalls', when US aircraft bomb, say, a wedding party in Afghanistan), the United States has vowed to take more care with its 'targeted killings'. In June 2011, President Obama's top counterterrorism adviser, John Brennan, said that in over a year of drone strikes in Pakistan, 'there hasn't been a single collateral death because of the exceptional proficiency, precision of the capabilities we've been able to develop'.[21] This claim is contradicted by a report from the Bureau of Investigative Journalism which estimates that in 260 drone attacks in the first three years of Obama's presidency, 'between 282 and 535 civilians [were] credibly reported as killed, including more than 60 children'.[22] In one particular incident, US forces killed a Taliban member with a drone attack in a bid to draw out a higher-ranking commander at the funeral, and then bombed the funeral, attended by 5,000 mourners, killing 45 civilians and missing the intended target.

Civilians also pay a high price when the United States turns to terrorism outside of war. Take coercive diplomacy, an age-old instrument of statecraft. Its aim is to make non-compliance with a political demand so costly that the target nation is forced to reconsider its original position. The threat may be non-verbal or merely implied, but coercive diplomacy is nevertheless overt behaviour, with all parties fully aware of the stakes.[23] Examples include the threat of use and/or the actual use of limited military force, trade threats and retaliation, suspension of bilateral aid and credits, and blocking of credits from International Financial Institutions (IFIs) or private banks, although positive inducements and assurances can also be used alongside punitive threats to influence the target nation. It might be said that coercive diplomacy is an effective strategy in international relations since it has the potential to achieve political ends with little or no bloodshed. This underestimates the impact such pressures can have on a population, as in the case of nearly one million deaths due to US-led UN economic sanctions in Iraq. A declassified US Defense Intelligence Agency document shows that the United States was fully aware of the necessity of particular chemicals for water treatment, and the human cost sanctioning these chemicals would entail back in 1991.[24] It nevertheless went ahead with sanctioning them (having already intentionally destroyed Iraq's water treatment facilities in the Gulf War), thus exposing hundreds of thousands of children to potentially deadly diarrhoeal diseases. Is deliberately enacting a policy that deprives civilians of basic needs and causes mass disease and death not a form of violence? Is it any less indiscriminate, destructive or terrifying than, say, a biological weapon attack? While campaigning for the US presidency in 2008, Hillary Clinton said: 'I believe in coercive diplomacy. I think that you try to figure out how to move bad actors in a direction that you prefer in order to avoid more dire consequences'.[25] Clearly, a million deaths are not 'dire' enough.

Terrorism can also be intertwined with covert action. Turned into an art form by the CIA, covert action was discredited in the mid 1970s when highly embarrassing details were exposed by Congressional inquiries into CIA activities abroad. As a result, President Ford banned assassinations,[26] the CIA sacrificed a few veteran agents, and Congress imposed strict limits on covert activities. Covert action made a comeback in the 1980s (with great success in Soviet-occupied Afghanistan), lay low again in the 1990s (after the controversy of the 1987 Iran–Contra affair), and was unleashed with a vengeance after 9/11.[27] It is firmly outside the operations of traditional intelligence collection, and can include propaganda and disinformation campaigns, funding of opposition parties or media, sabotage, assassination, support for subversion, extraordinary rendition, and participation in coups d'état. 'Plausible deniability' (where the sponsor is able to deny his or her involvement in the action undertaken) is crucial to covert action, although (as in, say, the case of President Kennedy and the Bay of Pigs invasion in 1961) it is not always possible to maintain secrecy. Two of the many covert operations undertaken by the United States were in Guatemala (1954) and Chile (1973), both of which subverted democratic processes and brought to power right-wing dictatorships. Aside from the unsuccessful Bay of Pigs invasion, CIA agents also made numerous assassination attempts against Fidel Castro (including the infamous exploding cigar) and collaborated with exiled Cuban terrorists (including Orlando Bosch, who was implicated in the bombing of the Cubana airliner in 1976) to carry out terrorist acts on Cuban soil.

The United States has also used terrorism to advance its foreign objectives through sponsorship of other terrorist states. Throughout the Cold War, right-wing dictatorships were taken by the United States to be bulwarks against political instability and revolution, and thus received substantial assistance in spite of their undemocratic practices and shocking human rights records. The Nixon administration relied particularly heavily on dictators when it became clear that public disillusionment with Vietnam made further military interventions problematic. In what later became known as the 'Nixon Doctrine', the United States would provide economic and military assistance, but local governments had to take primary responsibility for their own defence without relying on American troops. Nixon's visit to Jakarta in 1969, where he praised General Suharto for the political and economic 'stability' he had brought to Indonesia, well illustrates US foreign policy at the time. It was a side issue that this 'stability' had come at the expense of more than 500,000 lives (as well as another 750,000 arrests) in less than a year.[28] In 1968, a CIA report had claimed that the 'massacres in Indonesia rank as one of the worst mass murders of the twentieth century, along with the Soviet purges of the 1930s, the Nazi mass murders during the Second World War, and the Maoist bloodbath of the early 1950s',[29] but Nixon had not come all the way to Jakarta to discuss mass murder. Indeed, the United States had welcomed the 'clean-up' of the Indonesian Communist Party (to use the words of the undersecretary of state, George Ball),[30] contributing to the bloodshed by providing intelligence information on communists and supplying Suharto's troops with weapons and state-of-the-art communications equipment to help coordinate the killings.[31] Once Suharto had totally crushed all opposition, the United States (and its close allies such as the United Kingdom, as well as IFIs) opened the purse strings to ensure that the 'New Order' would survive.[32] Following Nixon's visit to Jakarta, the decision was made to increase military assistance to Indonesia from $5.8 million to $25 million, in accordance with the 'Nixon Doctrine'.[33] This helped Indonesia purchase new combat weapons and aircraft, which must have come in handy when Suharto launched the near-genocidal invasion of East Timor in December 1975.

Overall, between 1950 and 1979, US military aid programmes transferred $107.3 billion in equipment and services to friendly powers, in addition to $121 billion in arms sales.[34] Did these arms transfers promote state terrorist activities in those countries? Can it be said that without these arms transfers state terrorism would not have occurred or would have occurred at a much lower level?[35] It can certainly be argued that state terrorism rarely requires sophisticated weaponry. If a government wants to use repressive measures against its people, it can easily do so with a reasonably sized army and police force with access to small arms, armoured vehicles and counter-insurgency equipment. Also, as far as military sales are concerned, there are always alternative sources of supply for those governments intent on arming themselves.[36] However, it is not a recognised defence to say, 'If I didn't do it, someone else would', and there are clear cases where imported arms have allowed a repressive government to remain in power when it would otherwise have been overthrown by an internal rebellion. In El Salvador, for instance, US military aid helped the armed forces and allied right-wing death squads defeat the Farabundo Marti National Liberation Front (FMLN). True, the FMLN received support from Nicaragua and Cuba, but the massive US aid that poured into this tiny country (about

$6 billion, or an average of $100,000 for each member of the Salvadoran armed forces)[37] meant that the guerrillas could never win. An estimated 75,000 people were killed between 1980 and 1991, with the Salvadoran army and the death squads reported to be responsible for 95 per cent of these deaths.[38] This could have been prevented had the United States not supplied the Salvadoran regime with the weapons to crush its adversaries.

More importantly, arms transfers are usually accompanied by economic assistance and training, which more explicitly connects the assisting state to the political crimes of the assisted state. For example, when the socialist Salvadore Allende was elected president in Chile in 1970, Nixon famously ordered the CIA director, Richard Helms, to 'make the economy scream'.[39] Consequently, Washington reduced bilateral aid (from $35.4 million in 1969 to $1.5 million in 1971), cut credits (US Export-Import Bank credits went from $28.7 million to zero in the same years), and pushed IFIs to cut Chile off.[40] At the same time, US military aid was significantly increased (from $0.8 million in 1970 to $15 million in 1973) to retain close contact with the Chilean military.[41] The military training programme was also expanded: the number of Chilean officers trained at the notorious School of the Americas (SOA) in Panama rose from 181 to 257 during the Allende years.[42] After the military coup, led by the staunch anti-communist General Augusto Pinochet in 1973, US economic assistance resumed ($5.3 million in economic aid and $98.1 million in Export–Import Bank credit were given in 1974, in addition to $15.9 million in military aid). Chile was also able to secure previously denied loans from the World Bank and Inter-American Development Bank (totalling $111.2 million again in 1974).[43] So it has to be asked whether the Pinochet dictatorship could have taken power and lasted long enough to cause the deaths of thousands of men, women and children without such backing.

*   *   *

Why should we single out US state terrorism in particular? Is it not the case that practically every state has been guilty of some form of state terrorism in the past? Indeed, in all of the cases where the United States has supported state terrorism, the *primary* responsibility must fall on the state committing the terrorism. Complicity is criminal, but there is no doubt that Suharto or Pinochet should have been held accountable for the unimaginable terror they unleashed on their own people. However, this book focuses on the United States in recognition of the impact it has made on the international community over a sustained period of time. We all know that the United States is the only current power with a global reach, politically, economically, militarily and culturally. It is an undisputed leader in international affairs, with huge influence in NATO, and in the United Nations through its permanent membership in the Security Council. It has hundreds of military bases all around the world, with a military budget that is some 43 per cent of the world's total, five times larger than its nearest rival, China.[44] It also has control over the policies of major IFIs, such as the World Bank and the IMF, and many of the largest and most influential multinational corporations and private financial institutions are based in its territory, funding and lobbying political decision makers. Of course, all this does not make the United States some shadowy, omnipotent force whose hand guides all major international decisions. It is quite clear, for instance, that it has run into serious difficulties in its attempts to control Afghanistan and Iraq, and it also did not call the shots in the early days of the 'Arab Spring' – not to mention that its extremely high levels of military expenditure weigh heavily on the state budget, and have compounded the current economic crisis. There is nothing timeless or inevitable about current power relations.

Even so, US hegemony means that criticising its foreign policy is a matter of restoring balance. In many countries, US political and popular culture feature heavily in broadcast media, so American elites (or their products) have a voice around the globe. We have all grown to understand the potential import of US political reactions, so when, say, revolution erupts in Tunisia or Egypt, everyone has one eye on America's response. Meanwhile, a deluge of entertainment media, mostly propagating a specific glamorised aspect of American culture, finds its way through sheer financial weight into the homes of billions of people. Consequently, to measure the kind of media presence the United States has in other countries against that of, say, China, is to identify a colossal difference. In the British 'quality' media in early 2012, minor developments in the US Republican Primaries made the news daily, while coverage of China's approach to its crucial Communist Party congress was almost non-existent.[45] Indeed, it is rare in the West to hear about Chinese politicians at all, and most reporting on China is reduced to its human rights abuses. This is not to say that China does not deserve criticism. The problem is that this criticism becomes skewed because either we do not hear about similar US abuses, or we experience them alongside a continually reiterated US rhetoric of democracy, freedom, justice, and counter-terrorism. To focus on *US* state terrorism therefore has the distinction of challenging common perception.

Most importantly, however, we want to emphasise the consistency of purpose behind US foreign policy. This book concentrates on US actions since the Second World War, an important moment of American ascendency. Our argument is that the motivation behind these actions has predominantly been to spread an economic model conducive to American business interests. In other words, what the United States calls 'free markets' (which is effectively 'freedom' for the wealthy nations to exploit the natural resources and restructure the economies of poor nations according to strict Western dictates) has always formed the core of its foreign policy objectives. There is even continuity in the face of apparent change: the end of the Cold War mainly presented a problem of propaganda, demanding new narratives and enemies to act as alibi for US interventions abroad. State terrorism is not the preserve of particular presidents, or particular political parties, operating under extraordinary circumstances. Indeed, the personality traits and intentions of individuals can quickly be sidelined as the realities of US power structures become apparent.

The best way to illustrate this point is by considering the US administrations with the least aggressive reputations, most notably those of Carter and Clinton. It is often convenient to blame US state terrorism on 'madmen' such as Nixon (who, incidentally, used the 'madman theory' to make the North Vietnamese think that he was capable of anything),[46] Reagan (who, some critics claim, was already in the grips of Alzheimer's disease during his presidency), and more recently George W. Bush. There appears to be an understanding that Republicans are more inclined to dismiss human rights considerations and place what they call 'national security interests' above all else. This might be a valid point, but it refuses to take into account how even well-meaning Democrats operate within hegemonic structures. Carter, for instance, refused to undertake military interventions, but still continued to interfere in the internal affairs of other states by supporting repressive regimes. However much we may want to call Carter's foreign policy 'benevolent hegemony' or 'empire lite', it must be recognised that the United States was still an accessory to state terrorism at the time.

When Carter became president in 1977, he promised to advance the principles of human rights and non-intervention, and thus distance the United States from right-wing dictatorships. In his inaugural address to the nation, he declared that 'our moral sense dictates a clear-cut preference for those societies which share with us an abiding respect for individual human rights'.[47] Two years later, on the 30th anniversary of the signing of the Universal Declaration of Human Rights, he reiterated that

> our deepest affinities are with nations which commit themselves to a democratic path to development. Toward regimes which persist in wholesale violations of human rights we will not hesitate to convey our outrage nor will we pretend that our relations are unaffected.

Clearly aiming at his many critics, Carter also highlighted the achievements of his human rights policy:

> In some countries, political prisoners have been released by the hundreds, even thousands. In others, the brutality of repression has been lessened. In still others, there's a movement toward democratic institutions or the rule of law when these movements were not previously detectable.[48]

How serious was Carter about human rights? How did he act when human rights principles clashed with national interest? Take Iran, for example. In the late 1970s, when the Shah of Iran's repressive rule was finally met with an outburst of popular anger, Carter found himself in a difficult position. Ever since the CIA had deposed the democratically elected prime minister, Mohammad Mossadegh, in 1953, Iran had been supported by the United States. Back on his Peacock Throne, the Shah had received more than $1 billion in US aid in the decade following the coup,[49] even though the torture chambers of his notorious security services, SAVAK, were among the Middle East's most terrible institutions. When Carter visited Tehran in December 1977, he praised the Shah for turning Iran into 'an island of stability in one of the more troubled areas of the world'.[50] Countless reports had by that point emerged on a SAVAK torture method called 'cooking' where the victim would be strapped to a bed of wire that would then be electrified to become a red-hot toaster.[51] But Carter made no mention of this. Instead, the Shah was told that 'the cause of human rights is one that is also shared deeply by our people and by the leaders of our two nations'.[52] When the Shah's soldiers responded to the ever increasing unrest by murdering thousands of people in a demonstration in Tehran in 1978, Carter still refused to withdraw support from Iran's ruler. As it became clear that the Shah could no longer cling on to power, Carter was urged by his National Security Advisor, Zbigniew Brzezinski, to take military action to prevent the Shah's downfall. But he refused. Just a day after the Shah left Iran, Carter told a news conference that 'we have no desire nor ability to intrude massive forces into Iran or any other country to determine the outcome of domestic political issues'. Remember: 'We've tried this once in Vietnam. It didn't work well, as you well know'.[53]

Carter's human rights policy never really rose above rhetoric. In both Iran and Nicaragua (where Anastasio Somoza's repressive regime was challenged by the National Sandinista Liberation Front), he resisted calls to cut aid and arms deliveries to dictators accused of human rights abuses, only withdrawing support when their rule became untenable. Declassified documents show that Carter also continued to back the Suharto regime, providing military assistance to the Indonesian armed forces at a time when near genocidal violence was taking place in East Timor.[54] Further, he increased aid and arms transfers to many other repressive governments (South Korea, the Philippines, El Salvador and Morocco are just a few examples), particularly towards the end of his presidency.[55] In an interview with the *Observer* in 2011, Carter was asked what he was most proud of when he made a reassessment of his presidency. He replied: 'We kept our country at peace. We never went to war. We never dropped a bomb. We never fired a bullet. But we still achieved our international goals'.[56] True, Carter refused to undertake military interventions, even when he came under fire for not preventing the downfall of Somoza and the Shah of Iran. But it is unlikely that many administrations would have taken the military road when Americans were still in the grips of the so-called 'Vietnam Syndrome'. According to Stephen Cohen, deputy assistant secretary for human rights and security assistance during the Carter administration, Carter 'exhibited a remarkable degree of tentativeness and caution, so that the pursuit of human rights goals was anything but single-minded'. The result was that in many cases 'other US interests were found to outweigh human rights concerns under the exception for "extraordinary circumstances"' and money continued to flow to repressive regimes.[57]

It could still be said, of course, that the Cold War was a time that necessitated extreme foreign policy. It is important to examine the validity of this justification. The orthodox version of the Cold War paints a picture of a bipolar world in which one of the poles (the Soviet Union) is an inherently hostile and expansionist power while the other (the United States) is a benign and democratic power that has no choice but to respond to this grave threat to its national security and hold back the former by any means necessary. This formed the basis of the US policy of 'containment', often credited to George Kennan, who argued that the Soviet Union aimed to fill 'every nook and cranny available to it in the basin of world power' and called for 'a long-term, patient but firm and vigilant containment of

Russian expansive tendencies'.[58] NSC-68, the formerly classified report issued by the National Security Council in April 1950 and signed by President Truman in September 1950, reflected Kennan's assessment when it claimed that the Soviet Union sought 'to impose its absolute authority over the rest of the world'. In stark contrast, the 'fundamental purpose of the United States' was 'to assure the integrity and vitality of our free society, which is founded upon the dignity and worth of the individual'. This 'free society' was open to 'diversity', and in fact 'derives its strength from its hospitality even to antipathetic ideas'. It was also marked by 'generous and constructive impulses' and 'the absence of covetousness' in international relations. But the 'Kremlin design' had put 'the integrity and vitality' of the 'free society' in 'greater jeopardy than ever before', and thus it was critical that the United States should contain this 'aggressive threat' by maintaining 'a strong military posture'. This meant that the United States had to allocate more of its resources to defence and investment in war-supporting industries, although public relations demanded that the military build-up be explained as solely defensive.[59] Shortly after NSC-68 was completed, US military spending soared on the grounds that the North Korean invasion of South Korea in June 1950 had set in motion the Soviet takeover of the world. In just a few years, US military production had increased sevenfold, the army had grown by 50 per cent, NATO had been strengthened, West Germany had been rearmed, and military aid to the French army fighting anti-colonial forces in Indochina had been stepped up, paving the way for the Vietnam War.[60]

A more realistic historical interpretation of the Cold War, however, is that US foreign policy was overwhelmingly driven to promote the expansion of American capitalism into every corner of the world. Indeed at the start of the Cold War, Kennan had written: 'We have about 50% of the world's wealth, but only 6.3% of its population ... Our real task in the coming period is to devise a pattern of relationships that will permit us to maintain this position of disparity'.[61] This required that the South, along with its highly prized markets and cheap sources of labour and raw materials, be fully incorporated into a free market system and brought under the control of the capitalist economies of the North. The planned economy of the Soviet Union challenged US plans to build a free-market world order dominated by its own corporations. Moreover, Soviet support for the targets of US interventions in the South imposed unacceptable limits upon US hegemonic power.[62] Thus, the Soviet threat was overstated because it served as a highly convenient pretext for justifying US interventions, which were necessary if nationalist and left-leaning governments considered inimical to US economic interests were to be stifled or overthrown. Many formerly classified documents reveal how the United States considered 'radical nationalism' in the South as a major threat. To take one example: in 1953, NSC 144/1 warned that there was 'a trend in Latin America towards nationalist regimes' due to the 'increasing popular demand for an improvement in the low living standards of the masses'. Its advice was that action had to be taken to 'arrest the drift in the area toward radical and nationalistic regimes', including 'encouraging Latin American countries to recognize that the bulk of capital required for their economic development can best be supplied by private enterprise'.[63] 'Encourage' is an interesting word here, since in most Latin American cases this involved replacing the democratically elected government with a right-wing dictatorship brutal enough to implement US-friendly policies using any means necessary.

We concede that it is not always helpful to interpret US interventions in terms of capitalist expansionism, and there is something to be said for the 'commie hysteria' which sometimes provoked the CIA into action. But this does not change the fact that economic interests were the primary motivation for US relations with the South at the time. Since the end of the Cold War, the United States has reduced its reliance on right-wing dictatorships (mainly because the state terrorism exercised by most of these dictatorships was so successful in destroying practically all opposition during the Cold War), but it still continues to undertake military and non-military interventions to preserve a world order conducive to American capitalism. Take President Clinton, whose liberal internationalist grand strategy never shied away from reinforcing US hegemony.

Indeed, his promotion of democracy, free trade, and multilateral institutions, ostensibly to help maintain peace and security, always worked hand in hand with his support for repressive regimes. Under Clinton, the Colombian government continued to receive economic and military assistance even though it was widely known to be engaged in state terrorism. Israel, Egypt and Saudi Arabia were also backed by him, and Turkey (whose military actions in the Kurdish-dominated regions had killed tens of thousands of people, destroyed 3,500 villages and created over two million internally displaced persons and refugees) was given more US military aid in 1997 than in the entire Cold War period.[64] For much of the South the Cold War never really ended.

Colombia in particular demonstrates the continuities between the Cold War and post-Cold War US foreign policy. Doug Stokes explains how during the Cold War, Colombia was one of the largest Latin American recipients of US military aid (it was only surpassed by El Salvador when President Reagan came to power in the 1980s), primarily for anti-communist counter-insurgency.[65] Yet, Stokes continues, in the post-Cold War era, US funding of the Colombian military has remained extremely high (with more than $2 billion given between 2000 and 2002 alone),[66] although new reasons like the 'war on drugs' and the 'war on terror' have replaced the 'red scare'. Between 2000 and 2001, the Clinton administration made a commitment to Plan Colombia, a $1.3 billion US military aid package to the Colombian military, making Colombia the world's third-largest recipient of US military aid after Israel and Egypt at the time. The stated objective of Plan Colombia was the eradication of coca plantations and the targeting of the leftist Revolutionary Armed Forces of Colombia (FARC) rebels, who were accused by the United States of funding their campaign against the Colombian government through the coca trade.[67] It did not matter that the Colombian military had one of the worst human rights records in the western hemisphere, and had forged close ties with well-funded and well-armed right-wing paramilitary groups, such as the AUC (United Self-Defence Forces of Colombia).[68] And even though the United States's own agencies, such as the Drug Enforcement Agency (DEA), have stated on the record that the right-wing paramilitaries are more heavily involved in drug cultivation and trans-shipment to the United States, the only targets have been the coca plantations within the FARC zones of control.[69] AUC's involvement in a campaign of terror against thousands of teachers and lecturers, journalists, human rights investigators, community activists, and indigenous leaders have also been brushed aside by Colombia's US backers.[70]

Colombia is the United States's seventh-largest oil supplier, and the discovery of vast oil reserves within its territory make it invaluable as the United States tries to decrease its reliance on Middle Eastern oil and shift its purchasing to Latin America.[71] Since the FARC has consistently bombed major oil pipelines (which prompted the Bush administration to request $98 million for a Colombian military counter-insurgency force devoted to protecting the US-owned Occidental Oil's Cano Limon oil pipeline in Colombia),[72] and has destabilised the Colombian government through its decades-long campaign, it constitutes the primary threat to US interests in Colombia. It is also the case that the FARC's alternative socio-economic project is an unacceptable challenge to the US-led neoliberal restructuring of Colombia's economy, which makes FARC's destruction all the more necessary.[73] Plan Colombia represents the continuation of US interventionism in Latin America, with American economic interests still acting as the main motivating factor. It is a classic counter-insurgency war, and shares many characteristics with the strategies employed during the Cold War, including the targeting of civilians whose only crime is to demand political reforms.

The transition to the post-Cold War era can be understood through the lens of neoliberalism, which since the late 1970s has taken the economic exploitation of the South to new levels. The market crash of 1929 and the Great Depression that followed had made laissez-faire capitalism and opposition to state intervention in the economy unpopular in public-policy circles. But in the economic turmoil of the 1970s, neoliberalism's three-part formula of deregulation, privatisation and cutbacks to social programmes became orthodoxy. Neoliberalism was very effective in restoring (or, in the case of China or Russia, say, creating) the power of economic elites everywhere. For example:

in the United States, the share of national income of the top 1 per cent of income earners increased from 8 per cent to 15 per cent (which was very close to the pre-Second World War share) after the implementation of neoliberal policies.[74] Neoliberalism rapidly spread around the world, opening up new commercial frontiers and tearing down the barriers that stood in the way of the free movement of capital at the level of the global economy. The South paid a particularly heavy price. When the neoliberal vision could not be implemented democratically, it relied on right-wing regimes to force it upon unwilling populations. The 'hidden hand' of the market was often accompanied by the 'iron fist' of the dictator.

Neoliberals claim to distrust all state power, but in reality they require a strong and, if necessary, coercive state 'to protect our freedom both from the enemies outside our gates and from our fellow-citizens: to preserve law and order, to enforce private contracts, to foster competitive markets', in the words of Milton Friedman.[75] Friedman himself visited Chile with his wife in March 1975, and later wrote a letter to Pinochet, advising him that the Chilean economy needed a 'shock treatment', by which, as Naomi Klein has shown, he meant a rapid and no-holds-barred adoption of free-market policies.[76] The fact that the 'shock treatment' was inextricably linked to the torture and disappearance of thousands of Chileans did not unduly concern Friedman. 'In spite of my profound disagreement with the authoritarian political system of Chile', he claimed in *Newsweek*, 'I do not consider it as evil for an economist to render technical economic advice to the Chilean Government.'[77] Since then the mission to force this 'shock treatment' on countries around the world has continued through strong US-led initiatives, backed up by economic and military pressures when necessary. The extreme 'structural adjustments' that neoliberalism demands from national governments are forced on unwilling populations through pliant or corrupt governments and conditional IFI credits. In the South, the majority of people have sunk deeper into poverty than ever before, with vast areas of the Earth's surface turning into slums. And even in the affluent North, subjected to much milder forms of neoliberalism, people have begun to suffer, burdened with massive debt, and facing increasing class disparity and the destruction of the welfare state. State terrorism pays, but only for the few.

*   *   *

The 13 interviews that comprise the rest of this book expand on many of the issues raised here. Those interviewed are all leading academics in the areas they have been called upon to discuss. Our aim is to analyse US state terrorism from as many perspectives as possible, and the interview format has allowed us access to authoritative views on a hugely varied range of subjects, including politics, law, philosophy, economics, and social theory. Importantly, each interviewee is asked not simply to reiterate positions they have already published, but to expand on, clarify and defend those positions. In each case, however, we ultimately aim to demonstrate one aspect of our claim that the United States is the most consistent perpetrator and supporter of state terrorism in post-war history.

The chapters are ordered according to theme. In Chapters 2 to 5, we attempt to develop our concept of state terrorism and illustrate certain norms of obligation, both legal and moral, that may act as standards of judgement over US policy. Chapters 6 to 8 examine how the dominant discourse of terrorism is reproduced in the public sphere through both media representation and academic research. In Chapters 9 and 10 we focus on the core motivations behind US state terrorism, showing how the dominant discourse often hides the economic objectives. The final four chapters are case studies which demonstrate in greater detail the nature and impact of US interventions in particular geographic areas. The interviews were conducted either in person, by telephone, or by email, and took place between October 2010 and April 2012. Those interviews conducted in the early stages were also revisited and updated in 2012.

Chapter 2: The Definition of Terrorism   Following some of the issues raised in our introductory chapter, we discuss with Noam Chomsky the different definitions of terrorism (particularly the varied and ever shifting official US definitions), and show how the dominant conceptions that ignore state violence and repression often aim to legitimate US foreign-policy practices. Chomsky explains that the definitions available when he first started researching the subject in the early 1980s when President Reagan declared a 'war on terrorism' were generally adequate to the task, and the range of clauses inserted and/or deleted since are mostly cynical exercises designed to exclude US state actions from liability. Even so, Chomsky convincingly concludes that it is difficult for the United States not to fall foul of its own definitions.

Chapter 3: International Law and Human Rights   With Richard Falk we explore the standards set by international law for the behaviour of states, with particular emphasis on US attempts to exempt itself from liability or punishment. Falk explains how international law often acts to maintain hegemonic interests (for instance, in the way that the United Nations Security Council is set up), but also underscores the very real possibilities for a progressive counter-hegemonic turn in international law. We also discuss how the United States employs a limited concept of human rights which excludes social and economic rights, and evaluate the ideological support it receives from apparently neutral international human rights groups. Finally, we turn to the idea of terrorism, and consider how the international community's inability to agree upon a definition has impacted international law. The importance of including states and their authorised agents in any future legal definition of terrorism is stressed.

Chapter 4: Torture as Terrorism   Our discussion of torture with Marjorie Cohn begins with its definition in the Convention against Torture and Other Cruel, Inhuman or Degrading Treatment or Punishment, which the United States has signed and ratified, thus making it part of its body of laws. We then discuss the more recent use of torture by US agents in Afghanistan and Iraq, and more broadly in the 'extraordinary rendition' programme, and evaluate the inability of domestic and international courts to bring those responsible to account. Other issues explored with Cohn include the connection between race and torture (with questions such as, 'Is it really easier to torture a person who is considered to be racially or culturally inferior?' intended to broaden our understanding of the horrific images which emerged from Abu Ghraib in 2004), as well as the media representations of women as both victims and perpetrators of torture. Finally, Cohn explains how the US prison system is also guilty of cruel and inhuman punishment, thus making torture part of US domestic policy.

Chapter 5: Morality, Justification and Responsibility   In this interview, we discuss with Ted Honderich the philosophical issues surrounding the morality of terrorism and questions of democratic responsibility. We question Honderich's understanding of state terrorism in regard to legality, and examine whether acts such as unilateral or covert intervention should be considered wrong in and of themselves. Honderich argues that they need not be, and, following consequentialist philosophical theory, insists that even self-interested, violent acts may be justified if they accord with his 'Principle of Humanity'. However, it is made clear that many US actions have not been justifiable under the rules of this principle. What is more, this is unlikely to change under the 'hierarchic democracy' of the United States, in which certain political and economic interests disproportionately control decision-making processes.

Chapter 6: The Media Image of Terrorism   This interview with Edward Herman examines the role played by the corporate news media in propagating dominant ideas of terrorism. In choosing to cover only particular kinds of terrorism, the media tacitly accept that state terrorism (especially by the United States) does not count. Furthermore, Herman argues, they actually contribute to terror by exaggerating terrorist threats against the United States and pushing for aggressive foreign policy, including appeals to racism and other ideological hatreds, to encourage public support. We also return to Herman and Chomsky's famous media 'Propaganda Model', first published in the 1980s, to re-evaluate its relevance in coverage of recent conflicts, particularly in light of controversies such as Abu Ghraib in Iraq.

Chapter 7: The Discourse of Terror   Following on from our discussion with Herman, we examine with Judith Butler the ways in which dominant visual and linguistic representations of terrorism affect public perception and debate on the subject. Butler's concept of 'framing' shows how wars and political situations may come to be understood as conflicts demanding allegiance to sides rather than principles. We also explore the psychological impacts of the discourse on terrorism, especially after 9/11, including how the state and media use fear to heighten demand for greater security and shut down critical analysis. Finally, we turn to Guantanamo Bay, discussing the way in which it acts as a clear warning, and potential source of terror, even to US citizens.

Chapter 8: Terrorism Studies and Academia   In this interview, Richard Jackson explains why state terrorism is not widely researched in the academic field of terrorism studies, pointing to factors such as its development from an orthodox Cold War perspective, the lack of critical-skills teaching in universities, and the lack of institutional support for criticism of (Western) state crimes. Instead, a good academic career is defined by its adherence to predefined pathways, leading to promotion, research funding, and supplementary government or media work. For the most part, Jackson argues, it is institutional structure that guides scholars in this direction. We finish by examining the growing sub-discipline of critical terrorism studies, and evaluate the possibilities of resisting the tide.

Chapter 9: International Financial Institutions and the Economics of Terrorism   This interview with Patrick Bond demonstrates how US state terrorism functions in parallel with IFIs, in particular the IMF and the World Bank, to further economic objectives. Bond explains how, under US influence and behind a rhetoric of poverty reduction, these IFIs allow the global North to appropriate the resources of the South. Repressive regimes are encouraged to borrow funds (provided they act in accordance with neoliberal interests), creating a double impact – first strengthening the regime's capacity for terror, and then crippling subsequent democratic governments with a demand to service the debts incurred. Using South Africa during and after apartheid as an example, we show how a kind of economic terror has replaced direct violence in the continuing repression of Southern populations.

Chapter 10: The Guiding Force of US Militarism   Here we discuss with Ismael Hossein-zadeh his work on the military–industrial complex. Hossein-zadeh explains how, to a great extent, US wars, military aid, and security demands are ends in themselves, the product of an increasingly 'parasitic' imperialism allowing a global military and corporate elite to siphon off national wealth. Accordingly, he disputes various official reasons for US military interventions, both during and after the Cold War, and demonstrates the economic drives behind them. At the same time, we challenge Hossein-zadeh on the importance of other critical interpretations of US policy, most notably that of oil, in order to demonstrate a range of corporate interests competing to shape state actions.

Chapter 11: The United States in the Middle East   In this interview, Gilbert Achcar provides a brief history of US involvement in the Greater Middle East. We examine the importance of the US presence in the Saudi Kingdom, and its alliances with fundamentalist Islam against progressive nationalism, before moving on to US support for the dictatorship in Iran before the Islamic revolution, and the motivations behind more recent military interventions in Afghanistan, Iraq, and Libya. A pattern emerges in which the United States has consistently sought to maintain regional control, regardless of the human cost. Achcar also emphasises the central role of oil in Middle East policy, thus forming a counterpoint to Hossein-zadeh's thesis. We feel that together these arguments highlight the complex network of influences on US political processes.

Chapter 12: US Support for Israeli State Terror   This interview with Norman Finkelstein deals with the history of US–Israeli relations since the beginning of their close alliance in the 1960s. We examine specific events in which the Israeli military has been responsible for committing or facilitating terrorism, such as the Sabra and Shatila massacres in Lebanon, and the 2008 invasion of Gaza. We show how continued US support, particularly with the vetoes cast to United Nations resolutions, has allowed these widely condemned acts to go unpunished, and ask to what degree Israel is reliant on the United States, economically, ideologically, and politically. Finkelstein expertly explains how, despite its regional military dominance, Israel would be unable to maintain its aggressive stance without such consistent backing.

Chapter 13: The United States in Latin America   Our interview with Greg Grandin investigates a number of cases of US involvement in the horrific violence that swept through Central and South America during the Cold War. We begin with Guatemala, the United States's first full-scale intervention in that period, with Grandin explaining how the communism it sought to destroy was precisely the driving force behind the nation's progressive democracy. We next turn to the 1959 Cuban Revolution, the important lessons Castro and his comrades learned from the Guatemala experience, and how, in turn, the United States reacted to the possibility of more revolutionary Cubas by talking up nation-building social programmes on one hand, while employing stronger terror tactics on the other. Finally, we show how, in Colombia, terroristic US foreign policy continues, with a concerted effort to destroy progressive movements, long after the Cold War's end.

Chapter 14: NATO's Secret Armies in Europe   This interview with Daniele Ganser centres on how a network of clandestine anti-communist armies was set up in western Europe by the CIA and the British secret service MI6 (in close collaboration with NATO and other European secret military services) after the Second World War. Initially designed to build a resistance in the case of a Soviet invasion of western Europe, the network rapidly developed into a force fighting internal enemies, such as communist and socialist political parties. Although no official documents have been declassified (despite repeated requests by scholars working on the subject), Ganser provides an excellent analysis of these secret armies through his knowledge of reliable secondary sources, and explains how the United States turned Europe into a secret battleground, with devastating consequences.

Cihan Aksan and Jon Bailes
Nicosia, April 2012

NOTES

All online references in the book last accessed 16 April 2012.

1. Herbert Marcuse, *One-Dimensional Man* (Boston: Beacon Press, 1964), p.87.
2. See: Mark G. Stewart and John Mueller, 'Acceptability of Terrorism Risks and Prioritising Protective Measures for Key Infrastructure', paper presented at the First International Conference of Protective Structures, Manchester, UK, 2010, <http://polisci.osu.edu/faculty/jmueller/stewprst.pdf>.
3. Jonathan Barker, *The No-Nonsense Guide to Global Terrorism*, 2nd edn (Oxford: New Internationalist, 2008), p.72.
4. The terms 'the United States' and 'US' refer to the nation as political actor in international relations.
5. *US Code*, Title 22, Section 2656f, <http://tinyurl.com/cwe4anr>.
6. Robert E. Goodin, *What's Wrong with Terrorism?* (Cambridge: Polity Press, 2006), p.7.
7. Ibid., p.55.
8. *Code of Federal Regulations*, Title 28, Section 0.85, <http://tinyurl.com/cyljc6j>.
9. Goodin, *What's Wrong?* p.57.
10. Christopher Mitchell, et al., 'State Terrorism: Issues of Concept and Measurement', in Michael Stohl and George A. Lopez (eds), *Government Violence and Repression: An Agenda for Research* (New York: Greenwood Press, 1986), pp.1–25 (p.13).
11. *Operations: US Army Field Manual*, FM 3-0, 9-37, 14 June 2001, <http://tinyurl.com/cuod9w2>.
12. Walter Laqueur, *No End to War: Terrorism in the Twenty-First Century* (New York: Continuum, 2007), p.238.

13. Harlan Ullman and James Wade, *Shock and Awe: Achieving Rapid Dominance* (Washington: NDU, 1996), p.xi, <http://www.dodccrp.org/files/Ullman_Shock.pdf>.
14. Ibid., p.xii.
15. Ibid., pp.55–6.
16. Ibid., p.50.
17. Ibid., p.39.
18. Ruth Blakeley, *State Terrorism and Neoliberalism: The North in the South* (Abingdon: Routledge, 2009), p.36.
19. Ullman and Wade, *Shock and Awe*, p.xxvi.
20. Cihan Aksan and Jon Bailes, 'An Interview with Dahr Jamail', *State of Nature*, Spring 2006, <http://www.stateofnature.org/dahrJamail.html>; see also Dahr Jamail, *Beyond the Green Zone: Dispatches from an Unembedded Journalist in Occupied Iraq* (Chicago: Haymarket, 2007).
21. Scott Shane, 'C.I.A. Is Disputed on Civilian Toll in Drone Strikes', *New York Times*, 11 August 2011, <http://tinyurl.com/4x89dmv>.
22. Chris Woods and Christina Lamb, 'Obama Terror Drones: CIA Tactics in Pakistan Include Targeting Rescuers and Funerals', *The Bureau of Investigative Journalism*, 4 February 2012, <http://tinyurl.com/bsvog57>.
23. Michael Stohl, 'The Superpowers and International Terrorism', in Stohl and Lopez, *Government Violence and Repression*, pp.207–34 (p.213).
24. Thomas J. Nagy, 'The Role of "Iraq Water Treatment Vulnerabilities" in Halting One Genocide and Preventing Others', 12 June 2001, <http://www.casi.org.uk/info/nagy010612.pdf>.
25. 'Transcript: Democratic Debate in Los Angeles', *New York Times*, 31 January 2008, <http://tinyurl.com/c8le6tw>.
26. The prohibition of assassination is an executive order, and remains in place because no subsequent president has revoked it. However, the president is within his or her rights to circumvent and nullify executive orders, and indeed President George W. Bush authorised the CIA to use previously prohibited means to attack Osama bin Laden and al-Qaeda on the grounds that executive order bans do not apply during wartime. The subsequent assassination of bin Laden on the orders of President Barack Obama shows that Bush's policy remains firmly in place. See Kristen Eichensehr, 'On the Offensive: Assassination Policy Under International Law', Harvard International Review, Vol.25, Issue 3, 2003, <http://hir.harvard.edu/leadership/on-the-offensive>.
27. Max Boot, 'Covert Action Makes a Comeback', *Wall Street Journal*, 5 January 2011, <http://tinyurl.com/89pf9ox>. Boot is a fan of covert action. In the above article, he advises the Obama administration against opening negotiations with Iran because a covert action programme would better serve US interests.
28. The exact number of people killed in Indonesia is difficult to determine. Estimates range from over 100,000 to over a million, but the most reliable studies place the figure at 500,000 people. See: David F. Schmitz, *The United*

States and Right-Wing Dictatorships, 1965–1989 (New York: Cambridge University Press, 2006), p.48.

29. Ibid., p.48.
30. Ibid., p.47.
31. John Pilger, *The New Rulers of the World* (London: Verso, 2002), p.30.
32. 'Memorandum. Subject: Djakarta Visit: Your Meetings with President Suharto', 18 July 1969, <http://tinyurl.com/cktsrcq>.
33. Schmitz, *The United States and Right-Wing Dictatorships*, pp.76–7.
34. Edward S. Herman, *The Real Terror Network: Terrorism in Fact and Propaganda* (Boston: South End Press, 1982), p.127.
35. Deborah J. Gerner, 'Weapons for Repression? US Arms Transfers to the Third World', in Michael Stohl and George A. Lopez (eds), *Terrible Beyond Endurance* (Westport, Conn.: Greenwood Press, 1988), pp.247–79 (p.248). It is worth nothing that, if applying current US legal standards, as stated in the PATRIOT Act, such questions are not even necessary to demonstrate responsibility. The Act describes as a 'terrorist' the person 'who pays for a bomb' as well as 'the one who pushes the button'. See United States Department of Justice, 'The USA PATRIOT Act: Preserving Life and Liberty', <http://www.justice.gov/archive/ll/highlights.htm>.
36. Gerner, 'Weapons for Repression', p.256.
37. Frederick H. Gareau, *State Terrorism and the United States: From Counterinsurgency to the War on Terrorism* (Atlanta: Clarity Press, 2004), p.41.
38. Ibid.
39. 'Covert Action in Chile, 1963–1973', Staff Report of the Select Committee to Study Governmental Operations with Respect to Intelligence Activities (US Senate), 18 December 1975, <http://foia.state.gov/Reports/ChurchReport.asp>.
40. An exception was the International Monetary Fund (IMF), which 'extended Chile approximately $90 million during 1971 and 1972 to assist with foreign exchange difficulties', ibid.
41. Ibid.
42. Gareau, *State Terrorism and the United States*, p.70.
43. 'Covert Action in Chile'.
44. *SIPRI Yearbook 2011* (Oxford: Oxford University Press, 2010), <http://www.sipri.org/yearbook/2011/04/04A>.
45. Martin Jacques, 'Why do we continue to ignore China's rise? Arrogance', *Observer*, 25 March 2012, <http://tinyurl.com/7m6oane>.
46. Schmitz, *The United States and Right-Wing Dictatorships*, p.75.
47. 'Inaugural Address', 20 January 1977, <http://tinyurl.com/canyabn>.
48. 'Universal Declaration of Human Rights: Remarks at a White House Meeting Commemorating the 30th Anniversary of the Declaration's Signing', 6 December 1978, <http://tinyurl.com/bw8q8ne>.
49. Stephen Kinzer, *All the Shah's Men: An American Coup and the Roots of Middle East Terror*, 2nd edn (Hoboken, N.J.: John Wiley & Sons, 2008), p.202.

50. 'Tehran, Iran: Toasts of the President and the Shah at a State Dinner', 31 December 1977, <http://tinyurl.com/cxrbnkt>.
51. Robert Fisk, *The Great War for Civilisation: The Conquest of the Middle East* (London: Fourth Estate, 2005), pp.120–1.
52. 'Tehran, Iran: Toasts of the President'.
53. 'The President's News Conference', 17 January 1979, <http://tinyurl.com/br86gsq>.
54. 'Memorandum. Subject: Summary of Vice President's Meeting with Suharto', May 1978, <http://tinyurl.com/d4gwqyu>.
55. Gerner, 'Weapons for Repression', p.255.
56. Carole Cadwalladr, 'Jimmy Carter: "We never dropped a bomb. We never fired a bullet. We never went to war"', *Observer*, 11 September 2011, <http://tinyurl.com/c76rnlq>.
57. Quoted in Michael Stohl, David Carleton, and Stephen E. Johnson, 'Human Rights and US Foreign Assistance from Nixon to Carter', *Journal of Peace Research*, Vol.21, Issue 3 (1984), pp.215–26 (p.223).
58. George F. Kennan, 'The Sources of Soviet Conduct', in James F. Hoge, Jr., and Fareed Zakaria (eds) *The American Encounter: The United States and the Making of the Modern World* (New York: Basic Books, 1997), pp.155–69 (p.163).
59. 'NSC-68: United States Objectives and Programs for National Security: A Report to the President Pursuant to the President's Directive of January 31, 1950', 14 April 1950, <http://www.fas.org/irp/offdocs/nsc-hst/nsc-68.htm>.
60. Michael Cox and Doug Stokes, *US Foreign Policy* (Oxford: Oxford University Press, 2008), p.78.
61. Quoted in Doug Stokes, 'Why the End of the Cold War Doesn't Matter: The US War of Terror in Colombia', *Review of International Studies*, No.29 (2003), pp.569–85 (p.575).
62. Noam Chomsky, *Deterring Democracy* (London: Vintage, 1992), p.27.
63. 'NSC 144/1: US Objectives and Courses of Action with Respect to Latin America', 18 March 1973, <http://tinyurl.com/bsvdf8g>.
64. Noam Chomsky, 'Prospects for Peace in the Middle East', lecture delivered at the First Annual Maryse Mikhail Lecture, University of Toledo, 4 March 2001, <http://www.chomsky.info/talks/20010304.htm>.
65. Stokes, 'End of the Cold War', p.577.
66. Ibid.
67. Ibid.
68. Only a quarter of the US military aid to Colombia is attached to human rights conditions. Thus when Congress recently froze $55 million in US military assistance due to the rise in extrajudicial killings, it was hardly noticed by the Colombian government. Blakeley, *State Terrorism and Neoliberalism*, p.130.
69. Stokes, 'Better Lead than Bread? A Critical Analysis of the US's Plan Colombia', *Civil Wars*, Vol.4, Issue 2 (2001), pp.59–78 (p.65).

70. Blakeley, *State Terrorism and Neoliberalism*, p.130.
71. Stokes, 'End of the Cold War', p.582.
72. Ibid.
73. Stokes, 'Better Lead than Bread?', p.72.
74. David Harvey, *A Brief History of Neoliberalism* (Oxford: Oxford University Press, 2005), p.16.
75. Quoted in Naomi Klein, *The Shock Doctrine* (London: Penguin, 2007), p.5.
76. Ibid., pp.80–1.
77. Quoted in Orlando Letelier, 'The Chicago Boys in Chile: Economic Freedom's Awful Truth', *The Nation*, 28 August 1976.

2

Noam Chomsky
The Definition of Terrorism

How would you define terrorism?

Noam Chomsky: I started writing extensively on terrorism as soon as the Reagan administration came in. One of the first acts of the Reagan administration in 1981 was to declare a 'war on terror', although that has kind of been forgotten because the outcome was so horrendous; nobody wants to talk about it. The administration stated that the focal point of their foreign policy would be the war against state-directed international terrorism, which they called a return to barbarism in our time and the plague of the modern age. So I started to write about it, and I used the official definitions: the ones in the US Code, the army manuals, the British government definition. They're all pretty much the same, but essentially it is the calculated use of violence or threat of violence against civilians for the purpose of intimidation or coercion or changing government policy. It's stated more explicitly, but that's the gist of it.

But if you use that definition there is a problem. It immediately follows that the United States is one of the leading terrorist states in the world, if not *the* leading terrorist state. But that's an unacceptable conclusion for them, so the reasoning is that there must be something wrong with the definition. In fact there is a huge academic literature on terrorism, but they don't use the official definitions, and the reason they don't use them is because of this 'flaw'. So, there have been many attempts to define terrorism, and discussions about whether it is definable, how it can be defined, and so on. But the basic problem is quite simple: it's necessary to find a definition of terrorism that will include *their* terror against *us*, but exclude *our* terror against *them*, and that is a difficult, if not impossible, task. So you have elaborate literature trying to define terror, basically to overcome this problem.

But if you look at the US record, the kindest judgement is that it is a record of terrorism. Maybe a more accurate judgement is that it's a record of aggression, which is a much more serious crime than terror. For example, take the state that has been the target of more terror than any other in the world, maybe more than all of them put together: Cuba. Within a few months of the Castro government taking over, the Eisenhower administration had a formal, internal plan to overthrow it, and the planes started bombing Cuba. Then Kennedy came in shortly after, and there was the Bay of Pigs invasion. When that failed, the Kennedy administration became hysterical. The internal records describe how they couldn't deal with the fact that this small country, which had been the first target of US foreign policy back in the 1820s, was refusing orders and beating back an invasion.

So, Washington initiated a programme of terror, and it wasn't even hidden internally. The assignment to run the campaign was given to Robert Kennedy and he took it as his highest priority. According to his biographer, Arthur Schlesinger, the Kennedy administration historian, he said the goal was to bring 'the terrors of the Earth' to Cuba. And if you look at the record it was pretty ugly: murders, sabotage, attacking ships in the Cuban harbour, probably even biological warfare attacks. It peaked with the blowing up of the Cubana airliner in 1976, killing 75 people or so. The perpetrators are known; in fact they are living happily in Florida, although one, Orlando Bosch, died in April 2011.

So this is not considered as the harbouring of terrorists, which is what the Taliban regime in Afghanistan was accused of?

NC: It's interesting because according to the Bush Doctrine those who harbour terrorists are as guilty as the terrorists themselves. There is no question that the United States is harbouring terrorists. To begin with, for a long time, terrorism was carried out by CIA agents, but later it was farmed out to people like Bosch and others in Florida. That they were terrorists was not in question. During the first Bush administration, the Justice Department wanted to deport Bosch because they said that he was a terrorist who was a threat to the security of the United States. The Justice Department and the FBI listed about 30 acts of terror committed by him, but Bush pardoned him.

It's a sort of point of principle that you don't investigate your own crimes. So we don't know how many people were killed in Vietnam, for example. On the other hand in, say, Kosovo, every bit of earth is uncovered to see if you can find a bone that could be attributed to a Serb crime. In East Timor at the same time there was great care to assure that there would be no serious investigation of crimes for which we shared primary responsibility. In fact, in 1984 the US was brought to the World Court on a charge of either terror or aggression against Nicaragua – to be nice to the United States, let's call it terror.[1] The case was presented by a distinguished Harvard University international lawyer, but most of it was thrown out for straightforward reasons: when the United States accepted the jurisdiction of the World Court in 1946, it added a reservation that the United States cannot be charged under any international treaty, which includes the UN Charter, which bans the use of force in international affairs except under conditions that certainly do not apply to the US war against Nicaragua, or the OAS Charter, which bans any interference in any country of the hemisphere. So the United States is immune to international treaties. The Nicaragua case nevertheless went through on very narrow grounds. The court had to consider just the bilateral treaty between Nicaragua and the United States and common international law. And on those narrow grounds they charged the United States with 'unlawful use of force', which is either terror or aggression, depending on how you see it.[2]

Doesn't this undermine the argument that some scholars put forth, that it's unnecessary to define state terrorism or make laws against it, because state agents have alternative liabilities like War Crimes Tribunals?

NC: They have liabilities only if they accept jurisdiction. The United States does not. In fact, the United States is self-authorised to carry out genocide. That actually came to the World Court. In the case that Yugoslavia brought against ten NATO countries in 1999, one of the charges was genocide. The United States withdrew from the case, and the court accepted that,[3] because when the United States signed the genocide convention, after 40 years, it added a reservation excluding the United States. In fact, in international agreements generally – the enabling conventions for the Universal Declaration of Human Rights and so on – the United States always adds a reservation excluding themselves. The United States does not surrender sovereignty, in courts or for anybody else.

Let's return to the official US definitions of terrorism. The one you quoted earlier was from the *US Army Manual*.

NC: That's the brief one; there's a longer one in the US code.

Yes, the US code 22, section 2656 f (d): 'terrorism means premeditated politically motivated violence perpetrated against noncombatant targets by subnational groups or clandestine agents'.[4]

NC: That's a later one, that's not the one I quoted. The one I quoted has nothing about subnational groups. Because remember that Reagan was claiming to be carrying out a war against state-directed terrorism. But when it became understood that the original definition also implicated the United States, they used their various tricks to try to get around it, and one of them was to restrict it to subnational groups.

Also the definition refers to 'clandestine agents', but most state terror isn't clandestine, so that appears to exclude state terrorism too.

NC: That's the idea. There is a problem as I said that you cannot have a definition which applies to the United States, so this is one of many devices to try to get around it. That's a revision.

So you would not use the US Code definition as it stands?

NC: I wouldn't, but in fact the US government doesn't either. That's why it has a list of states allegedly supporting terror, which have to be punished. Like Iran right now, which is accused of being a major sponsor of terrorism.

The current list of 'state sponsors of terrorism' according to the US State Department is Cuba, Iran, Sudan, and Syria.

NC: What is interesting is that, in 1982, Reagan wanted to support Saddam Hussein's attack on Iran, and they gave lavish aid to fight the war. In order to do that they had to remove Iraq from the list of states supporting terror because there is congressional legislation saying you can't give aid to such states. So they had a gap on the list, and they put in Cuba in recognition of the fact that it was the main target of terrorism. The cynicism of this is just indescribable.

Also during the 1980s, Reagan was supporting South Africa, which was by then already in violation of congressional sanctions that they had to get around. There was a UN study later which estimated that about a million and a half people were killed by South African atrocities just in Mozambique and Angola, not to speak of South Africa, and the US administration was supporting the apartheid regime. In 1988 the Pentagon declared the African National Congress was one of the 'more notorious terrorist groups' in the world; in fact Nelson Mandela was only removed from the terrorist list in 2008.

Perhaps we could look at the definition closely and focus on the meaning of 'innocents', 'civilians', or 'non-combatants'. Some scholars refuse to use the word 'innocent' because it opens up too many more questions. For instance, how do you define the guilt or innocence of a victim, or if terrorism is simply about killing innocents how is it different from murder?

NC: OK, let's take that. In October 2010, for example, there was a major trial under the revised Military Commissions Act of a young man, Omar Ahmed Khadr, who was 15 years old when he was captured and charged with killing an American soldier invading his country, Afghanistan. And he was charged with terror. He spent a year in Bagram, then seven more in Guantanamo Bay. Finally he was given a choice: plead guilty and serve eight more years, or plead innocent and the roof will fall in.

The term 'non-combatant' is also interesting as it is stretched to include a soldier when he or she is not actively engaged in combat.

NC: Non-combatant means somebody who Ed Herman refers to as a 'worthy victim', which is somebody on our side. Whereas if we attack somebody else, they are combatants or terrorists.

Who should count as a civilian then, if we focus on that word? Particularly thinking about state terrorism, if we restrict the definition to civilians, what about non-civilians such as members of the armed forces or police officers within a country or even members of armed resistance? Would they be legitimate targets?

NC: That raises another question. If you invade another country, is the resistance to your invasion terrorist? So, for example, was George Washington's army terrorist after they uncontroversially carried out all sorts of acts of terrorism? The fact they were withstanding a foreign occupation means we would not consider that terrorism. And, for example, the United States and the West do not say that the USA was engaged in terrorism in Afghanistan in the 1980s, because it was supporting resistance to the Russian invasion. They say, 'Well, it was an invasion, people have the right to resist.' But it doesn't work the other way round. I mean, say, when Israel invades Lebanon, it's the Lebanese who are terrorists.

What about if it's not an invasion? Take Chile, for example, and the kidnap and murder of General René Schneider, the commander-in-chief of the Chilean army, to clear the way for the military coup. Or if we think about Turkey, throughout the

70s and 80s, where army and police officers were also arrested and tortured. There was also armed resistance by people who called themselves an army, and therefore they wouldn't have considered themselves non-combatants. So was the fact that they were tortured, murdered and massacred still terrorism?

NC: But we are talking about a different phenomenon, we are talking about something internal to the state.

But the US was supporting that, so was it funding terrorism, if the targets were what we would regard as non-civilians?

NC: I would say so. But it's not as clear a case as the ones I mentioned. I feel in this discussion it would make sense to keep to the crystal-clear cases, but there are a lot of ambiguous cases. The only respect in which the ones I mentioned are not crystal clear is that we are bending over backwards to give the benefit of the doubt to the United States by calling it terror. The more natural definition for many of these cases is aggression.

How would you distinguish terrorism from aggression?

NC: Aggression, which is reasonably well defined in international law, if you believe international law and the Nuremburg judgement, is the supreme international crime, which differs from other war crimes in that it includes all the consequences that follow. So, for example, in the *New York Times* there was an article about the revival of sectarian conflict in Iraq, which says that sectarian conflict is one of the consequences of democratisation.[5] It's not a consequence of democratisation. It's a consequence of the cruel, vicious occupation, where the leadership should be hanged according to the standards of Nuremburg. But that's not discussable in the mainstream media.

Let's take Iran. The worst threat at the moment is supposed to be the Iranian threat, so that is the leading focus of foreign policy. That's accepted in the United States and in Europe, which is a kind of vassal of the United States, virtually without comment. So it does raise the question of exactly what the Iranian threat is. Actually, we have an authoritative answer to that, but there isn't any discussion and it's never cited. Every year the Pentagon and the intelligence agencies present an analysis to Congress of the global security situation. The most explicit recent report is from April 2010 (a later one is less specific and adds nothing new). It says there is really no military threat from Iran. Iran has very low military spending even by the standards of the region, and only limited capacity to deploy force abroad. Iran's strategic doctrine is designed to deter an invasion; to try and hold back an invasion long enough so that diplomacy can set in. The analysis says that if Iran is developing a nuclear capability, it would be part of their deterrent strategy. And of course the reason they have a deterrent strategy is that two countries on their borders are occupied by a brutal, vicious, hostile superpower which is constantly threatening an attack (which is a violation of the UN Charter, if anybody cares). Obama especially is building up offensive forces, so if anyone in the world needs a deterrent, Iran does.

So the US official estimate is that if Iran is developing a nuclear capability, it would be for deterrence, so there is essentially no military threat. But then the report goes on to say Iran is the major threat in the world. Why? Well, primarily because they might be a deterrent to the free resort to force by the US and its clients. And furthermore, they are trying to extend their influence into neighbouring countries. So if we invade the neighbouring countries and occupy them, that is called stabilisation, but if they try to extend their influence, say in Iraq and Afghanistan, the latter in a traditional area of Iranian influence, that's destabilisation. One of the crimes they are charged with is supporting the resistance in Iraq. Whether they did actually support it or didn't support it, I think the whole thing is surreal – *we* invade a country, and somebody else is charged with supporting the resistance. Once aggression takes place, the discussion is in a different dimension because that is such a severe crime anything else pales beside it.

Just to go back to one of the other definitions, in the *US Army Manual* it actually says that terrorism is 'intended to coerce or

intimidate governments or societies', and that 'terrorists usually pursue political, religious, or ideological goals'.[6] Is there any reason for distinguishing ideological or religious from political goals? Aren't all state terrorist goals political?

NC: To give you the honest truth I don't really see much point in that because the definitions are political acts. Going back to what you're quoting, which is probably the late 70s or early 80s, terrorism was given the obvious definition. It was in the 80s that they had to re-craft it, redesign it so you could sort of parse that and ask whether it was ideological or religious or different. But what it really means is that something we don't like is terrorism.

It's the same story with aggression. For example, when the Kennedy administration invaded South Vietnam in 1962, Adlai Stevenson, the UN representative at the time, said they were defending Vietnam from 'internal aggression', and Kennedy added they were defending it from 'the assault from within'. The Joint Chiefs of Staff had given their own definition of aggression, which included unarmed aggression, namely by political warfare. So if there's a political party which is not doing what the state wants, then by US standards that's aggression, the worst international crime which justifies anything in self-defence. If we were on Mars looking at this, we'd figure it was a comic strip, it's so ridiculous. But it has to be taken seriously by elite opinion; the task is to create some kind of ideological structure which will justify state crimes.

Some definitions also mention social objectives as well as political ones. Is that not effectively leaving the definition open to almost any interpretation?

NC: If you take that definition literally and you're serious about it, it completely falls apart. What follows is that the most powerful states, like the United States, are the worst terrorist states.

Take the US sanctions against Iran. There was an interesting document – it doesn't have official status but it is important –

by five former top NATO generals, defining what the strategies should be, and their recommendations for a strike and so on.[7] They also had a definition of 'acts of war', and one of the acts of war that they defined was threats to the financial system. Well, the US is trying to force all financial institutions out of Iran with threats; it's threatening to close off the American market to those who violate US unilateral sanctions against Iran. So that's an act of war according to Western concepts. Obviously, they don't say that.

One important example is the pressure on Belgian-based SWIFT, the international communication centre for international banks, demanding that they exclude Iran, an unprecedented step. As always, the US arrogates the right to dictate to others, including international institutions, what they must do. No other state can do so, and others must obey or there are sharp penalties. Another example is China, which observes the UN sanctions on Iran, which are pretty toothless, but does not observe the US sanctions, which have absolutely no status. But even though the US has no right to issue international sanctions, the State Department issued stern warnings to China – if they want to be accepted into the international community, they have to meet international responsibilities, namely to obey US sanctions. And within imperial ideology that makes sense. Essentially it says, 'Look, we own the world, and we decide what your responsibilities are. And you meet them, or else you're in trouble.' And the imperial ideology is so deeply rooted that Westerners can't even see this.

Would you distinguish conceptually between non-state terrorism and state terrorism? There are those who argue that they are conceptually different, and therefore equating them just spreads confusion. I am talking about people like Walter Laqueur, who's no fan of yours. How do you respond to that?

NC: Of course, they're different, but there are other kinds of terrorism which are also different.

Do they require different definitions then?

NC: They don't require different definitions. Any definition you have is going to have many different types of action that fall under it.

So it's a matter of all the actions sharing core characteristics?

NC: That's right. Now Laqueur, who is a very strong advocate of terrorism – he thinks it's wonderful – has to find a definition of terrorism that meets the primary condition of excluding the states that he serves and incorporating anything they don't like. And that's the same difficult problem I mentioned earlier. But it doesn't make sense to take any of this seriously. It's like asking Iranian clerics what they say about terrorism. Who cares?

I want to quote from your book, _The Washington Connection and Third World Fascism_: 'The basic _fact_ is that the United States has organised under its sponsorship and protection a neo-colonial system of client states ruled mainly by terror and serving the interests of a small local and foreign business and military elite.'[8] This was written in 1979. Would you say that this is still the case?

NC: It's there, but it's a little harder to spell out the details. The world has become more diverse. So, for example, a lot of that book was about Latin America and Indochina, and we didn't fully know how terrible things had been there at the time; a great deal has come out since. Some of it is really mind-blowing. But the US can no longer do what they did in Latin America. Latin America, just in the last ten years, has drifted out of US control. Take, say, Brazil. The first major national security state, or neo-Nazi terrorist state, in Latin America was installed in Brazil in 1964 where there was a military coup that overthrew the democratic government, organised by the Kennedy administration. Actually, the coup took place shortly after the Kennedy assassination, but the groundwork was laid by Kennedy. It was a pretty awful terrorist state. And so the wheels were in place, and that was when the dominoes started to fall. There was this huge plague of repression all over Latin America, ending up in South America with Argentina, which was Reagan's favourite, the worst of the terrorist states. And then it centred in Central America, after this long period. But the government that the US overthrew in Brazil – the Goulart government – was not all that different from Lula's. At that point if anyone dared make policies that went against US liberals like Kennedy, we'd say, 'OK, time to institute a neo-Nazi state.' But in the case of Lula, he was their fair-haired boy, most of the time. But it's not that the attitudes have changed, it's just that the capacity to overthrow governments has changed.

Take, say, military coups. In the last decade the US has been involved in three. The first was in Venezuela, where the US quite openly backed the forces that overthrew the government and kicked out the president, but it was overturned and he returned in a couple of days after an uprising that reversed the coup. The second was in Haiti, where France and the United States, the two traditional torturers of Haiti, moved in and basically invaded and kidnapped the president and sent him off to central Africa. For years the US insisted that he never must be allowed to return and his party must be excluded from elections. The reason is that he would almost certainly win. Finally they permitted him to return, but barred his party from elections, presumably for the same reason. The third coup was in Honduras. There was a military coup that threw out the president. At first the US joined the international condemnation, tepidly to be sure, but slowly it shifted position and became one of the few countries to recognise the coup regime, ignoring the crimes it committed and the destruction of Honduran democracy. The US then supported an election under the coup regime.

Venezuela of course is one of the main targets of Western demonisation. Take, for example an article in the *New York Times* by Simon Romero, their Latin American correspondent, about the terrible homicide rate in Venezuela. Of course it is pretty bad – it's safer to be in Iraq than in Venezuela – but the idea is, 'Look what a demon Chavez is!'[9] What he didn't bother saying is that by far the worst rate of homicide in Latin America is in Honduras, the second is in El Salvador, and the third is Jamaica. So, yes, Venezuela is high, but there are a few other things to say.

So it's as though murder in Venezuela is directly related to Chavez, but in Honduras it's just something that happens?

NC: Yes, it's just the 'Latin American temperament'.

Do we still need a definition of terrorism after all this?

NC: I think the early definitions in the US Code and Army Manuals and British law are pretty good definitions.

But again, don't those definitions contradict each other?

NC: In detail, but you have to be careful about the concept of definition. Even in mathematics, definitions came along only when they were needed to advance understanding. Take, say, the concept of proof, which is essential to mathematics. There wasn't really a clear definition of it until about a century ago. All the great mathematics was done with just an intuitive concept of proof. If you take a look at Newton, his work on calculus was internally contradictory. So, for example, in one line of the proof, zero would mean zero and then a couple of lines later zero would mean as small as possible. That's not the same thing. It was pointed out that the proofs just didn't follow through. But there was an interesting split at that time – the British mathematicians tried to fix up the definitions and didn't get anywhere because not enough was understood, whereas the European mathematicians ignored the contradictions and created the great mathematics. They were working with self-contradictory notions; they knew it but they just went ahead. Finally by the mid-nineteenth century, things had reached a point where you really needed a clear concept, so leading mathematicians developed the notion of limit clearly and provided a good definition which is the one that you learn in graduate school today.

But the point is, even in mathematics definitions come along when you need them. You can't take the terms of domestic or international affairs, or any human affairs, and give them clear definitions. Definitions are internal to explanatory theories and short of a real explanatory theory, which we just don't have for any aspect of human affairs, there's not much point in truly sharpening a concept.

What about for legal purposes? Should there not be a precise definition of terrorism for legislation and punishment?

NC: The definitions in legal systems are very far from precise, in the technical sense. They are supposed to be good enough for the purposes at hand.

You say in *Perilous Power* the task is not necessarily 'to find a sharp definition but to identify a concept'.[10]

NC: Clear enough for the purpose at hand. But to try and sharpen them up would be like doing an experiment to the seventeenth decimal place, when you don't understand the second decimal place. You do things to the point where they contribute to understanding. In the case of terrorism, the early definitions are perfectly adequate to the situations we have. Though ever since there has been this huge project to try to find a new definition because the consequence of the official definitions is unacceptable. But it's nothing that people on the outside should take seriously. We should understand the social and political meaning of these efforts to develop a notion of terrorism which will apply to them but not to us.

The US Department of State currently lists, as we said earlier, Cuba, Iran, Sudan and Syria as state sponsors of terrorism. If you were compiling your own list, who would be on it?

NC: The United States would be on top of the list. Britain would maybe be second. France is high up there, and so is Israel. With Israel, take, say, the Mavi Marmara crime, which is by no means the worst act of terror, but it was piracy, kidnapping in international waters and brutal murder. If Cuba had done that, we'd practically have a nuclear war. But in this case, it's just defence. And in fact what's rarely discussed is that Israel has been doing this for 30 years. They've been hijacking boats in international waters between Cyprus and Lebanon – killing, kidnapping, and taking people to prisons in Israel. Some of them are kept as hostages for long periods; they have disappeared into the Israeli secret prison system and we don't know what's happened to them. But it's all authorised by the godfather, namely the US, so therefore it's OK. And if you want to be honest about the talk about wars and definitions and so on, although we shouldn't dismiss it, as it's of some interest, the fact of the matter is that international affairs are run like a mafia. The godfather decides what counts, and the intellectual classes are there to justify it.

NOTES

1. See International Court of Justice, 'Case Concerning the Military and Paramilitary Activities in and against Nicaragua (*Nicaragua* v. *United States of America*)', <http://tinyurl.com/y5tn5s4>.
2. Ibid.
3. International Court of Justice, 'Case Concerning Legality of Use of Force (*Yugoslavia* v. *United States of America*) (Provisional Measures)', <http://www.icj-cij.org/docket/files/114/14129.pdf>.
4. US Congress, 'US Code, Title 22, Section 2656f (d)', <http://tinyurl.com/6m5f532>.
5. Steven Lee Myers, 'Iraqi Festival Falls Prey to the Forces of Democracy', *New York Times*, 4 October 2010.
6. *Operations: US Army Field Manual*, FM 3–0, 9–37, 14 June 2001, <http://tinyurl.com/cuod9w2>.
7. Klaus Naumann, John Shalikashvili, et al., 'Towards a Grand Strategy for an Uncertain World', <http://tinyurl.com/6t3ttce>.
8. Noam Chomsky and Edward S. Herman, *The Washington Connection and Third World Fascism: The Political Economy of Human Rights, Volume 1* (Boston, Mass.: South End Press, 1979), p.ix.
9. Simon Romero, 'Venezuela, More Deadly Than Iraq, Wonders Why', *New York Times*, 22 August 2010.
10. Noam Chomsky and Gilbert Achcar, *Perilous Power: The Middle East and US Foreign Policy* (London: Hamish Hamilton, 2007), p.5.

3
Richard A. Falk
International Law and Human Rights

What do you understand by 'hegemony'? Should the United States be categorised as a 'hegemon' or an 'empire'?

Richard Falk: To be a hegemon is inherently ambiguous, usually implying some mixture of dominance and legitimacy, that is, being seen as contributing global leadership in a generally benevolent manner. As such the meaning of hegemony is subject to varying interpretations depending on how the historical role of the United States is interpreted. After the Second World War, facilitating the establishment of the UN and aiding the reconstruction of Europe, the United States was widely viewed, at least in the West, as a benevolent hegemon. In the non-West, the US was often perceived as a supporter of the colonial powers in their struggle to maintain control over their colonial possessions, and was viewed far more critically, especially by emerging elites that were more inclined to socialist development paradigms than to the capitalist ethos favoured by Washington. More recently the US has more accurately been viewed as a militarist 'empire' that fights destructive wars and intervenes in a variety of societies, especially in the Middle East to retain control over oil reserves, and lends crucial support to Israel that not only oppresses the Palestinian people but threatens to convert the entire region into a war zone. At present, the United States, with over 700 foreign military bases, navies in every ocean, a programme to militarise space, and drone bases planned for all regions of the world, is increasingly perceived in relation to its hard power diplomacy, a threat to political independence and stability for many countries. It is perhaps best viewed as an 'authoritarian democracy' within its own territory and as 'a global state' of a new kind when considered internationally.

Although the UN General Assembly passed a resolution entitled 'Inadmissibility of the Policy of Hegemonism in International Relations' in 1979 (which, incidentally, was opposed by the United States), international law has still repeatedly been used to legitimate hegemonic power. To what extent is international law intertwined with the geopolitical priorities and interests of the West? And, perhaps more importantly, is there any scope for turning international law into a counter-hegemonic tool of resistance?

RF: Throughout its history, from its modern origins in the seventeenth century, international law has served the interests of the powerful and wealthy, but also contained the potential to protect the weak and vulnerable. It is truly both a sword and a shield, and this double reality has persisted up until the present era. Historically, international law lent a measure of legality to the colonial system, and allowed the West to set the rules for participation as a sovereign state on a global level. It also protected the interests of foreign investment in countries of the global South even when these were exploitative, and deprived countries of the benefits of resources situated within their territories. At the same time, international law was also appropriated by counter-hegemonic forces to contend that existing international arrangements were immoral and needed to be supplanted by new legal rules and procedures. The struggle against the international slave trade resulted in an international treaty that made slave trading unlawful and eventually led to the international condemnation of slavery as an institution.

More recently, the idea of self-determination was gradually given credibility by international law, and it lent strong emancipatory support to movements of liberation struggling against a West-centric world order. Latin American countries used international law creatively, both to limit the protection of foreign investment by establishing the primacy of national sovereignty in relation to natural resources, and by building support for the norm on non-intervention in internal affairs. Recently, both Israel and the United States have mounted attacks on 'lawfare', that is, counter-hegemonic uses of international law to question policies associated with the occupation of Palestine and criminal tactics of warfare.

Human rights and international criminal law both illustrate the contradictory potential of international law. On one level, the imposition of human rights norms is a restraint on interventionary diplomacy, especially if coupled with respect for the legal norm of self-determination. But on another level, the protection of human rights creates a pretext for intervention as given approval by the UN Security Council in the form of the R2P (responsibility to protect) norm, as used in the 2011 Libyan intervention. The same applies with international criminal accountability. In the Goldstone Report, Israeli perpetrators of possible crimes against humanity were made subject to prosecution and punishment, although the geopolitical leverage of the United States within the UN prevents implementation. At the same time, several African leaders are being prosecuted for their crimes against humanity and participation in genocide: a double standard of sorts, given the impunity accorded to the West and Israel.

The UN Charter upholds 'the principle of the sovereign equality of all its Members'.[1] But how can this article be taken seriously when the Security Council, whose five permanent members are armed with the power of the veto, constitutes a collective hegemony?

RF: The issue of permanent membership and the veto is somewhat complicated. There was a deliberate decision after the failure of the League of Nations to make the next attempt to establish a global political actor sensitive to geopolitical realities. The underlying idea was to provide major states, defined in 1945 by reference to the winners in the Second World War (now an anachronism), with assurance that they could take part in the UN without jeopardising their national interests. In this regard, the UN has succeeded, as none of the big countries has withdrawn, and the Organisation has managed to achieve virtually universal membership of all sovereign states. Of course, during the Cold War this was a somewhat hollow victory as the two superpowers used their vetoes to block Security Council decisions that were opposed to their interests, and a demoralising gridlock resulted.

As matters now stand, the veto seems inappropriate, given the absence of any deep ideological split between major states, and definitely constrains the war-prevention mission of the UN. Similarly, the present permanent five are out of touch with geopolitical realities, and constitute a remnant of a West-centric world order, casting a shadow of illegitimacy across the activities of the most important organ of global policymaking in the UN System. To achieve effectiveness and legitimacy it is time to scrap the right of veto given to permanent members, or at least severely restrict its use. It is also time to either abandon the idea of permanent membership or broaden it to reflect the rise of non-Western states to the status of global leaders (e.g. Brazil, India, Indonesia, Turkey, South Africa), and to downgrade European representation by either giving the European Union a single seat or rotating a European state among Germany, France, UK, and Italy.

But is this achievable in reality? Would the Western powers ever consent to such an assault on their collective hegemony?

RF: Despite years of effort to make adjustments in the permanent membership, it has not been possible to reach a compromise. Most attempts have not challenged the over-representation of Europe, but have tried to find ways to add countries from the global South. Opposition has surfaced regionally, with Pakistan opposing India being given a permanent seat, and similar problems surfacing between Brazil and Argentina, and Nigeria and South Africa. Other historical issues have also arisen in relation to the claims of Japan and Germany to be treated in a manner equivalent to the United Kingdom and France. There are also concerns that addressing the representation problem by adding permanent members, especially if also granted the veto, would make the Security Council unwieldy, and not capable of reaching decisions in most conflict situations. Some suggestions have been made either to abandon the veto, or restrict its availability. Another proposal would deny the veto to new permanent members of the Security Council. So far no formula has been found that is able to generate the consensus needed to amend the UN Charter, which would be necessary, and can be blocked if any of the five current permanent members is opposed.

In the case concerning 'the Military and Paramilitary Activities in and against Nicaragua' (*Nicaragua* v. *United States of America*), the International Court of Justice (ICJ) found in favour of Nicaragua and ordered the United States to make reparations for all injuries caused. When the US refused to comply with the judgement of the ICJ, Nicaragua brought the matter to the Security Council, where it was duly vetoed by the United States. What is the relevance of the ICJ when its judgements have to be enforced by the Security Council?

RF: The experience in the Nicaragua litigation illustrates the pervasiveness of a geopolitical veto that is more extensive than the Security Council prerogative. As a party to the ICJ, the US had an obligation to uphold adverse judgements, but was able to shift implementation to the Security Council where its veto was available. This experience reveals the primacy of geopolitics in relation to international law and international institutional authority. If the geopolitical wind had been blowing in the same direction as the findings in the Nicaragua judgement, that is, if the decision had been supportive of the US position, then the United States would have been quick to seek sanctions in the Security Council to reinforce its claims under international law. It remains important, however, to appreciate that even though such counter-hegemonic applications of international law can be neutralised, they are still significant. There is an impact on world public opinion and civil society forces. In the Nicaragua context, despite repudiating the decision explicitly, the US Government complied de facto with the main finding, the unlawfulness of blockading Nicaragua's ports. International law in its counter-hegemonic uses is very important in any domain where issues of legitimacy are significant, but is rarely able to have a corresponding behavioural impact. Similarly, the Goldstone Report establishes the credibility of the accusations directed at Israel with respect to its tactics used during the 2008–09 attacks on Gaza, but was not able to facilitate the next step that would have involved activating accountability mechanisms either within Israel or at the level of international society.

The legal scholar, Balakrishnan Rajagopal, claims that the international human rights movement has a 'birth defect' because it failed to mount a challenge to colonialism at the time.[2] Indeed, many of the endorsing governments of the Universal Declaration of Human Rights (UDHR), which was adopted by the UN General Assembly in 1948, were European colonial powers, some of which exerted incredible pressure at the drafting stage of the document to block any reference to the right of self-determination. Has the international human rights movement outgrown its 'birth defect'? Has it now developed a discourse that can also represent those countries and social movements which resist hegemony?

RF: I think the Rajagopal birth defect reflected the geopolitical realities that existed at the time the Universal Declaration was drafted and endorsed, in a manner parallel to the birth defect embedded in the overall constitutional structure of the UN, as most dramatically expressed by the operating procedures of the UN Security Council discussed above. It needs to be realised that a framework document such as the UDHR is a living legal organism that evolves over time, incorporating changes in the global climate of opinion. At the time, due to the concerns of the colonial powers the right of self-determination was not included among its provisions, yet by 1966 when the two human covenants were negotiated, the right of self-determination was elevated to the status of a common Article 1, and understood to be both inalienable and to inform the interpretation of all other rights. At the same time, the UDHR has some truly radical provisions that have been ignored, but remain authoritative if the political climate encourages their actualisation. For instance, Article 25 confers upon all persons the right to have a standard of living sufficient to meet the basic material needs of an individual and family. Article 28 goes even further, mandating the establishment of an international order that has the will and capacity to realise all other rights set forth in the Declaration. In passing it is worth noting that even in these idealistic provisions the UDHR was captive of the patriarchal language prevalent at the time, referring in Article 25, for instance, to the right of everyone 'to a standard of living adequate for the health and well-being of *himself* and of *his family*'.[3] It is inconceivable that such phrasing would be used if the UDHR were to be redrafted in 2012, as women have managed to change the normative atmosphere at least enough to render unacceptable discriminatory language of this sort.

There is another point to observe here. The UDHR has become an iconic document over the course of more than six decades, the starting point for discussions of whether or not the rights as set forth are truly universal or slanted to reflect the hegemony of Western values, especially those associated with liberal individualism. In 1948, when the majority of governments were actually in their domestic practices hostile to human rights, it was only possible to get approval for the Declaration because it was understood to be *unenforceable*! This feature of the process was underscored by calling the document a 'declaration' rather than a 'statement of principles' or a 'treaty' with obligatory implications. What led to the rise of human rights, and expressions of respect for the provisions of the UDHR, were three main developments: the activism of human rights NGOs that viewed UDHR as obligatory and were able to embarrass many governments in ways that induced unexpected degrees of compliance; the US 'discovery' of human rights during the Carter presidency in the late 1970s as part of an effort to restore America's moral reputation after its humiliating experiences in the Vietnam War; and perhaps most important of all, the degree to which human rights allowed the global anti-apartheid campaign to become a political project that contributed to the collapse of the racist regime in South Africa.

Western human rights groups, such as Amnesty International (AI) and Human Rights Watch (HRW), refused to take a stand on the legality of the Iraq War, in spite of widespread protests around the world. No such 'neutrality' was evident in an HRW report on Venezuela (2008), which was criticised in an open letter by 100 experts on Latin America as a 'politically motivated essay'.[4] To what extent do you think these human rights groups are politically motivated? And should those who are engaged in counter-hegemonic struggle, particularly in the global South, dissociate from them completely?

RF: This issue is tricky. There is no doubt that the private-funding base of these leading human rights NGOs leads to some biasing of their agendas, and that it is necessary to make this deficiency visible through critical reflection. At the same time, it is important to have such organisations dependent on voluntary contributions, rather than being like Freedom House and the two pro-democracy groups funded in the United States by Congress and aligned with the two main political parties (the International Republican Institute (IRI) and the National Democratic Institute for International Affairs (NDIIA)). In this respect, in most cases collaboration still seems to be desirable on a North/South basis, provided those NGOs in the global South do so with eyes wide open, and those of us in the North do our job of exposing and criticising. In my experience there has been some progress, although the problem remains serious. For instance, in the early period, the work of the main human rights NGOs was overwhelmingly concerned with the human wrongs of the Soviet system, and then secondarily with 'prisoners of conscience' held in captivity by governments in the global South. Gradually, in reaction to criticism there has been more self-criticism directed at American patterns of abuse, and a greater willingness to report critically on Israel. Often the criticisms are too mild, but in the United States they have been helpful in opening space for a more balanced dialogue, especially outside the governmental centre of authority in Washington, where closed minds preclude any kind of truthful accounting with respect to human rights in relation either to American military activities around the world, or with respect to Israel's consistent defiance of international law.

Since 1989, the United States has shifted its attention to democracy promotion and human rights, both of which have been irrevocably linked with free-market economics. As a consequence, 'democracy' has become synonymous with free trade and 'human rights' have been reduced to political and civil rights (with economic and social rights, which were also included in the UDHR document, sidelined). But are democracy and human rights even compatible with free-market economics?

RF: This is an important issue that is rarely discussed intelligently. I would respond in two different ways. First, there are degrees of incompatibility, and there are more factors relevant to upholding democracy and human rights than the operation of neoliberal markets. Perhaps this point can be initially made by reference to the decline of democracy and the erosion of human rights within the United States since the 9/11 attacks. The atmosphere of fear and security manipulated by the government has converted American citizens into terrorist suspects who are all subject to arbitrary and unreviewable detention and surveillance. Cumulatively, American society is sliding toward a new form of 'authoritarian democracy'. Elections continue, free speech is generally protected, institutions operate in accordance with the Constitution, but the reality of state–society relations is dramatically altered by the counter-terrorist claims of emergency rule and the right of exception. Even our sense of the free market is variable, shifting from a more welfare-oriented model after the Great Depression to a capital-driven market after the collapse of socialism as a viable alternative. That is, post-1989 capitalism was far more unfriendly to economic and social rights than was the prior capitalism seeking to win public approval as a more compassionate economic arrangement than that which prevailed in state socialist economies. The deliberate weakening of the labour movement by the machinations of market fundamentalists, gaining momentum during the periods when Margaret Thatcher led the United Kingdom and Ronald Reagan governed in the United States, also contributed to the decline of human rights. In effect, the systemic incompatibility between free-market capitalism and the quality of democratic life and respect for human rights has to be modified to take account of such contextual variables as wartime, security threats, and the societal balance between entrepreneurial and working classes.

At the same time there are systemic incompatibilities that should be acknowledged. The capitalist priority is efficiency of capital and profitability, which is generally inconsistent with protecting the vulnerabilities of people and nature. In the current setting the situation of the poor is neglected despite the grotesque wealth of the capitalist elites, and the dangers to the well-being of humanity associated with climate change are ignored despite a strong scientific consensus warning of the adverse, and possibly irreversible, consequences of further delays in reducing the level of greenhouse gas emissions, especially carbon. Nothing more vividly illustrates this incompatibility than the millions being devoted by the oil and gas industry to sponsoring climate sceptics, which, with the complicity of the media, have induced public confusion and indifference, with likely serious effects on future human well-being. In these regards capitalism is in crisis both morally, due to widening disparities of income and wealth and disclosures of abusive practices, and ecologically, due to its refusal to make business adjustments in accounting procedures that pass the consequences of emissions to the public and the future.

When Spain requested the extradition of the former Chilean dictator, General Augusto Pinochet, from the United Kingdom to face charges relating to torture, terrorism and genocide in 1998, it invoked the principle of Universal Jurisdiction (UJ). This was later attacked by Pinochet's close ally, Henry Kissinger, the former US secretary of state and national security advisor, who called the legal case against Pinochet 'a dangerous precedent', warning that states with authoritarian governments could now also exercise universal jurisdiction and try foreign nationals in domestic courts with limited or no judicial independence.[5] You have also stated that you are unsure 'whether the world as a whole is ready for universal jurisdiction in criminal proceedings based on Pinochet-like cases'.[6] Should domestic courts refrain from making judgements on serious breaches of international criminal law until more general guidelines are established?

RF: This question raised difficulties for me. On the one side, I welcome prosecutions of individuals such as Pinochet, and would welcome the indictment, prosecution, and punishment of Kissinger. On the other side is the geopolitical reality that only those in the global South are likely to experience the impact of UJ. The problem is not one of the absence of 'general guidelines', as these exist in various places, maybe most authoritatively in the list of international crimes given in the Statute of the International Criminal Court (ICC). As elsewhere in my responses, the main challenge is what to do in the face of double standards. Those who should be rendered accountable under international criminal law, the Kissingers of this world, enjoy de facto impunity, while those who come from countries that have long been targets of hegemonic abuse are used as poster children of accountability.

Pinochet is a kind of hybrid case as his ascent to power and his abuses enjoyed the support of and encouragement from Washington, and especially from Kissinger. It is of course amusingly self-serving for Kissinger to be the one warning of the pitfalls of UJ! One of these pitfalls that actually exists is the sense that the liberal democracies of the North would occupy the high moral ground by making the main culprits of the world all appear to be situated in the South. This pattern is already part of the first decade of experience in the ICC, which goes after a series of African leaders, but tells Palestine that it has no standing to pursue its claims concerning Israel's Gaza attacks because Palestine has not been recognised as a state within the United Nations. This issue of expanding the reach of international criminal law by reliance on the use of UJ by domestic courts needs to be balanced against the injustice of according impunity to those with strong geopolitical backing. It is notable that several western European countries backtracked on UJ after threats of retaliatory moves by the United States and

Israel. There is no doubt that the domain of UJ is a geopolitical battleground.

Indeed, war crimes and torture charges were also filed against the former US Secretary of Defense Donald Rumsfeld and other senior officials in German courts in 2006, but led to nothing. Does what you say about the impunity of figures like Kissinger and the influence of the US in Europe suggest that UJ is a dead end? What can be gained by charging US state representatives?

RF: At this stage there exists de facto impunity for such Western international political personalities from the perspective of formal legal mechanisms. But the fact that UJ exists in relation to serious international crimes does convey two important aspects of the global reality: first, that such individuals would be held accountable if international law was applied without regard to geopolitics, and second, that there is enough ambiguity about the reach of UJ that it inhibits such individuals and conveys an impression of de facto criminality.

There are several considerations that bear on an appraisal of UJ. The weaknesses and biases of the international mechanisms of accountability make it seem desirable to extend the domain of accountability by empowering domestic courts to act as agents of the world legal system. Even if there is no consistent application of UJ, it still leads those who might be prosecuted to alter their travel plans to avoid even the complication of waiting for a complaint to be dismissed. It has been reported that both George W. Bush and Dick Cheney are reluctant to travel to democratic countries where the UJ provision exists. Also, even the dismissal of a complaint as took place with regard to Rumsfeld calls attention to his criminal record, alerts civil society to this fact, and may produce indirect pressures that disrupt the comfort level of unindicted war criminals.

On the cautionary side, UJ could be used to achieve some kind of ideologically motivated criminalisation of 'the other' that would discredit and derail a constructive effort to develop a credible meta-law that governs the behaviour of leaders of sovereign states. It should be appreciated that this whole effort to hold leaders of states criminally responsible is a rather radical challenge to territorial sovereignty and a repudiation of the whole related ethos of 'sovereign immunity'. Such an undertaking assumed seriousness after the Nuremberg and Tokyo trials of surviving German and Japanese political and military leaders, and although tainted by its character of being 'victors' justice' it did set up a series of expectations that the legal status of these undertakings would be determined by whether in the future those who sat in judgement would accept the same standards being applied to themselves. In fact, this 'Nuremberg Promise' has been broken and the trials to some extent invalidated.[7]

My conclusion is that it is on balance desirable to encourage UJ, and to create pressure from below to make application of such jurisdiction as consistent as possible. I think this will act as a deterrent in some situations, although this impact will never be acknowledged by those affected as it would only embolden civil society to intensify its pressures. There may come a future time when the ICC provides a sufficiently comprehensive and consistent regime for the enforcement of international criminal law against state crime as to make UJ redundant, but such a circumstance is not likely to emerge in the near future.

The Chilean government considered the Spanish proceedings as 'an illegitimate invasion of the jurisdiction of the Chilean courts'.[8] Should the foreign domestic courts not have respected the primacy of Chilean jurisdiction in the Pinochet case, particularly since Chile was a constitutional democracy at that point? Or did Chile in fact require such international pressure in order eventually to act against Pinochet by stripping him of his immunity from prosecution?

RF: I think this is a question that is difficult to answer aside from the specifics of a given situation. In the Pinochet context it seemed that Chile was honouring its amnesty law, and was unlikely to prosecute Pinochet when Spain issued its extradition request and Britain detained Pinochet during a visit for medical examinations. At the same time, there is a sense that to avoid partisanship in relation to the application of international criminal law, it is desirable to defer to the country where the crimes took place if there exists a reasonable prospect that justice will be rendered. It is also likely to be true that the evidence and witnesses will be more readily available, but it may also be true, as was the case in Chile, that there were fears that the transition to democracy might be blocked if the amnesty compromise was suspended and accountability imposed on Pinochet. In the end, given international pressures and the British legal determination that Pinochet should be held accountable for violations of the Torture Convention, the Chilean government shifted its position and initiated several prosecutions of Pinochet, although none were carried to a legal conclusion due to his failing health and subsequent death.

Although the Convention on the Prevention and Punishment of the Crime of Genocide (1948) defined genocide as 'acts committed with intent to destroy, in whole or in part, a national, ethnical, racial, or religious group',[9] the Spanish courts extended the concept to include 'political groups'. Is it now time to move beyond the present text of the Genocide Convention? Should the crime of 'political genocide' be recognised under international law?

RF: I think if there is to be a crime of 'political genocide' it needs to be formulated with great care and precision to avoid unpopular views from being criminalised. As matters now stand, the combination of genocide, as conventionally understood, and crimes against humanity, seems sufficient to cover the criminality of political leaders, and the lethal consequences of totalising ideologies. With Islamophobic tendencies in Europe and North America it is quite possible that Islamic leaders could be charged with 'political genocide'. An extremist American pastor in a small Florida church held a trial that convicted the Koran of encouraging the murder of non-Muslims and of being responsible for the 9/11 attacks. It is this sort of outlook that would be encouraged to claim that Islam embodied 'political genocide', a development that would have many negative effects on inter-civilisational relations within and among countries.

The Spanish courts also charged Pinochet with terrorism, which is interesting because there is still widespread disagreement within the international community over whether states or their authorised agents should even be included in the definition of terrorism. How important is it that this definitional stalemate is resolved? What are the obstacles to its resolution?

RF: It was a step forward to charge Pinochet with terrorism, and to acknowledge that the essence of the crime is the use of political violence to induce great fear in society and against those who are innocent, and not just such violence that is directed against the state by opposition groups. It may be that there is so much ambiguity and ideology attached to the term 'terrorism' that it is best to avoid its use altogether, as it is likely to be twisted in public discourse to demonise the enemies of the established order, while exempting state violence from legal and moral scrutiny. As powerful interests have a large stake in the one-sided conception of terrorism it is unlikely that the welcome Spanish departure from this pattern will be often repeated.

The ICC can only prosecute terrorist acts if they fall within the categories of genocide, crimes against humanity, or war crimes. Do you think that its jurisdiction should extend to terrorism specifically? And if so, would this make the participation of the United States in the Court all the more unlikely?

RF: Of course, this raises questions that were partially addressed in the prior response. It would not be desirable to include 'terrorism' among international crimes subject to ICC jurisdiction if defined to apply only to anti-state acts of violence. The failure to include terrorism as a distinct crime was due to the inability to agree upon its proper definition. In this regard, if the Spanish approach in the Pinochet case were to be adopted by the ICC, then it does seem that this would be an additional impediment to US participation, but it would be a delegitimising mistake to tempt the United States to become a party to the Rome Treaty by agreeing to define terrorism narrowly in the manner favoured by the American government. With a reactionary US Congress there is, in any event, no likelihood of securing American participation even if the current parties to the treaty were to go along with Washington's views on terrorism.

NOTES

1. *Charter of the United Nations*, Article 2(1).
2. Balakrishnan Rajagopal, 'The International Human Rights Movement Today', *Maryland Journal of International Law*, Vol.24 (2009), pp.56–62 (p.57).
3. 'The Universal Declaration of Human Rights', Article 25(1), <http://tinyurl.com/n68aou> (emphasis added).
4. For the full text of the letter, see <http://nacla.org/node/5334>.
5. Henry Kissinger, 'The Pitfalls of Universal Jurisdiction', *Foreign Affairs*, July–August 2001.
6. Richard Falk, *Achieving Human Rights* (New York: Routledge, 2007), p.120.
7. See Karl Jaspers, *The Question of German Guilt*, trans. E.B. Ashton (New York: Fordham University Press, 2000).
8. *When Tyrants Tremble: The Pinochet Case*, Human Rights Watch, Vol.11, No.1 (1999), <http://www.hrw.org/reports/1999/chile/>.
9. 'Convention on the Prevention and Punishment of the Crime of Genocide', Article 2, <http://www.hrweb.org/legal/genocide.html>.

4

Marjorie Cohn
Torture as Terrorism

What is the definition of torture?

Marjorie Cohn: The United States has ratified the Convention against Torture and Other Cruel, Inhuman or Degrading Treatment or Punishment (the Torture Convention), making it part of US law under the Supremacy Clause of the Constitution, which says that treaties shall be the supreme law of the land. The Torture Convention defines torture as the intentional infliction of severe physical or mental pain or suffering by someone acting in an official capacity, in order to obtain information from the person being tortured or a third person, or for purposes of punishment, or discrimination, or intimidation.

Is it ever justified to torture a person?

MC: No. The Torture Convention says, 'No exceptional circumstances whatsoever, whether a state of war or a threat of war, internal political instability or any other public emergency, may be invoked as a justification for torture.'[1]

But considering that it is sometimes justified to kill people (for instance, just war theorists would grant that it is justified to kill combatants under certain conditions in war), why is it never justified to torture?

MC: The prohibition against torture is a *jus cogens* norm. *Jus cogens* is Latin for 'higher law' or 'compelling law'. This means that no country can ever pass a law that allows torture. There can be no immunity from criminal liability for violation of a *jus* *cogens* prohibition. Other *jus cogens* norms include genocide, slavery, and waging wars of aggression.

What about morally speaking? Some people might accept that torture is illegal, but argue that it could be morally justified in certain extreme circumstances, for instance, to prevent a greater crime. How would you respond to this type of argument?

MC: As philosopher John Lango explains in his chapter in *The United States and Torture: Interrogation, Incarceration, and Abuse*,[2] 'Terrorism can never warrant terroristic torment.' Also, he debunks the so-called 'ticking time bomb' scenario as a fantasy. There is no guarantee that we will know who the terrorist is who knows where the ticking bomb is located, and that torturing him will lead us to the bomb and save millions of lives. Torture is immoral in all circumstances.

As you said, the United States is a signatory to the Torture Convention, which was adopted by the United Nations General Assembly in 1984. Article 3.1 clearly states that outsourcing torture to proxies is illegal, and yet the US has been involved in 'extraordinary rendition', whereby suspects are transferred without legal proceeding for interrogation to countries with a record of using torture. Has rendition always been US-led? How have EU states and private companies contributed to this process? And how do you evaluate the impotence of international law in the face of such blatant violations of legal norms and obligations?

MC: The United States has not only signed, but has also ratified the Torture Convention. That makes it a party to this treaty and it is therefore bound by the treaty's mandates and prohibitions. Another treaty the United States has ratified is the International Covenant on Civil Political Rights (ICCPR), which prohibits 'states parties' from subjecting persons 'to torture or to cruel, inhuman, or degrading treatment or punishment'.[3] The Human Rights Committee, which is the body that monitors the ICCPR, has interpreted that prohibition to forbid states parties from exposing 'individuals to the danger of torture or cruel, inhuman or degrading treatment or punishment upon return to another country by way of their extradition, expulsion or *refoulement*'.[4]

The United States has participated in extraordinary renditions for more than 20 years. Before the terrorist attacks of 11 September 2001, however, this practice was usually limited to people subject to foreign arrest warrants. Since 9/11, US involvement in extraordinary renditions, sometimes called 'outsourcing torture', has increased dramatically. Terrorism suspects in Europe, Asia, Africa, and the Middle East have been rendered to foreign countries such as Egypt, Syria, Morocco, and Jordan, all notorious for torture. The Council of Europe has identified 14 European states which have apparently cooperated with the United States in extraordinary renditions. For example, Sweden assisted the United States in rendering prisoners to Egypt where they were then subjected to torture. There are secret CIA prisons, called 'black sites', in many countries, including Romania and Poland, in which prisoners have been tortured after having been rendered there. There are reports that Turkey, Germany, Spain, and Cyprus provided 'staging posts' and the United Kingdom, Greece, Portugal, and Ireland served as 'stop-off points' for persons being rendered to other countries, where they were tortured. Private companies, such as Jeppesen Dataplan, Inc., a subsidiary of Boeing, have provided flight planning and logistical support services to aircraft and crews used by the CIA to forcibly render prisoners for torture.

Legal proceedings have occurred in the United States and several European countries to secure redress for victims of torture after extraordinary rendition. Lawsuits have faced judicial and political obstacles, such as the 'state secrets privilege' that George W. Bush and Barack Obama have successfully used to prevent litigation of these cases in the United States. Criminal cases have also been filed in Europe, with some success. For example, an Italian judge convicted 22 CIA operatives and a US Air Force colonel of arranging the kidnapping of a Muslim cleric in Milan in 2003, then flying him to Egypt where he was tortured. Hassan Mustafa Osama Nasr told Human Rights Watch in 2007 that he was 'hung up like a slaughtered sheep and given electrical shocks' while in Egypt. 'I was brutally tortured and I could hear the screams of others who were tortured too', he added.[5] The convicted Americans face arrest if they travel outside the United States, although they will not be likely to face the consequences of their convictions unless they travel to Italy, or to another country which then extradites them to Italy. This is an unusual case, as any political pressure the United States may have exerted on the Italian government did not prevent the conviction. On the other hand, some European cases investigating US officials under universal jurisdiction have been dismissed after the US government applied political pressure to governmental authorities in those countries, notably Belgium during the Bush administration and Spain during Obama's tenure. However, approximately 70 countries worldwide have enacted freedom of information laws, notably the United States, Albania, Macedonia, Poland, and Romania. Freedom of information cases can reveal important information and educate the public about rendition cases. They can also strengthen ongoing criminal and civil investigations.

Some theorists distinguish between 'interrogational torture' and 'terroristic torture'. The latter is considered to be 'torture used as a deterrent, a statement of intent by the State. [It] is meant as a signal to those who defy the legitimacy of State authorities'.[6] Guatemala can be used as an example here. During the counter-insurgency campaign in Guatemala (1960–96), the army targeted rural populations with the aim of cutting off the support to guerrillas. The bodies of torture victims would be displayed to relatives and neighbours or simply left on the side of the road for everyone to see. Newspapers would also publish photographs of mutilated bodies, which often acted as a warning to citizens not to oppose the ruling regime. We want to ask: First, is the distinction between 'interrogational torture' and 'terroristic torture' helpful? And, if so, would you classify the more recent use of torture in, say, Guantánamo Bay or Abu Ghraib, as terroristic torture?

MC: The distinction is relevant. Torture is sometimes used during interrogations to secure information from the person being tortured. This kind of torture and cruel, inhuman, and degrading treatment – both illegal under US law – was widespread during the Bush administration's 'war on terror'.[7] Interrogational torture took place in Iraq, Afghanistan, Guantánamo Bay, and the secret CIA 'black sites'.

Interrogators agree that torture is not efficacious to glean intelligence. Glenn L. Carle, who supervised the 2002 interrogation of a high-level detainee for the CIA, told the *New York Times* that coercive techniques 'didn't provide useful, meaningful, trustworthy information'.[8] Likewise, Ali Soufan, who interrogated Abu Zubaydah, testified before Congress that harsh interrogation techniques 'are ineffective, slow, and unreliable, and as a result harmful to our efforts to defeat al-Qaida'.[9] Soufan maintains that any useful information Zubaydah provided happened before the 'enhanced interrogation techniques' were utilised. Matthew Alexander, a former senior military interrogator who supervised or conducted 1,300 interrogations in Iraq, which led to the capture of several al-Qaeda leaders, echoes Soufan's sentiments. Alexander said, 'I think that without a doubt, torture and enhanced interrogation techniques slowed down the hunt for bin Laden'.[10] Indeed, a 2006 study by the National Defense Intelligence College found that traditional, rapport-building interrogation techniques are extremely effective even with the most hardened detainees, but coercive tactics create resistance and resentment.

When I testified in 2008 before the House Judiciary Committee's Subcommittee on the Constitution, Civil Rights, and Civil Liberties about Bush administration interrogation policy, one of the Republican congressmen asked me how I would fashion an interrogation statute. I replied that it would require humane, kind, respectful treatment to develop trust. As the questioner sniggered, Professor Philippe Sands, who also testified on the same panel that day, said I was correct, that the British got much better intelligence from the Irish Republican Army when they used humane techniques.

In her chapter in *The United States and Torture*, journalist Jane Mayer discusses Ibn Sheikh al-Libi, who was tortured in CIA custody. Al-Libi provided a link between Saddam

Hussein and al-Qaeda, which Colin Powell cited in his speech before the Security Council as he tried to secure a resolution authorising the invasion of Iraq. The CIA knew al-Libi's information was false; indeed, he later recanted, and died under mysterious circumstances.

On the other hand, terroristic torture has also been used widely, especially by dictatorships in Latin America during the 1970s and 1980s, when the United States was supporting those repressive governments. People would be 'disappeared' in broad daylight, for all to see, and then taken to locations where they were tortured within earshot of people in the community. This was designed to send a message to would-be dissenters not to challenge the powers that be. Sister Dianna Ortiz, a Catholic nun who went to Guatemala in the mid 1980s to teach English, was kidnapped and brutally tortured by Guatemalan authorities who were working with the US government. She writes in the preface to *The United States and Torture*:

> So often it is assumed that torture is conducted for the purpose of gaining information. It is much more often intended to threaten populations into silence and submission. What I was to endure was a message, a warning to others – not to oppose, to remain silent and to yield to power without question. In Guatemala, the Catholic Church sought to walk in company with the suffering poor. I was to be a message board upon which those in power would write a warning to the Church to cease its opposition or be prepared to face the full force of the state.[11]

Terroristic torture has also been used in the 'war on terror' to discourage critics of US policy, both at home and abroad.

The historian Eric Hobsbawm writes how during the Argentinean dictatorship (1976–83) all officers in a unit would be 'obliged to take part in torture in order to bond them together in what was recognised as shared infamy'.[12] Would you say that people lose their moral compass when placed within certain social contexts? Should the blame in these situations ultimately fall on senior officers and/or political leaders?

MC: Many people who are forced to participate in torture later suffer from post-traumatic stress disorder. This happened during Bush's 'war on terror'. Former FBI agent Dan Coleman told Jane Mayer, 'Brutalization doesn't work. We know that. Besides, you lose your soul.'[13]

Under the well-established doctrine of 'command responsibility', commanders are liable for torture (considered a war crime under the Geneva Conventions and the US Torture Statute) if they knew or should have known their subordinates would commit torture and they did nothing to stop or prevent it. Bush officials Dick Cheney, Condoleezza Rice, George Tenet, John Ashcroft, Alberto Gonzales, Colin Powell, and Bush himself, as well as their lawyers, including John Yoo and Jay Bybee, engaged in a common plan to authorise torture in violation of the Convention against Torture and the Geneva Conventions. They knew that interrogators would take action based on that authorisation. These officials and lawyers should be investigated and prosecuted for war crimes under US law.

But this has not happened. Why not?

MC: President Obama's Justice Department proclaimed its intention to grant a free pass to Bush officials and their lawyers who constructed the regime of torture and abuse. Attorney General Eric H. Holder, Jr. announced on 30 June 2011, that his office will investigate only two instances of detainee mistreatment. He said the department 'has determined that an expanded criminal investigation of the remaining matters is not warranted'.[14] Holder has granted impunity to those who authorised, provided legal cover, and carried out the 'remaining matters'.

Both of the incidents that Holder has agreed to investigate involved egregious treatment and both resulted in death. These two deaths should be investigated and those responsible punished in accordance with the law. The investigation must have a much broader scope, however. More than 100 detainees have died in US custody, many from torture. And untold numbers were subjected to torture and cruel treatment in violation of US and international law. General Barry McCaffrey said, 'We tortured people unmercifully. We probably murdered dozens of them during the course of that, both the armed forces and the CIA.'[15]

Some theorists find a connection between torture and race. It is claimed that it is much easier to abuse a person who is considered a racially or culturally inferior 'other', particularly if the discourse is framed along the lines of a 'civilising mission'. But torture also takes place domestically. During the Pinochet years (1973–90), for instance, Chileans tortured Chileans. Those tortured were considered to be communist subversives, or ideological 'others', but race was not an issue. To what extent is race or culture a motivating factor for torture?

MC: The overwhelming number of detainees who were tortured and abused by US forces during the 'war on terror' were non-white. I don't believe we would have seen such widespread cruelty against white detainees. But at the same time, the war against terrorism is the current incarnation of the war on communism, in which numerous human rights and civil rights violations were perpetrated during the Cold War. People were tortured for ideological reasons, for opposing those in power. People have also been tortured throughout history for religious reasons.

But why would we not have seen such widespread torture with white detainees, when as you say people are also tortured for ideological or religious reasons? Is there any reason to believe that, say, anti-Arab sentiment has made the torture in the 'war on terror' worse?

MC: I think so. For example, in the wake of the 11 September attacks, more than 1,200 Muslim, South Asian and Arab non-citizens were rounded up by the Immigration and Naturalization Service and the FBI in one of the most extensive incidents of racial profiling in the United States since people of Japanese descent were interned during the Second World War. None was ever charged with any connection to terrorism. A

December 2003 report by the Department of Justice's Office of the Inspector General investigated allegations of physical and verbal abuse of non-citizen prisoners by the Federal Bureau of Prisons' Metropolitan Detention Center (MDC) in Brooklyn, New York.[16] The report concluded that several MDC staff members slammed and bounced detainees into the walls, twisted or bent their arms, hands, wrists, or fingers, pulled their thumbs back, tripped them, and dragged them on the floor. The Center for Constitutional Rights filed a class action lawsuit in 2002, on behalf of people detained by the United States in the racial profiling dragnet after 9/11.[17] In November 2009, five of the seven plaintiffs settled their claims for $1.26 million from the United States. So, although torture is not only used against people of colour, the racial element creates an excess of abuse beyond that which may otherwise occur.

The horrific photographs from Abu Ghraib mostly involved male prisoners. And yet we know that there are also photographs of women prisoners being tortured, abused and raped, which, incidentally, have not been released to the public. Why have the experiences of women at Abu Ghraib not received as much attention?

MC: Many pictures taken at Abu Ghraib were shown to Congress but not released to the public. According to Major General Antonio Taguba, who conducted an inquiry into the Abu Ghraib scandal, 'These pictures show torture, abuse, rape and every indecency.'[18] At least one shows the rape of a female prisoner by an American soldier. In another photo, a female prisoner is having her clothes forcibly removed to expose her breasts. President Obama refused to allow them to be publicly released, saying they could put our troops at risk. Women held at Abu Ghraib begged their families to smuggle poison into the prisons so they could kill themselves because of the humiliation they suffered at the hands of US forces.

Former Navy General Counsel Alberto Mora testified before Congress that the two most effective recruiting tools for those who would do harm to US soldiers in Iraq were Abu Ghraib and Guantánamo. When people see the US government torturing detainees from their countries, they resent us even more. Indeed, an interrogator currently serving in Afghanistan, told *Forbes*:

> I cannot even count the amount of times that I personally have come face to face with detainees, who told me they were primarily motivated to do what they did, because of hearing that we committed torture ... Torture committed by Americans in the past continues to kill Americans today.[19]

Muslims are likely to be even more offended at the torture of women, who are often veiled and many covered with the burka to shield them from public eyes.

Of course, in Abu Ghraib, a woman was also one of the perpetrators of torture. In fact, Lynndie England, the female private who in one shocking photograph was seen posing with a naked and bloodied male prisoner on a leash, became the face of the Abu Ghraib scandal. She later claimed that she was an uneducated young woman who was unduly influenced by her lover, Specialist Charles Graner, but the general verdict appears to be that she was the 'monster' of Abu Ghraib. Why is it so disturbing when women torture? Why do they become infamous while women victims of torture remain anonymous and invisible?

MC: Lynndie England was apparently in love with Charles Graner and probably influenced by him. As former Brigadier General Janis Karpinski noted, England did not think of those torture methods on her own. The same methods were used by US forces in other places besides Abu Ghraib. Techniques of torture and abuse migrated from Guantánamo to Iraq via General Geoffrey Miller. General Miller oversaw interrogations at the United States prison at Guantánamo Bay, Cuba. He was sent to Abu Ghraib to transfer his interrogation system from Cuba to Iraq. It was on his watch that the worst mistreatment, depicted in the publicised photographs, occurred.

It is disturbing when anyone commits torture. The photos of England with detainees at Abu Ghraib became iconic, not only because she was a woman but also because she looked so young. Most people would be surprised and perhaps more offended that members of the 'fair sex' would engage in torture. On the other hand, although many women have been tortured, not only in Abu Ghraib, but during the 'dirty wars' in Latin America and by the Shah of Iran, for example, they are not widely reported in the media. Perhaps in both these cases this is because women are not generally thought of as soldiers, so it seems more shocking when a woman commits torture, but it is more shameful and repulsive to think of women as victims of torture, as they cannot simply be dismissed as 'enemy combatants' or terrorists.

You mentioned that torture methods were being used in locations besides Abu Ghraib. Is there clear evidence that US forces employed a *systematic* programme of torture throughout its detention centres, contrary to the idea that a few low-ranking rogue individuals were responsible?

MC: Bush admitted that he approved of high-level meetings of the National Security Council Principals Committee in which harsh interrogation techniques, including water boarding, were authorised by Dick Cheney, Condoleezza Rice, John Ashcroft, Colin Powell, Donald Rumsfeld and George Tenet.[20] Cheney has also publicly confessed to ordering war crimes. Asked about water boarding in an *ABC News* interview, Cheney replied, 'I was aware of the program, certainly, and involved in helping get the process cleared.'[21]

There is widespread use of stun guns, electric cattle prods, 'restraint chairs', chemical sprays, and dogs within the US prison system. Many prisoners have also reported being beaten, raped, and put in solitary confinement for long periods of time. Last year, prisoners at California's high-security Pelican Bay State Prison went on a hunger strike to protest what they called were 'torturous conditions', and similar protests have taken place in other prisons around the country. Would you say that the way in which the US treats its own prisoners also qualifies as torture?

MC: Yes. As journalist Lance Tapley points out in his chapter in *The United States and Torture*, cell extractions – where prisoners are dragged and beaten – as well as solitary confinement – which is considered torture as it can lead to hallucinations, catatonia, and suicide – are commonplace in America's supermax prisons. Inmates in Pelican Bay's Security Housing Unit (SHU) are confined to their cells for 22½ hours a day, mostly for administrative convenience. They are released for only one hour to walk in a small area with high walls. The cells in the SHU are eight feet by ten feet with no windows. Fluorescent lights are often kept on 24 hours per day.

The Commission on Safety and Abuse in America's Prisons (CSAAP), which is headed by a former US attorney general and a former chief judge of the US Court of Appeals, found that '[p]eople who pose no real threat to anyone and also those who are mentally ill are languishing for months or years in high-security units'. The Commission also stated: 'In some places, the environment is so severe that people end up completely isolated, confined in constantly bright or constantly dim spaces without any meaningful contact – torturous conditions that are proven to cause mental deterioration.'[22]

As of this interview, Bradley Manning has been held for 20 months in military custody. During the first eight months, he was kept in solitary confinement in the military brig at Quantico, Virginia. Manning was also humiliated by being stripped naked and paraded before other inmates. This treatment violates the Convention against Torture and Other Cruel, Inhuman or Degrading Treatment or Punishment. Juan Ernesto Mendez, United Nations special rapporteur on torture, said that 'Manning was subjected to cruel, inhuman and degrading treatment in the excessive and prolonged isolation he was put in during the eight months he was in Quantico'.[23]

NOTES

1. 'The Convention against Torture and Other Cruel, Inhuman or Degrading Treatment or Punishment', G.A. res.39/46, annex, 39 UN GAOR Supp. (No.51) at 197, UN Doc.A/39/51 (1984), art.2.

2. John W. Lango, 'Fundamental Human Rights and the Coercive Interrogation of Terrorists in an Extreme Emergency', in Marjorie Cohn (ed.), *The United States and Torture: Interrogation, Incarceration, and Abuse* (New York: NYU Press, 2011), pp.97–118.

3. 'International Covenant on Civil and Political Rights', art.7, G.A. res.2200A (XXI), 21 UN GAOR Supp. (No.16) at 52, UN Doc.A/6316 (1966), 999 UNTS. 171.

4. UN Human Rights Committee, 'General Comment No.20, Concerning the Prohibition of Torture and Cruel, Inhuman or Degrading Treatment or Punishment (Article 7)', UN Doc.A/47/40 (1992).

5. See Human Rights Watch, 'Italy/US: Ruling Expected in Historic CIA Rendition Case', 3 November 2009, <http://tinyurl.com/yk7awa4>; Rachel Donadio, 'Italy Convicts 23 Americans for CIA Renditions', *New York Times*, 4 November 2009, <http://tinyurl.com/yln7o62>.

6. Vittorio Bufacchi and Jean Maria Arrigo, 'Torture, Terrorism and the State: A Refutation of the Ticking-Bomb Argument', in David Rodin (ed.), *War, Torture and Terrorism: Ethics and War in the 21st Century* (Oxford: Blackwell Publishing, 2007), pp.115–32 (p.119).

7. 'War on terror' is a misnomer. Terrorism is a tactic, not an enemy. You don't declare war on a tactic. Yet under the guise of the 'war on terror', the Bush administration committed numerous violations of human rights and drastically weakened civil liberties both in the United States and abroad.

8. Scott Shane and Charlie Savage, 'Bin Laden Raid Revives Debate on Value of Torture', *New York Times*, 3 May 2011, <http://tinyurl.com/69pxlwt>.

9. Ari Shapiro, 'Interrogation Dissident Testifies On Methods', NPR, 13 May 2009, <http://tinyurl.com/pt7pm4>.

10. Dan Froomkin, 'Torture May Have Slowed Hunt for Bin Laden, Not Hastened It', *Huffington Post*, 6 May 2011, <http://tinyurl.com/4yy4g3t>.

11. Sister Diana Ortiz, 'Preface', in Cohn, *The United States and Torture*, pp.xi–xii.

12. Eric Hobsbawm, *Globalisation, Democracy and Terrorism* (London: Little, Brown, 2007), p.128.

13. Jane Mayer, 'Outsourcing Torture: The Secret History of America's "Extraordinary Rendition" Program', in Cohn, *The United States and Torture*, pp.137–60 (p.146).

14. 'TEXT: Statements from Holder, Panetta on Decision not to Investigate CIA Officials', *National Journal*, 30 June 2011, <http://tinyurl.com/6rxkq47>.

15. Scott Horton, 'The Bush Era Torture–Homicides', *Harper's Magazine*, 7 May 2009, <http://www.harpers.org/archive/2009/05/hbc-90004921>.

16. US Department of Justice, Office of the Inspector General, 'Supplemental Report on September 11 Detainees' Allegations of Abuse at the Metropolitan Detention Center in Brooklyn, New York', December 2003, <http://www.fas.org/irp/agency/doj/oig/detainees1203.pdf>.

17. 'Class Action Complaint and Demand for Jury Trial, *Ibrahim Turkmen, et al. v. John Ashcroft, et al.*, CV-02-2307 (EDNY, 17 April 2002)', <http://tinyurl.com/7rb3syd>.

18. Duncan Gardham and Paul Cruickshank, 'Abu Ghraib abuse photos "show rape"', *The Telegraph*, 7 May 2009, <http://tinyurl.com/qyqrjh>.

19. Osha Gray Davidson, 'Senior US Interrogator: Torture Talk Puts Troops at Risk', *Forbes*, 5 May 2011, <http://tinyurl.com/89qkjnh>.

20. See Jan Crawford Greenburg, Howard L. Rosenburg, and Ariane de Vogue, 'Bush Aware of Advisers' Interrogation Talks', *ABC News*, 11 April 2008, <http://tinyurl.com/4264a6>.

21. Richard Cheney, interview with *ABC News*, 15 December 2008, <http://tinyurl.com/6qhr7lz>.

22. Marjorie Cohn, 'Anti-Torture Strike in California Prisons', *Consortium News*, 19 July 2011, <http://tinyurl.com/6tde9pq>.

23. Ed Pilkington, 'Bradley Manning's treatment was cruel and inhuman, UN torture chief rules', *The Guardian*, 12 March 2012, <http://tinyurl.com/6u28fc9>.

5

Ted Honderich
Morality, Justification,
and Responsibility

You make a clear distinction between legality and what is right, and also insist that terrorism is violence that is 'not according to international law'.[1] Could you clarify why it is necessary for you to define terrorism in part by its illegality if that does not have direct bearing on its morality?

Ted Honderich: Terrorism is defined by me as (1) destructive violence or force usually including killing, (2) smaller in scale than war, (3) with a political and social aim such as the aim of an indigenous people with respect to a homeland, (4) not according to national or international law, and (5) prima facie wrong because it is destructive violence, but not necessarily wrong all things considered. The definition certainly includes state terrorism, considerable amounts of it by the United States in Latin America over decades, and arguably the killing of Osama bin Laden in Pakistan.

Are you implying in your question that it is odd or maybe mistaken and in any case not necessary to include in my definition of terrorism its not being according to law – because I take the illegality not to entail that terrorism is wrong? Well, there are lots of questions about definitions and their kinds – those aiming to capture primary ordinary usage, and those that are adequate initial clarifications or preoccupied or prescriptive or persuasive or loaded or lying definitions.

But I hadn't thought until now that anybody's definition of anything about which a moral question arises should have in it only what they or anybody else takes to have a direct bearing on its morality. Maybe that is arguable, but I don't quickly see how. Still, I do see that all the elements in my definition of terrorism can be thought to have such a bearing.

I defined terrorism as its being against national or international law in order to distinguish it from other uses of violence – somehow official ones by somehow authorised armies or security forces or police. I defined it that way partly to be in decent accord with one primary ordinary usage, part of one such usage. Also, of course, I didn't want to beg the question at issue by defining terrorism as wrong or implying that, but I did want to register something of the fact that terrorism is ordinarily thought of not as action carried out by a somehow accepted government or regime – a regime, by the way, being an imposed form of governing in the concealed interest of a minority, smaller or larger, maybe as large as an economic and social class.

You say I don't take the absence of legality to have a direct bearing on terrorism's morality – I take it you mean on the question of right or wrong. Well, I do indeed think and declare that the illegality of terrorism cannot in and by itself make it wrong. That seems to me obvious. There is terrorism now revered in many national histories, maybe as glorious revolutions. There was terrorism in the understandable and defensible founding of the state of Israel within its original borders in 1948, Zionism as I understand that term that is in several other ways used or abused or left vague.

There has also been terrorist war, the latter being the same as terrorism in my definition except larger in scale. Its illegality doesn't make it wrong either. But of course it can be wrong. The American and British invasion and occupation of Iraq is of course a recent case of terrorist war, grisly in its hypocrisy and in the effects of its hypocrisy.

The subject of definitions in serious discussion and to a lesser extent in ordinary propaganda is itself a problem, and you make me want to think more about my definition of terrorism. But let me end here by a bit of self-defence with respect to my definition. It is, I submit, superior to much else.

In distinguishing terrorism from somehow standard war and the like, it is better than the definition in *The New Oxford*

Dictionary of English, which says terrorism is just the use of violence and intimidation in the pursuit of political aims. In effect, given the definition of violence as physical force, that makes any effective nation state terrorist. Denmark is made terrorist, not to mention Somerset. I have lately been informed that Oxford has caught up with reality in this regard if not in all others – *Oxford Dictionaries* online defines terrorism as 'the unofficial or unauthorized use of violence and intimidation in the pursuit of political aims'.[2] Glad to see it.

Also, my definition and the new Oxford one stand above the stupidity and the moral stupidity that terrorism and presumably state terrorism is or includes the intentional killing of the innocent. The principal aim of that definition of terrorism is to distinguish it from somehow official war and the like by a government, by implication to distinguish terrorism from respectable war. But of course by any defensible idea of what it is to act intentionally, necessarily an idea of acting with foreseeable consequences, in fact the idea of any decent legal system, almost all war includes the intentional killing of innocents, more than terrorism, usually overwhelmingly more.

Does the way international law is set up not cause problems for your definition? For example, you describe what you call Israel's 'Neo-Zionism' as 'terrorism by a national state',[3] but many UN resolutions brought against Israel have not been passed, despite overwhelming international support, due to the US veto (14 votes to one in the Security Council). The point is therefore, whatever people may think of it, this Israeli violence against Palestinians is not technically illegal. Does your definition of 'not according to international law' account for this?

TH: This good question again takes me aback. How much should it do that? Maybe not much. One thing it makes clearer is that what is against international law is unclear and up for dispute – but we knew that. The murderous war criminals Bush and Blair, as they are in my view, invented international law with respect to the aggression against Iraq. They got corrupt and toadying lawyers, notably one Goldsmith, attorney general of England, to declare what they wanted. But surely the one and only test of international law cannot be Security Council decisions?

I take it that there are other grounds, precedents and sources of judgement. There is the UN Declaration of Human Rights. There are many resolutions of the UN General Assembly. There are the inclusions of the defensive principle of the just war in agreements of law.

I take it those grounds must include something that amounts to a people's right of self-defence – say the self-defence of the Palestinians against neo-Zionist rapine, the taking from the indigenous people of Palestine at least their autonomy in the last one-fifth of their homeland.

But might it be the case that I have to retreat in a new definition to an admittedly vaguer idea? That terrorism is violence that is against a certain international consensus of judgement, against an international fact of accreditation, beyond official tolerance? That, of course, could not and would not be an idea to the effect that states in their activities cannot engage in terrorism.

Such a new definition, of course, would face the problem of further specification. But, to come back to my main point, certainly there is sense and a need to distinguish terrorism from the actions of somehow established governments or regimes.

Can it ever be right, given the existence of international law, for a nation such as the United States to use military intervention unilaterally? What about covert support for terrorism abroad, whether state or non-state? Or aggression, that is, violence against a state other than in direct self-defence? Are such actions wrong *because* they are unilateral, covert or aggressive?

TH: My way of thinking about terrorism, war and so on is by way of the principle of right and wrong that is the Principle of Humanity – the principle of getting and keeping people out of lives of deprivation and suffering – and of course also by way of difficult or nearly impossibly difficult premises of fact, most saliently premises to the effect that particular action is a rational means to the end of the principle. This way of proceeding must leave open the possibility or at least the conceivability of rightful unilateral military intervention by a nation – or of course any other entity or organisation, say a resistance or liberation movement. The same way of thinking applies to support for terrorism abroad, aggression, and violence against a state other than in direct self-defence.

I am interested in your idea, in regards to, say, military intervention, that 'the right thing can be done with vicious intentions',[4] and also that 'the ends and the means justify the means'.[5] Using such ideas, one can perhaps morally justify a regime change being forced on a country from outside, even if the motives behind that are not altruistic, that is, the aggressor has something to gain itself (the installation of a government more favourable to its political or economic aims). But what counts as the 'ends' in such a situation? Arguments attempting to justify interventions tend to accept the regime change as the end, but should it not be considered as means? Does this affect the possible justification?

TH: It seems obvious to me that the right thing can be done out of bad motives. It seems obvious because what philosophers call consequentialism is true – actions, policies, institutions, societies, are made right or wrong by their probable consequences, nothing else. The alternative to consequentialism, that intentions make actions right, or that some things are right on account of the agent's integrity, or on account of personal relations, or virtues detached from consequences, or Kant's pure good will, or whatever – those suspect ideas are rightly in decline. Can you really dispute consequentialism? Even if you think, rightly, that intentions are among the guides to who needs punishment or the like, and of course guides to probable consequences?

Surely, to take even an extreme case, a child might rightly be saved from slavery and torture by someone moved only by sexual desires and intentions – rightly saved as a result of being far less badly off, in a life far less bad? As I say, that is not to say that the agent's desires, etc. are irrelevant to one's judgement of him, maybe action against him, and relevant to comparing the possible alternative consequences. I happen to think myself

that all our justifications of action are consequentialist, some
of them pretending to be otherwise. It is absurd to say, as non-
consequentialists do, that a mother cares for a child only or even
essentially because it is *her child*, because of that relationship
that is not a consequence of her action, meaning thereby that
her care is not motivated and defended by its consequences.

I note in passing that much regime change is importantly
change in the direction of what is too mildly called our hierarchic
democracy – including its monstrous denials of equality and
hence including for a start, far more importantly, violations
of various kinds of freedom. A question has to arise, whatever
its answer may be, of whether a regime change to hierarchic
democracy may in fact serve the end of the Principle of Humanity
less than certain alternatives to it. There are more freedoms than
political ones. I make bold to say that it is not yet settled that
the overthrow and murder of Colonel Gaddafi by means of our
air war will turn out best for Libyans.

This isn't idle wondering about hierarchic democracy and
alternatives. For a start, the Cuban regime has done better for
Cubans than the American regime has done for Americans.

**When a country such as the United States has a history of
(directly or indirectly) enforcing regime changes, or propping
up dictatorships, does it make sense to try and justify each case
in isolation, that is, whether Bosnia, or Iraq, or Libya were
'right?' Is it not more important to examine the continuity of
motivating interests – the ideology – behind such acts, and their
aggregate results? So if US interests coincide with humanitarian
goals or the opinion of the international community and save
lives in one case, that is not to their credit if the policy destroys
more lives overall.**

TH: You may anticipate that I certainly agree with the tendency
of this question. Anybody must agree who has actually read
the books of Noam Chomsky, the greatest judge in history
not only of the nature of human language but also of the
American regime's relations to the rest of the world. But I hope
we agree that the matter is not about motivation, intention, or

the concealment of it, or self-deception and so on. Of course there must be more than suspicion of every single American so-called humanitarian intervention, and now every British one – certainly every British one since the period of Blair and the New Labour Party – whatever is said of our earlier engagements in imperialism, etc.

You explore the possibility that terrorism can be justified, using such criteria as the impossibility of negotiation, realistic chance of success, and killing civilians only because no other means are available. And you say that '[s]ome ... terrorism, if very likely none of it by national states, can be regarded as directed to the end of getting people out of wretchedness and other distress'.[6] Are such justifications the preserve of the weak against the strong? Could the United States not also apply these criteria to justify its 'war on terror' – claims that negotiation appeared pointless, killing civilians was unavoidable, the intended ends were to stop suffering, and it was reasonable to anticipate success?

TH: I can give a decent answer to the question about the preserve of the weak only by saying something more of that principle of right and wrong according to me, the Principle of Humanity. In my opinion it's the principle of the Left in politics when the Left is true to itself. In brief it is that we must get and keep people out of lives of deprivation and suffering – out of what you can call bad lives.

Those are lives denied or deprived of the great human goods, frustrated in the fundamental desires of our human nature. These six great goods or desires, in my judgement, are for a decent length of conscious life, bodily well-being, specified kinds of freedom and power, respect and self-respect, the goods of relationship, and such goods of culture as literacy and religion.

The Principle of Humanity, fully stated, is as follows. The right thing – action, practice, institution, government, society, possible world – is the one that according to the best judgement and information at the time is the rational one in the sense of being effective and not self-defeating with respect to one end –

the end of getting and keeping people out of bad lives. Certainly a consequentialism.

No metaphor there, no ambiguity, no oratory, no help with evasion, no cant about 'the American way of life', no tripe of a low English prime minister about *The Big Society*, nothing about undefined 'freedom', no inane pretences of economic necessity and impossibility, no ignorant and dim piety about desert, no stuff from a wretched political party's advertising agency. Nothing vacuous or absurd about socialism or capitalism. No pretence of avoiding the question of right and wrong, say by talking of the acceptable and the unacceptable. No leading of the innocent into thinking they know the answer to the question of right and wrong without thinking about it. No avoidance of the true proposition that the aim of selling is never truth. Maybe as important as anything else, no invitation to the self-deception in which conservative governments live and breathe.

As I say there is nothing in the principle about desert, that falsehood of such use or rather misuse by the money-grubbers. It is not a principle of equality either. Its end, whatever side effects there would be of achieving its end, is not the end of making people equal, making them the same. Its end is getting people out of misery, whatever role can be played in that by practices and institutions of equality, and, as I say, whatever side effects of equality go with achieving its end. It is, I suppose, a necessary articulation of the Golden Rule, and of the best of private religion, and of other great instructions in the highest human culture, those declarations of sympathy, empathy and generosity.

You do indeed know more of a thing, know more of a principle of right and wrong, by knowing what it is not. What is the tradition of conservatism, originally the tradition of a political party in England, now of both the Republican and the Democratic Party in the United States?

Both American and British conservatives used to say they were against change but for reform, which they never distinguished. Even their main and almost only thinker Edmund Burke didn't do it. Anyway they're patently not against change when it suits them, as Reaganism and Thatcherism and Britain's New Labour Party demonstrated. The very short story of conservatism is not that it is selfish but that it has no principle of right and wrong at all to defend the self-interest it shares with the rest of us. Who can see this and feel able to learn from what conservatism says of terrorism or state terrorism?

And what is liberalism in both England and America? What is this politics that is making possible the conservative and liberal coalition government in Britain as we speak? What is this politics that may actually be allowing the party of conservatism to be more vicious than it would be without the fig leaf provided by their coalition partner?

Liberalism is good intentions without resolution, maybe not so much intentions as just an uneasy conscience. It lacks the resolution of a determinate principle. It is true to its principal founder, John Stuart Mill. His politics are summed up by the fact that he most famously declared in *On Liberty* that there is to be no state intervention in the life of an individual against his will unless he harms another individual not an agreeing partner – and then failed to say what harm is, even to try.[7] A thing I seem to have learned lately from the coalition government and its further violation of the poor and the weak is that liberalism has had too much respect from the likes of me in having been given very little of it.

Partly because the coalition government in question, like conservatism in America and elsewhere, is relevant to matters of terrorism and state terrorism, let me say a word more of comparison. The Principle of Humanity has in it none of the lying by culpable self-deception on particular issues that is part of the tradition of liberalism. I have in mind in particular a muddied lie by the Baroness Shirley Williams, one of the 'gang of four' who tragically weakened the Left in Britain by leaving the Labour Party. The lie, in discussion with the exemplary perceiver of reality Polly Toynbee, was that the greatest achievement of civilisation in British history, the National Health Service, is well enough preserved by opening up to 49 per cent of it to profitisation.[8]

But to come round at last to your question, that was whether the Principle of Humanity is the preserve of the weak against the strong, and whether this makes it useable against me and others like me on the Left. In effect, since bad lives are in general those of the weak as against the strong, the principle will indeed make its justifications the preserve of the weak against the strong. So, you ask, can American imperialism make use of the principle?

It is unlikely, to say the very least, that the principle could justify US actions as we know them – the actions of what is dignified by being called hierarchic democracy in and outside of the United States. That democracy is in fact not only a regime but also truly described as the organisation of the strong in America against the weak. There seems to me no chance that the Principle of Humanity and well-argued minor premises, factual premises, could give a general justification of, say, America's 'war on terror'. It is all-important to me that the principle is not plastic rhetoric, not plastic in the contemporary sense of the word and also the original one – easily shaped to whatever end.

But I admit that your question is one that brings into focus the difficulty of arguing not for the rightness of the Principle of Humanity itself, but for the necessary further factual premises in any case. Most relevant in the present discussion, there is the factual question of whether terrorism or terrorist war or other action is in fact rational with respect to the end of the principle. The factual questions are much harder than the principal moral question, the general question of right and wrong.

There is another hard question, smaller, which this discussion between us brings to mind. It is the question which someone will have called a choice of rhetoric, a choice of a mode of address. The Principle of Humanity calls for a rational decision in this matter as well. How in these darkening days should we supporters of the principle talk, talk in different places? Parliamentary language? Academic restraint? Tolerance in speech of all opinions? Mutual respect? According anonymity to the adversaries of the principle, adversaries by commission or omission? Or the expression not only of condescension but also contempt?

I find the answer difficult, even for this very interview. Certainly our conventions of speech and discussion are of wonderfully more use to some of us than others. They keep truth and moral truth quiet if heard at all. One quick thought in this neighbourhood is that there must be contexts in which propositions about what is in fact stupidity and moral stupidity are to be preferred to quiet allusions to class-government, self-deception, and hierarchic democracy.

In trying to justify any terrorism – state terrorism, non-state terrorism, or what you call 'terrorist war' – it has to be taken into account that the death of 'innocents' will be a consequence, whether directly targeted or not. The question is how to judge (and who has the right to judge) at what point such deaths, as part of the means, become too great for the desired end. However, does it not simply become relative according to one's perception of the end, which, as Igor Primoratz argues, being 'the ultimate goal' for the potential terrorist, by definition 'overrides all other values that might conflict with it, all considerations that might stand in the way of its realisation'?[9]

TH: Maybe there is something about the question that I don't get. Maybe I misunderstand it. I take it that the question presupposes that a moral position, mine in particular, may involve a single principle of right and wrong that overrides all other considerations. Indeed a moral position, certainly mine, may do that. So does such a principle of anyone else. Moreover, it is my confident conviction that it is exactly such a principle, an overriding principle of the kind attempted by Plato, mediaeval Christians, Kant, Mill, and so on, indeed attempted by all reflective moralists, that is an absolute requirement both of morality and of rational reflection. There is no decision procedure worth the name without such a principle.

It is exactly the absence of a principle, and of course also a principle of such literalness and determinateness as to prevent or at any rate resist self-deception and worse, that is the failure of most thinking about right and wrong. It is the absence of such a principle, most importantly in conservatism and liberalism, that has contributed so plainly to the viciousness of American foreign policy – and, to take another salient example, the barbarism of neo-Zionism in its ongoing rape of the Palestinians. It is the absence of a principle that has contributed so much to failing to see that the Palestinians have a moral right to their terrorism against neo-Zionism within all of historic Palestine. It is the absence of such a principle that helps so much to make for an absence of discrimination with respect to terrorism and in particular state terrorism.

Nothing in all that excludes secondary considerations that turn up elsewhere in good thinking, including that of Igor Primoratz. You will remember that I do not take such a principle to make things easy. It doesn't. The facts are harder to judge.

But, to return to the US, even if some utilise wars and terror for pure cynical economic expansion, for others is there not genuine belief in the righteousness of what they are doing – a sense, no matter how delusional, that they are bringing the world freedom and opportunity, based on a moral principle?

TH: Again I agree. So what? There is no doubt that our wretched coalition government here in Britain, in which I cannot resist saying again that the main sham of the tradition of liberalism is exposed – our coalition government is persuaded of its own rectitude, rationality, etc. Even of its humanity. Even its humanity in terms of the clear-headed Principle of Humanity. I remember being on television once with a dim minister-to-be who pretended he would embrace it when put in charge of the universities – David Willetts. When such things are said, they are half listened to. This is a further proof of the lowering of the level of intelligence in public debate first achieved by Thatcher.

It seems to me possible that if you take into account relative good and bad, which is certainly yet more important than absolute good and bad – remember freedoms for a start – there is about as much argument now, in so far as the existing state of a society is concerned and nothing else, for violent revolution against hierarchic democracy – as much argument in this respect as there was for revolution in the circumstances of, say, the English Revolution of the seventeenth century, such as it was, and the French Revolution, and the Russian Revolution, and the Cuban Revolution. That is, there is as much argument in terms of inhumanity in the existing state of a society – the denial of the great goods and great human desires, the making of misery.

Of course, as you have heard, that cannot be the end of the story. There can be no justified violent action that is not rational – not rational in terms of means and ends, certainly the costs of means in terms of humanity. To a judgement of the state of a society you must add what is harder, a judgement of whether an attempt at revolution will work. It does not matter that governmental and class resistance will of course be what will make the revolution wrong, that this resistance will be more responsible for the wrong than the revolutionary action of the revolutionaries. What matters is that the governmental and class defence with its great costs is likely to be successful.

In the 'Arab Spring', it seems that the demand for democracy encapsulated all needs, including basics such as food and jobs, which initially triggered the strikes and protests. Effectively then, democracy anticipates the opportunity to determine society as a whole. Your Principle of Humanity is about taking decisions to help realise the goods of life as widely as possible. Do you think democracy has the power of a single good that contains within it the possibility of realising all other goods, and is therefore a worthy overriding cause in itself?

TH: I don't know the ideologies, loyalties, ambitions and self-interests of the protestors and fighters of the Arab Spring. I don't think you do either. We are not told by even the decent part of our press. And frankly, I am tired of thinking of adding excuses of any hierarchic democracy, American or British or any other, to the condemnation of it that is a consequence of the Principle of Humanity. I am more than tired of contemplating the value of what is simply called 'democracy' without consideration of what thing is being contemplated, let alone the trivial and dismal incantation of 'freedom'.

Hierarchic democracy in America, Britain and elsewhere, as I should have said before, and am free and obliged to judge in the absence of work by those economists and others who should have carried it out, is such that the top economic decile has such wealth and income as to issue in its having more than a thousand times the political influence and power of the bottom decile. With this inequality, of course, goes exactly such a disparity in all freedoms and the other great goods.

It is ludicrous to suppose that the American and English regimes of hierarchic democracy, given their history, and especially the present response in England to the global economic situation and the national economic situation, will serve the end you mention of the Principle of Humanity. Even only a cursory reading of the decent English newspapers, say *The Guardian* and *The Independent*, makes the supposition ludicrous.

Those newspapers by their omissions make something else clear. It is that it can be guessed, despite our ignorance, that it is probable that the aims of the Arab revolutions must be judged to have been, in sum or in the main, hierarchic democracy. That reduces my enthusiasm for the Arab Spring. I admit, however, although without benefit of knowing anything of Marx, that what I think he properly called bourgeois revolutions may have in them a little more hope with respect to humanity than most of the regimes they are replacing.

The general question you raise is maybe the largest and most terrible question about governments and kinds of democracy. I don't know a general answer.

You have previously used the phrase 'cowardly war' to describe conflicts in which soldiers are distanced as much as possible from danger with the result that greater civilian casualties are inevitable. Is it reasonable to expect the leaders, especially of a democracy, in which they represent only their own people by mandate, not to put the lives of their own people first in war?

TH: I remember the philosopher Richard Wollheim, no revolutionary he, saying to me in the early 1960s that he was surprised that patriotism was still considered a virtue – or anyway so considered among the members of enlightened people. The philosopher and still Marxist Jerry Cohen said the same. No doubt there is some reflection about division of labour in life – parents having a special obligation with respect to their child and so on, leaders of a nation having a paternal obligation. But it really cannot be the case that leaders in a hierarchic democracy, on the premise or rather the dream that they represent all the people, should put some of humanity first in the way they do.

There are secondary questions about killing from a great height, by drone, frying to death the intended victims and the rest. We shouldn't forget, though, that it turns stomachs in a particular way. That it does so is not irrelevant to further reflection. Horror counts. If the Principle of Humanity necessarily is general, it is unique in being in direct touch with such realities.

Regarding the aftermath of 9/11 and the invasion of Afghanistan, one point you make is that '[h]uman nature exists', and 'it puts limits on our reactions to such horrors as 9/11. What we have little choice but to do, having been attacked, is not all that would be right if we were not so human.'[10] However, while of course mass public anger is expected, is it not reasonable to expect at least our leaders not to stoke the fires, to avoid a cycle of vengeance? And, in the case of Afghanistan, given the initial period of rational negotiation, and the planning of the invasion prior to its execution, is the idea of instinctive reaction even appropriate?

TH: I say thanks for the question. I hereby change my mind about that excusing of the United States in its war against Afghanistan, and so I accept your objection. It must remain true that 'ought' implies 'can', that no person or nation can be blamed for doing what is the only course open – where that is partly a matter of the limits of human nature. I now take it, in brief, that two facts about the United States, facts that do not distinguish it from other hierarchic democracies, are better put in place of my excuse.

One is of course the mass-produced stupidity and the moral stupidity of the United States, the first of those being supportive and creative of the second, a stupidity and moral stupidity owed fundamentally to the inequalities and therefore denials of freedom touched on earlier. The second is the culpability with respect to those stupidities of deciles towards the top of the American population.

Although we can question the quality of US democracy (unequal social and political influence, narrow political spectrum, imbalanced voting system, lack of engagement), it is still a fact that, simply because it is democracy, people collectively select their political representatives. Nobody, for example, has to endorse major, corporate-funded parties that are likely to support military interventions. Given that, to what extent are people, in even what you call a 'hierarchic democracy', responsible for their government's state terrorism, or even terrorist attacks against themselves?

TH: To be relevant, there is room for reflection on the proposition that 'nobody ... has to endorse major, corporate-funded parties that are likely to support military interventions'. If there is no party of intelligence and moral intelligence with the slightest chance of winning the election, I take it there is some argument for the conclusion that people have to endorse another party. The least bad. That may be better than not voting, I take it.

What is now to be done by those who are of the Left, are of the Principle of Humanity? The answer is civil disobedience, any civil disobedience in accord with the Principle of Humanity, any such civil disobedience in the hope of being followed by mass civil disobedience. In particular any such civil disobedience with respect to American and now British state terrorism.

It is inhumanity that the Occupation movement, most notably in Wall Street and outside St Paul's Cathedral in London, has had the great honour to resist. Do you wonder if the present governments of the United States and Britain, as against the Occupiers, will maintain a respectability in future, have a decent place in history, even in the minds of ordinary readers of history? They will not. The Occupiers will have such a place, as certainly as one is had now by those who have resisted inhumanity throughout history. The Occupiers are not kiddies. They have a rank above money-grubbers, the political class, right-wing historians, the lesser press, all those kiddies in thinking and feeling about what is right.

Such civil disobedience is morally necessary. So are further gestures of it. Speaking of England, maybe one by another English army colonel today, true to Colonel Rainborough of the Civil War in the seventeenth century? Rainborough said, you may remember, the greatest thing in the political history of England: 'For really I think the poorest he hath a life to live, as the greatest he.' Maybe a tank now in Parliament Square to support the big strike or the march? No shells in the colonel's tank. After the television cameras arrive, back to barracks in Pimlico to accept the penalty for his civil and military disobedience.

You say that omissions, such as not sufficiently protesting, are to be considered in a judgement of responsibility, even that 'in connection with the wrongs of September 11, our omissions were a necessary context for the particular intentions on the part of the killers'.[11] Is a lack of knowledge and accessibility of knowledge in, say, the United States an excuse for omission? What about feelings of the disempowered, the inability to affect anything? Where do our obligations to protesting perceived wrongs, and then responsibilities for violence perpetrated by our states, begin and end in a hierarchic democracy?

TH: Yes, it must be that the omissions in question are on the part of those who have some level of knowledge and judgement. To take one easy example, the omissions are paradigmatically culpable on the part of those in the top economic deciles in our societies. Their responsibility for the ignorance of a large part of the population, by way of the media, is out of all proportion to that of those on the bottom. We are not all wretched Murdochs and New Labour spin doctors.

At the moment we are having this conversation it is hard to see that President Obama, that once great hope, so welcomed by the likes of me, is not among the culpable. It depends on some of those hard premises, one about getting a second term of office.

NOTES

1. Ted Honderich, *Terrorism for Humanity: Inquiries in Political Philosophy* (London: Pluto Press, 2003), p.155.
2. 'Terrorism', *Oxford Dictionaries*, <http://tinyurl.com/7jmhxbe>.
3. Ted Honderich, *Humanity, Terrorism, Terrorist War* (London: Continuum, 2006), p.102.
4. Jon Bailes and Cihan Aksan, 'Humanity and Terror: An Interview with Ted Honderich', *State of Nature*, Autumn 2007, <http://www.stateofnature.org/tedHonderich.html>.
5. Honderich, *Humanity, Terrorism*, p.80.
6. Honderich, *Terrorism for Humanity*, p.172.
7. John Stuart Mill, *On Liberty* (London: John W. Parker and Son, 1859), p.22.
8. 'Who is right on the NHS? You decide', *The Guardian*, 16 March 2012, <http://tinyurl.com/7mllpwq>.
9. Igor Primoratz, 'The Morality of Terrorism', *Journal of Applied Philosophy*, Vol.14, No.3 (1997), 221–33 (p.223).
10. Honderich, *Humanity, Terrorism*, p.141.
11. Ted Honderich, *After the Terror* (Edinburgh: Edinburgh University Press, 2002), p.125.

6

Edward S. Herman
The Media Image of Terrorism

Margaret Thatcher referred to publicity as the oxygen of terrorism, and this is quite a widely accepted idea; the implication being that terrorism requires mass media coverage to gain support, legitimacy, and sympathy. What would you make of this point in regards to state terrorism?

Edward Herman: First, I should note that Mrs Thatcher's point is very misleading. For one thing it obscures the fact that terrorists often resort to violence, and seek publicity, in response to grievances of marginalised and weak people that cannot be addressed through the mainstream media or existing political or judicial processes. So they may need that publicity 'oxygen' to gain desperately needed attention and to breathe at all. A second point that Mrs Thatcher evades is that the state often uses the terrorism of the weak (which I have labelled 'retail terrorism', as opposed to 'wholesale' – large-scale – terrorism, carried out by the state) in order to create fear, so as to divert the population from unpopular economic policies or to justify the abridgement of civil liberties and arms build-ups and war. The George W. Bush administration in the United States was notorious for regularly using terrorist scares for electoral advantage or to justify some military or political action, scares that were in virtually every case based on trivial, out-of-date, or manufactured incidents. It is also not true that retail terrorist actions usually create support or legitimise those who engage in them – almost always the publicity given to the terrorists is negative and their cause is not advanced by these acts.[1]

State terrorism may be used either at home or to pacify people abroad, the latter often done indirectly through proxy forces. If a state is using terror to crush its own people, it needs to make the threat known to the populace to make them acquiesce through fear. So in this case a certain amount of publicity 'oxygen' would serve state terror, although the state may deny and limit information on its terror in order to avoid damaging publicity abroad. At home not much publicity may be required, given that policy actions, such as people being shot or dragged out of houses and 'disappeared', and word-of-mouth information flows, may suffice to alert and terrorise the populace.

Where state terrorism is carried out abroad, directly or through foreign proxies, publicity in the home country is of course undesirable. Supporting state terrorism abroad, if described honestly, would be deemed immoral, so truthful publicity would be avoided by the state and discouraged for the media. The publicity itself would be deemed 'unpatriotic', and in the case of the Reagan administration's support of the terrorising Guatemala government in the 1980s, human rights organisations such as Amnesty International and Human Rights Watch were harshly condemned by administration officials for alleged exaggeration, but also for providing aid to the enemy insurgents and populace under terrorist siege.[2]

State terrorism, direct or through proxy, is also defended by claiming that it is not terrorism at all but 'retaliation' or 'counter-terrorism'. By this means the real terrorism is ignored or explained away, and the publicity serving as 'oxygen' is the actions of the retail terrorists or resistance to the wholesale terrorism. In short, the state terrorism is kept in low key as regards publicity, and greater attention and indignation is given to those supposedly inducing the retaliation. By this means US sponsorship of a system of National Security States in Latin America between the 1950s and the 1980s, with a huge rise of death squads and organised torture, was given little publicity, and the US image of opposing terrorism was successfully maintained.

It may be noted that the Argentinean military regime of 1976–83, which was supported by the United States, was allowed by the US mainstream media to be fighting 'terrorism', but not to be engaging in terrorism itself. But following the ousting of that regime an Alfonsin government-appointed

'National Commission on Disappeared Persons' concluded that 'the armed forces responded to the terrorists' crimes with a terrorism infinitely worse than that which they were combating'. But this was ex post facto, and this important estimate of relative terrorisms was barely mentioned and never reflected on in the mainstream media of the United States.[3]

Do the media play a role in spreading terror (perhaps we could say terrifying as opposed to terrorising) when it comes to coverage of terror attacks against the US and its allies? Do they help to promote anti-US terrorist aims in this regard, or US interests?

EH: The media play a key role in producing fear in the case of actual or allegedly threatened terrorist attacks. In fact, they play such a role perhaps most importantly on the basis of alleged *plans* of terrorist attacks. There have been very few foreign-sponsored terrorist attacks against the United States – in fact, none within the United States itself since 9/11. But there have been numerous claims of plots that never materialised, and which were often disclosed just in time to meet some kind of political need (an election, a planned escalation of a war). The Bush administration's political successes were built heavily on this willingness to use alleged terrorist threats to make 'security' a major issue and to suggest Bush's prowess in meeting these threats. In a number of cases the evidence of the plot was stale or the plot was clearly encouraged by paid government informers,[4] but the plots and threats are invariably treated seriously and intensively by the mainstream media. The media cooperate because this is cheap and easy 'news' that feeds into already conventional and institutionalised fears, and the media do not want to be charged with excessive liberalism or lack of patriotic ardour.

   The United States has evolved into a permanent war economy and polity, and the media are an integral part of this system. Stoking fear and normalising war in the minds of the public are essential to justifying the enormous outlays of the permanent war system; the government, both major political parties, and the media simply take that spending for granted and do not debate the trade-offs involved. The permanent war system has been relabelled a 'war on terrorism', but this is ideology and propaganda. It is arguably a war 'of' terrorism – of state terrorism fighting against recalcitrant states or insurgents, quickly labelled terrorists, often brought into action by the primary terrorism. So yes, the policies and media actually provoke terrorism. This serves some US interests, but not that of the underlying population which bears the human and economic costs of militarisation and permanent warfare, just as it does the costs of the recent and ongoing economic crisis.

How do you see the relationship between 'mainstream' news media coverage of terrorism (at home and abroad) and the US government? Do the media influence government decisions and policy (the so-called 'CNN effect')? Does the government gain more leverage to dictate what should and should not be reported under a threat of terrorism?

EH: The mainstream media are part of a closely integrated corporate and political system, and they consistently serve as a propaganda arm of the state on foreign policy issues. There is in fact a steady revolving door between news media personnel and government foreign policy agencies, and there is a class and structural commonality and a sharing of interests that profoundly affect media performance. The United States is now an openly imperial power, projecting power across the globe with its huge military establishment and its global system of bases, and through its domination of a reinvigorated NATO. The media follow in the wake of this expansionism.

There is no doubt an interactive process at work between government and media, with the media sometimes affecting government responses, usually pushing it toward more aggressive external actions, especially with the increased importance of the right-wing media. We should perhaps speak more of a 'Murdoch–Fox effect' rather than a 'CNN effect', although both tend to push the government in the same (readier resort to force) direction. There is also little doubt that the fear of terrorism, or rather fear of appearing soft on terrorism and insufficiently hard on terrorists, gives the government more leverage both to suppress information and to publish information that is highly problematic and doesn't pass the smell test.

The Wikileaks disclosure of vast details on the United States's death and torture dealing in Iraq, and the media's response to these revelations, have been enlightening. For one thing, much of the material made available was of events and decisions that the media shouldn't have missed if they were serving the public interest. For another thing, the major media treated this disclosure too briefly, too selectively (often stressing claims of Iranian intervention in Iraq), and with hostility, assailing and denigrating the author, Julian Assange. This led one commentator to note that whereas Nixon had had to organise an attempt to discredit Dan Ellsberg, who with the help of the *New York Times* released the Pentagon Papers in 1971, in 2010 the media itself, led by the *New York Times*, took on that attack-dog responsibility.[5]

Would you go as far as to say that, in some cases, the media has pushed harder than the government for military intervention? Are we talking about the kind of influence which could drum up demand for action that could force the government's hand in a case where it might not otherwise intervene militarily?

EH: The government is often far from united in decision making on war, and it is true that the media may strengthen the hand of one or another decision-making faction. It is also true that there is a long history of media pushing hard for military intervention or creating the moral environment in which it happens. This is still true in the cases of Iran and Syria where the mainstream media have been either pushing for war or making it easier to do so by featuring and demonising the target governments. The *New York Times* has had almost daily articles about civilian victims of government action in Syria, showing not only crowds of people protesting but more pictures of dead bodies within a few weeks than they have shown of dead Palestinians or Afghanis over the past decade.

If fear of the Soviet threat was the greatest weapon for gaining public consent for military interventions and sponsorship of state terror during the Cold War, during the 1990s we had a period in which the more positive narrative of 'humanitarian intervention' became dominant. Yet after 9/11 the media and government have both seemed all too keen to abandon that and again adopt the threat narrative. Is terror an important part of US democracy?

EH: It is true that 'humanitarian intervention' and 'responsibility to protect' took something of a back seat after 9/11, when al-Qaeda, Afghanistan and the Taliban, and the new 'war on terror' rose to top propaganda service. 9/11 was a 'big bang', a new 'Pearl Harbor' that the war party had longed for and got in September 2001. It has been used relentlessly, and actually has provided the basis for a new 'war *of* terror', capped recently by the US administration's declaration of the right to kill 'terrorists' anywhere by administrative–military fiat. This in effect makes the entire world a US 'free-fire zone', and also, in effect, a global terrorist state.

But it should also be noted that 'humanitarian intervention' and R2P (responsibility to protect) are not dead, and made a major comeback in the run-up to the NATO war on Libya, justified in PR and by the UN and ICC authorities by the need to protect Libyan civilians. Similar arguments, and a huge volume of selective government–media propaganda are being used to push for international intervention in Syria – but not in Yemen, Saudi Arabia or Palestine!

So, in general has there been a shift away from the rhetoric of 'war on terror', at least tentatively, under Obama and after the publicity failure of the Iraq and Afghanistan wars? Indeed, have the so-called Arab Spring and the 'humanitarian' justification for intervention in Libya *forced* a change in narrative? In other words, has 'terrorism' as an idea lost any of its propagandistic purchase?

EH: These are all verbal weapons of propaganda that move into and out of service depending on circumstances. The 'war on terror' would not easily apply to the Arab Spring cases, unless one were to oppose state terror, which the West could not do as the terrorists in leading governments like those of Egypt, Tunisia, Bahrain, and Yemen were our old allies. But humanitarian intervention and R2P could be used, discretely and selectively, against Arab governments engaging in repression who are on the Western hit list. This has worked very well, with the important cooperation of repressive Arab governments who are Western allies. The Western media have also done a fine job of playing dumb on this selectivity, inflating the charges against the hit-list governments and ignoring the very substantial civilian costs of supporting the 'resistance' (often yesterday's 'terrorists').

But 'terrorism' is still very much in the Western propaganda arsenal and is even now employed to justify drone and secret operations murders in the global free-fire zone.

In *The Politics of Genocide* you describe the history of crimes against humanity, war crimes, ethnic cleansing and genocide as showing 'the centrality of racism to the imperial project'.[6] But is there any racial motivation in US state and state sponsored terror where the only discernible pattern seems to be military and economic interests? Is, for example, the anti-Arab Muslim slant in certain state and media discourse any more than the propaganda designed to legitimise terrorism by demonising the Other?

EH: It is perhaps an axiom of human affairs that when one group inflicts great suffering and harm upon another, the perpetrator group automatically regards the victim group as somehow inferior, and less good or less human than the perpetrator. Even if it could be shown that 100 per cent of a state's conquest and subjugation of another territory or group was driven solely by its interests in stealing the oil or rare mineral deposits from that territory's inhabitants, no conquest and subjugation would occur without the perpetrator group convincing itself of the justness and rightness of its actions. Throughout history, this has meant that the subjugated group must become an incarnation of everything the conqueror is not – that is, the racial, ethnic, religious, or 'civilisational' inferior of the conqueror.

Racism was not the main motivation in the long history of colonial conquest and the slave trade, but with the white North technologically more advanced than the non-white South, conquest, exploitation, enslavement, and extermination were practicable and highly profitable, and racial differences were quickly made the basis for contempt, hatred, and mistreatment. It is easier to treat harshly people who have been converted into some equivalent of the US Declaration of Independence's 'merciless Indian savages'. As John Ellis has noted: 'At best, the Europeans regarded those they slaughtered [in Africa] with amused contempt.'[7]

Racism is also not a main motivator in today's anti-Arab Muslim campaigns in the West, as the West has excellent relations with 'well-behaved' Arab Muslims such as the Saudis, Kuwaitis, and Egyptians on the US dole (Mubarak for decades, and the Egyptian military leaders), and even Saddam Hussein in the years before his invasion of Kuwait. It is even a bit awkward to have segments of the media and political leadership engage in general accusations about the terroristic proclivities of Muslims and Koran-bashing with so many friends in the Arab and broader Muslim world. But given the Western warfare against Arabs in the Middle East and Africa, along with Muslims in Afghanistan, Pakistan, and elsewhere, and Arab and Muslim resistance and responsive terrorism, it was inevitable that anti-Arab and anti-Muslim demonisation would take hold in the West and make it easier to slaughter their civilian populations.

One other factor that has been of some importance is that Israel has been striving for years to dispossess Palestinians in the interest of a greater Israel. To provide the moral justifications for this systematic ethnic cleansing, the portrayal of Palestinians and Arabs as terrorists is helpful. Ditto for demonising the Iraqis and Iranians. Israeli influence has caused this to be fed into the Western political media views about Arabs.

But is it really *inevitable* that racial demonisation takes hold in such circumstances? For example, did it play a part, say, against Latin Americans when US hostilities were centred there? Is it not that a particular racism like that against Arabs and Muslims either has to be already present culturally, or needs to be deliberately incited by the media?

EH: It certainly emerged in the colonial period, but not so much in more recent times because we were always fighting on the side of the local elites, not combating and enslaving the entire population. As I mentioned, the Israeli interest in mobilising Western sentiment toward justifying anti-Arab warfare has probably been important, and the US vested interests in permanent war have also found anti-Muslim and anti-Arab demonisation useful. The politicians and media follow in the wake of these powerful initiators.

So are we talking about racism as an *effect* of imperial expansionism – an attempt to rationalise it where other rationalisations are absent – rather than a *cause*, with the media playing an important role in this process?

EH: That is putting it too strongly and making it too calculated. There probably was some element of racism in Western imperial expansion and colonialism from the beginning, and it grew along with the imperial process of conquest, so was in a sense continually causing it, or making it more easily justified throughout the entire process of conquest and occupation.

Your 'Propaganda Model', first published in 1988, explains how media are filtered to make criticism of the established system less likely, through ownership, funding, sourcing, flak and dominant political ideology.[8] Do you think there have been any breakthroughs in media coverage that go against the model in recent years? Do criticism of Iraq, the Abu Ghraib photos, stories about rendition flights, and so on add up to any kind of change in media approach?

EH: *No* – there haven't been any 'breakthroughs in media coverage that go against the model in recent years'. In fact, the extent to which the media collaborated with the Bush administration in the run-up to the Iraq War in 2003, in the face of massive street protests on the part of ordinary citizens, was a media regression from the Vietnam War experience. The *New York Times* and *Washington Post* both semi-apologised for their failures of 2002–03, but they had hardly finished these when they were doing the same in preparing the public for a possible war against Iran. As I noted above, some important elements of the media have even taken over the task of protecting the war-makers from exposures like that of Wikileaks by serving as enforcers assailing the authors of such efforts.

It should also be stressed that the Propaganda Model rests on structural facts, and these have, on balance, tended to reinforce the applicability of the model. The media have become more centralised, competition for advertising has intensified, sourcing has become even more focused on power centres that can provide news cheaply and whose claims require less investigative expense, and the flak of those power centres has become more sophisticated and compelling. Flak from within the media has become more important with the rise of Fox and greater importance of right-wing blogs and talk shows. The possible offset in Internet modes of communication has not materialised in practice, much of it dominated by mainstream media, right-wing blogs, diversionary social media, and small, underfunded and fragmented non-right-wing entities. As regards ideology, anticommunism retains some force, free-market ideology has grown greatly in importance with the decline of social democracy and the increase in inequality and consolidation of upper-class power, and permanent warfare under US and NATO auspices has made for quiescence in the West.

So how does something like, say, Abu Ghraib, go from being ignored to becoming a major news story? What do you see as the conditions and limits on such critical coverage that stops it from contradicting overall support for the war?

EH: The Iraq War was major news, and serious torture by US forces, with dramatic pictures, could not be indefinitely avoided any more than the My Lai Massacre could be kept under the rug in another war that commanded lots of attention. In both cases the evidence was ignored for many months. Even in the Soviet Union nasty things coming out of Afghanistan couldn't be entirely kept out of the media, and the Soviet secretary of defence complained bitterly about the media's unpatriotic behaviour.[9] But the media in both places are 'patriotic' and follow and emphasise a party line that features the positives, the benign intent of the government, and Abu Ghraib as a regrettable deviation, and the evil intent and acts of the enemy.

So, we might say the limit of criticism is the point at which particular events might be connected as examples of something more universal – that can't be done?

EH: I believe it can't be done. The elements of the propaganda model that make elite opinion prevail and allow elite decisions to fend off challenge are stronger than in 1988. The permanent war economy is more firmly entrenched, money-dominated elections are assured, and connecting critical points into a universal for the majority is not on the cards.

You mentioned the 'semi-apologies' of certain media organisations for their war support leading up to Iraq. Indeed, there is an interesting narrative that has become popular in the more 'liberal' media, almost using the devastation of 9/11 as an excuse – the idea that the government was given more leeway than usual due to the shock of the events, and more critical journalism was temporarily 'put on hold'. Given what you've said about coverage of wars before and since failing in the same ways, do you see this as a cynical and cowardly excuse, scapegoating the then government to deny responsibility?

EH: These apologies were never complete, and were offered because it was so evident that these media institutions had failed to do their job, that they had to say *something*. I don't think they were blaming the government, but there was a certain cynicism in that they didn't really explain why, they didn't fire the leading editors who had been responsible for swallowing and propagandising lies and who should probably be in jail as collaborators in war crimes, and they didn't put in place reforms that might prevent a repetition of this gross malperformance. And they immediately began to do the same as regards Iran.

Could we really expect the mass media in a liberal capitalist society *not* to resemble the media described in the propaganda model? Is it a virile right wing or neoliberalism that refuses to name and vilify US state terror, or a fundamental deficiency in the forms or systemic structures of liberal media?

EH: Again, the answer is *no* – both on institutional as well as historical grounds. The model is built on the structural characteristics of a liberal capitalist society and it has evolved in a manner that looks very much built-in. We would not expect such media to name and vilify US terror as that is their own terror, which needs protection by institutions that are part of the corporate establishment and system. We and our clients only retaliate, we do not terrorise. This can involve the media in really serious contortions, applied double standards, and suppressions, but it has operated in this fashion for many years and, as the propaganda model suggests, flows from basic structural characteristics of the media. The right wing helps reduce any deviation from this kind of apologetics for our own terrorism, but the main thrust is independent of the work of these enforcers.

It seems that even when atrocities are revealed in the media as being directed or supported by the United States this does not lead to delegitimisation of the overall foreign policy project. The state can even admit to something as horrific as what you have referred to as the 'sanctions of mass destruction' in 1990s' Iraq and still not provoke a mass outcry. Why is this? Do you think the media, and the state via the media, define the parameters and language of debate on subjects such as terrorism to the point where it is difficult to conceive anything the US does as terrorism? Is the idea of US righteousness so strong and so

enforced culturally that even its terrorism seems as if it's done for the right reasons?

EH: Actually, the phrase – an entirely appropriate one – 'sanctions of mass destruction' was the title of a 1999 *Foreign Affairs* article co-authored by the brothers John and Karl Mueller. They made the reasonable point that the US–UK-engineered sanctions on Iraq, then in their ninth year, 'may well have been a necessary cause of the deaths of more people in Iraq than have been slain by all so-called weapons of mass destruction throughout history', and added how 'interesting' it was that 'this loss of human life has failed to make a great impression in the United States'.[10] Or, to return to what I said in answer to your earlier question, in this case, the perpetrator group not only didn't care about the monumental loss of Iraqi lives, but, in the then US ambassador to the United Nations Madeleine Albright's notable phrase (1996), this loss of Iraqi lives was 'worth it'.

In the case of the 'sanctions of mass destruction' applied to Iraq (1990–2003), and the subsequent case of the actual second war waged by the United States and Britain in the conquest of Iraq, plausible estimates place the combined Iraqi death toll at somewhere between 1 and 2 million persons. With human losses on this scale occurring as the result of deliberately crafted policies, we are not just talking about 'terrorism', but rather more realistically a *genocidal* campaign. Yet, as David Peterson and I showed in *The Politics of Genocide*, the establishment media were extremely reluctant to use the term 'genocide' to describe these Iraqi deaths, whether caused by the sanctions or by the war and occupation.[11] If anything, the notion that if the United States and the United Kingdom (or *our* side) perpetrate great atrocities it never really happens extends far beyond acts of US and UK state terrorism to the gravest atrocities conceivable.

The parameters of discussion do flow from state interest. Officials like Madeleine Albright are treated with great deference, and if she says the consequences of the sanctions of mass destruction are 'worth it', the media do not and will not challenge this; and if the Bush administration says that the invasion–occupation of Iraq is justified, even on grounds that at the time seemed highly questionable, the mainstream media are prepared to ignore the lies, extreme law violations, and violence far beyond 'terrorism'. So the combination of structure, patriotism, self-righteousness, deference to state interest and official claims rules out the use of the plain word terrorism in application to US terrorisation. The United States can only wage a 'war on terror'!

NOTES

1. See: Edward S. Herman and Gerry O'Sullivan, *The 'Terrorism' Industry* (New York: Pantheon, 1989), pp.42–4.
2. See Edward S. Herman and Noam Chomsky, *Manufacturing Consent* (New York: Pantheon, 1988, 2002; Bodley Head, 2008), pp.72–4.
3. See Herman and O'Sullivan, *The 'Terrorism' Industry*, Chs 3 and 8.
4. On entrapment in the so-called 'war on terror', see Amy Goodman, 'Entrapment or Foiling Terror? FBI's Reliance on Paid Informants Raises Questions about Validity of Terrorism Cases', *Democracy NOW!*, 6 October 2010, <http://tinyurl.com/28yrdwu>.
5. For one example of this attack-dog function, see John F. Burns and Ravi Somaiya, 'WikiLeaks Founder on the Run, Trailed by Notoriety', *New York Times*, 23 October 2010; and for a criticism of the *Times*'s performance of this role, see Glenn Greenwald, 'The Nixonian henchmen of today: at the NYT', *Salon.com*, 24 October 2010, <http://tinyurl.com/2uvj4le>.
6. Edward S. Herman and David Peterson, *The Politics of Genocide* (New York: Monthly Review Press, 2010), p.22.
7. John Ellis, *The Social History of the Machine Gun* (New York: Pantheon, 1975), p.101.
8. Herman and Chomsky, *Manufacturing Consent*, ch.1.
9. Bill Keller, 'Soviet Official Says Press Harms Army', *New York Times*, 21 January 1988.
10. John Mueller and Karl Mueller, 'Sanctions of Mass Destruction', *Foreign Affairs*, Vol.78, No.3 (1999).
11. Herman and Peterson, *The Politics of Genocide*, p.35 and p.72.

7

Judith Butler
The Discourse of Terror

To what extent, in your view, do the ways in which mainstream media select and contextualise events determine the boundaries of public thinking? You have said on one hand, regarding the 'framing' of war and terrorism, that '[e]fforts to control the visual and narrative dimensions of war delimit public discourse by establishing and disposing the sensuous parameters of reality itself',[1] but also that 'specters are produced that haunt the ratified version of reality'.[2]

Judith Butler: There are surely many ways that this happens, but we can note at the most obvious level the way in which forms of resistance or violence get cast as 'conflicts' that assume two sides that are fighting only against one another. We are more often than not asked, for instance, to regard Israel and Palestine as in a conflict of this kind, a framing that sets each of them on equal footing, and implicitly analogises the political situation to a fist fight, a soccer match, or a domestic quarrel. So if, then, the only two intelligible political positions are 'pro-Palestinian' or 'pro-Israeli', the presumption is that one's position is determined by a sentiment that wants one side to win over the other. In the meantime, what is lost is any sense that the Palestinian resistance to Israeli colonial rule is waged from a situation of occupation or expulsion, that there is a military order that controls the boundaries of what would be a sovereign Palestinian state, that the land on which that state is now thinkable has been radically diminished by an ongoing practice of land confiscation and appropriation. So we set the actors on the scene through the banal discourse of 'conflict' in ways that fully deflect from the history and struggle of colonial resistance, refusing as well by that means to link the resistance to other forms of colonial resistance, their rationale, and their tactics.

Obviously, visual renditions of war not only establish what can be seen, and the audio track established what can be heard, but the photographs also 'train' us in ways of focusing on targets, ways of regarding suffering and loss. So photographs can be forms of recruitment, ways of bringing the viewer into the military, as it were. In this way, they prepare us for war, even enlist us in war, at the level of the senses, establishing a sensate regime of war.

Given that, do you think framing, or PR, or even concealment of facts in media and politics decisively damages public awareness on the means and ends of US foreign policy (particularly the implementation of neoliberal economic policies through unilateral war, and sponsorship of dictatorships or the overthrow of democratic governments)? Or is there a high level of awareness, which for some reason still does not lead to an outcry, and if so what ideological role does such coverage play?

JB: Perhaps we have to remember that there are forms of outrage that do not lead to any sort of mobilisation, and there are ways of 'registering the facts' that do not lead to outrage. So if we are trying to account for mobilisation, we have to ask, under what conditions do outraged forms of knowing lead to social mobilisations and movements? So awareness alone does not suffice, and neither does outrage. I think something happens only when people find that they are moved with others, find themselves linked or allied in new ways, showing up or speaking out in ways that resonate with one another. That resonating can be very compelling and lead to moving and speaking more emphatically and with sharper focus.

In your essay 'The Charge of Anti-Semitism: Jews, Israel, and the Risks of Public Critique', you make the point that labelling

as anti-Semitic those who protest Israeli state violence against the Palestinians, is

> to seek to control the kind of speech that circulates in the public sphere, to terrorise with the charge of anti-Semitism, and to produce a climate of fear through the tactical use of a heinous judgment with which no progressive person would want to identify.[3]

Is the word 'terrorise' here deliberately chosen to create resonance with the idea of terrorism itself? To what extent is this form of political correctness a 'linguistic terrorism' that, if effective, helps facilitate state terrorism?

JB: As I read that sentence, I wonder whether I might have meant 'terrify us'; but perhaps as well there was a less than conscious effort to show that the suppression of debate about Palestine and about the Boycott, Divestment, and Sanctions movement – within many academic circles – does seek to establish those who would address such issues in speech as already collaborating with 'terrorist' regimes, although now only Hamas is officially terrorist according to the US government and its allies. In any case, the idea that speaking at all on the topic, demanding public space in which to have that debate, is itself an act of complicity with violence, and violence against Israelis, understood as synonymous with Jews, and so violence against Jews, clearly stops the speech with an unspeakable allegation. If you speak, you are in an unspeakable place, have become a Nazi or its moral equivalent (if there is a moral equivalent). It certainly terrifies, but perhaps also it is a linguistic permutation of state terrorism, an assault that stops one in one's tracks, and secures the continuing operation of the regime and its monopoly on politically intelligible speech.

The dominant 'Western' political climate today seems to be one in which protecting sections of the population from danger, whether actual or predicted, takes precedence over considerations such as civil liberties or the lives of 'non-Western' people. Surely, however, garnering consent through fear has always been a part of politics, and this is not a specifically modern phenomenon. What, if anything, distinguishes its current form?

JB: Maybe we need to start with the rethinking of what is 'West' and what is 'non-West'. It seems to me that there are any number of populations which already cross that divide, and we could probably point to several existing states that belong exclusively neither to one category nor to the other. Do we use these terms to designate geographical realities, geopolitical ones, or perhaps sites of power, exploitation, orientalism that move through space and time in ways that have to be tracked historically.

In any case, it is true that non-governmental organisations working within strong human rights frameworks are now confounded by securitarian forms of logic and power that extend the paternalistic bias of their work in new ways. The state or global forms of power that seek to protect populations considered in danger may well extend their own power through those acts of protection. Where is democratic process or popular sovereignty for the endangered population? It cannot be 'given' or 'allocated' by some other power without that same power claiming the right to withdraw what it gives. And yet, popular sovereignty has to be given by a people to itself, and this is the important meaning of self-determination. So the question is whether NGOs that bring protection or aid or reparation therapies are furthering the possibility of self-determination or extending a form of managerial power and paternalism.

You have also pointed out that the notion of safety related to greater security is actually false, and entails great risk. To accept this security is to put oneself in the hands of authorities – state and corporate – as if they can be completely trusted to act purely in one's interests. In fact the less accountable they are the less likely they are to do so. What does support for such 'security'-focused policy indicate – is it fear again, or, say, naivety or desperation (a lack of perceived alternative)?

JB: There are doubtless all kinds of ways of explaining why people want security, but I do not think we can start with the psychological explanations. Even psychological states like fear or desire for safety are conditioned by social and political forms of intimidation and scaremongering that intensify those emotions, and even work to persuade people that nothing less than their survival is at stake. So we have to be able to track the ways in which fear, for instance, is monopolised by state and media institutions, ways in which fear is actually promoted and distributed as a way of bolstering the need for greater security and militarisation. I do not mean to say that such institutions act unilaterally on psychic life, or that they determine certain psychic outcomes. Rather, they exploit forms of fear and insecurity that are there for any population – no political organisation of life could ever fully do away with fear and insecurity; but some work to intensify, accelerate, and make more acute forms of fear, and to provide ideological focus for such intensified fears, at which point critical thinking has a fierce rival: the critical analysis that shows precisely how those forms of fear are promulgated, and for what purpose. If those forms of criticism are successful, then people can feel rage about having had their fear exploited, and form an analysis at the same time.

What, if any, have been the major shifts in US state discourse during the Obama presidency – especially, for example, given the events of the 'Arab Spring'? Has the United States softened its more aggressive post-9/11 rhetoric – even been forced to do so because peaceful uprisings like the one in Egypt in early 2011 successfully reappropriated the meaning of democracy?

JB: I do not follow this rhetoric closely anymore, since there is a limit to how much heartsickness one can bear. But it is clear that whatever language of democracy Obama and his administration use is very tactically deployed, and has as its main aim the extension of US power and interests. I am sorry to be so blunt, but I do not see much ambiguity here. Obama was late to affirm the Egyptian revolution as a democratic movement, and even then he was eager to have installed those military leaders who were known for their practices of torture. And now he is quick to make allies with the Muslim Brotherhood for tactical reasons as well (though earlier that same administration stoked Islamophobic fear about that very political party). Obama's failure to close Guantanamo is yet another instance where the rhetoric of democratic and constitutional rights proved not useful for his international relations, relations which are always pursued in ways that continue to link and fortify securitarian power with the opening of new markets.

In considering dissent, you say that the events of 9/11 'led public intellectuals to waver in their commitment to principles of justice and prompted journalists to take leave of the time-honoured tradition of investigative journalism'.[4] But was there really such a shift, or does this romanticise the situation before 9/11? Would public intellectuals and investigative journalists have made, say, a war on Iraq significantly more difficult if 9/11 hadn't happened?

JB: I certainly don't mean to suggest that all investigative journalism prior to 9/11 in the US was praiseworthy. But there were more examples to which one could point, and there were at last some activist photographers who understood that getting information into the public sphere in spite of military censorship was a right and obligation within democracy. That strain in war journalism did nearly vanish during that time.

But was it not precisely the complacency and attitude to reporting world affairs and US foreign policy, including US state terrorism, for years before 9/11 that made the reaction that followed it possible? The event itself, devastating as it was, effectively had no context. The government was free to write its own narrative because one had not been started earlier (for the most part), and it is far more difficult to undo that now. Effectively, it was the relatively small amount of critical academia and journalism *before* 9/11 that created a climate in which no other reaction was possible. Is that a fair analysis?

JB: I am not sure that I know enough about the pre-history of 9/11 to agree or disagree. But I did think at the time that the Bush administration took a number of cues from the Israeli government, not only by drawing on and intensifying anti-Arab racism, but by insisting that the attack on US government and financial buildings was an attack on 'democracy' and by invoking 'security at all costs' to wage war without a clear focus (why the Taliban?), and by suspending both constitutional rights and the regular protocol for congressional approval for declaring war. The Gulf War was a clear precedent as well, and it let us begin to understand how the US government would go to war to secure strategic oil reserves and potential markets.

Jean Baudrillard wrote about 9/11 'that we have dreamt of this event, that everyone without exception has dreamt of it – because no one can avoid dreaming of the destruction of any power that has become hegemonic to this degree', but that this 'is unacceptable to the Western moral conscience'.[5] What do you think of this idea, or the implications that follow from it – firstly, that 'we' must be almost relieved at the opportunity, given by the 'war on terror', to transfer our guilt to the 'terrorist'; secondly, that this relief brings its own guilt, and imbeds us even more deeply in a complex relationship with a power we become collectively responsible for, and must defend, despite understanding its inherent violence?

JB: Perhaps that view is too totalising. It is true that one was not allowed at the time to really ask, what would lead people to do this, from what sense of political outrage or injury? And in that way, the possibility of sympathetic identification was foreclosed. That does not mean that some people took quiet pleasure in certain icons of US capitalism coming down, even though they would oppose such action on moral and political grounds. So a different kind of pleasure surfaced in the aftermath, the pleasure of seeing the towers fall time and again, the experience of being entranced by the visual spectacle, and then also the very graphic forms of public mourning for exemplary citizens (taking place at the same time as the refusal to mourn the undocumented, the foreign, gay, and lesbian lives lost there, for example). I am not sure that the guilt over the pleasure reinstalled the good citizen. I think maybe the destructive pleasure got turned into the destructive pleasure of war (something we see still in the images of US soldiers urinating on the dead bodies of Taliban soldiers). Something of the pleasure in destruction gets unleashed, and then becomes part of war effort rationalised first as revenge (or justice defined as revenge). But then it takes new forms, as we see now. The pleasurable part of public mourning can also lead to a sense of self-sanctification that justifies in advance any war effort, whether or not the target and destruction are in any way related to the initial event.

Is it possible to imagine a non-violent response to something like 9/11? Is it not the case that with such an act of violence (inevitably taken as aggression, even if part of an ongoing cycle) the only response is self-preservation at the expense of the attacker, continuing the cycle? Or, is the claim of revenge more a systemic inevitability, that there is no way at least within the current model of capitalist global relations that the reaction could have been anything other than more terrorism?

JB: I think that many of the mobilisations against the wars waged by the United States and its allies since 2001 have been non-violent and massive. We have seen them throughout European capitals and in the United States, and in many other parts of the world as well. So it is not only imaginable, but already actual. If you are asking whether states and state actors can only respond through revenge, then you are suggesting that diplomatic solutions are hopeless. I wonder about economic sanctions, though, since that is a way that states engage in boycotts against one another. But because al-Qaeda has been a non-state-centred organisation, many of these scenarios do not exactly apply. These are not wars between states. And yet, it seems to me that we make a mistake if we accept the view that states are fighting terrorism, since we have abundant evidence for accepting the idea of state terrorism, and what is most urgent is to track and expose how state terrorism operates under the rubric of 'democracy'.

In discussing pictures of Guantanamo Bay from 2002, you point out that 'the DOD [US Department of Defense] did not hide these photos, but published them openly'. One conclusion you draw from this is that 'they published these photographs to make known that a certain vanquishing had taken place, the reversal of

national humiliation, a sign of successful vindication'.[6] However, do you think there was also an implied threat there too – a message that, as due process is no longer applicable to 'terror suspects', anyone is vulnerable if they do not conform?

JB: Yes, of course. The photographs are warnings, but also badges of pride. In other words, it is a way of saying that we will without any shame torture and kill you, and you should not forget that. It is also a way of establishing the national 'we' as one who not only has the power to torture and destroy, but who will not be destroyed, will emerge as indestructible. Of course, it is a fantasy at the same time that it is an instrumentalisation of power. And it lets us see the link between the photographs and the crafting of a national 'we', one which can be an important point of departure for a critical cultural practice against war, which would include another photography and another form of crafting the senses.

And the enemy in this case is not necessarily a foreigner. Is it fair to say here perhaps that the US state does *terrorise*, rather than *terrify*, its own population?

JB: Those it arrests without cause and imprisons without due process, those it stops on the borders or detains indefinitely in offshore prisons, are clearly terrorised by state power. Those who fear that such fates might become their own are terrified, but we can see how state terrorisation is already at work in the experience of being terrified.

NOTES

1. Judith Butler, *Frames of War: When Is Life Grievable?* (London and New York: Verso, 2010), p.xi.
2. Ibid., p.xiii.
3. Judith Butler, *Precarious Life: The Powers of Mourning and Violence* (London and New York: Verso, 2004), p.120.
4. Ibid., p.xi.
5. Jean Baudrillard, *The Spirit of Terrorism*, trans. Chris Turner (London and New York: Verso, 2002), p.5.
6. Butler, *Precarious Life*, pp.77–8.

8

Richard Jackson
Terrorism Studies and Academia

There has been a phenomenal rise in terrorism studies, particularly since 9/11. And yet state terrorism is hardly ever considered by terrorism scholars as an important area of research. What are some of the reasons for this in your view?

Richard Jackson: Terrorism studies has grown tremendously since 9/11, but with very few exceptions, has retained a narrow focus on non-state actors. In my view, there are a number of reasons for this. The first relates to the historical origins of the field in counter-insurgency studies. Emerging out of a state-centric, problem-solving perspective, the field first developed from a series of research activities which were aimed at better understanding and countering left-wing insurgent movements during the Cold War. In other words, terrorism studies had as its central focus from the very beginning the control of anti-state violence. Once a field has developed a central focus, scientific paradigm and set of key research questions, and incoming scholars are trained in the same approach and socialised into adopting the same paradigm, a process of sedimentation and institutionalisation sets in. In effect, the dominant approach becomes an enduring social structure which is exceedingly difficult – but not impossible – to alter.

At the same time, governments have quite effectively controlled the public language and popular understanding of terrorism, defining it in very specific ways in the legal system, and shaping its reporting and discussion in the media. In the late nineteenth century, anarchists used terrorism to try and create revolutionary conditions under autocracy, in the process assassinating several European heads of state. In response, the first international efforts were made to outlaw acts of terrorism, which was conceptualised solely as non-state violence against governments. Although there was a brief period at Nuremburg when Nazi leaders were condemned for the crime of terror, the term was thereafter used solely for describing insurgent groups and the state terrorism seen in the Second World War was largely forgotten. Since then, the media in all its forms – news and entertainment – has followed the governmental conceptualisation of terrorism as non-state violence, thereby helping to shape public understandings and common sense. Terrorism scholars have not been immune to these forces, and there is a strong correlation between depictions of terrorism in the popular media and academic descriptions within terrorism studies.

Of course, these processes intensified ever more greatly after 9/11, when every country in the world was required by the UN to update its anti-terrorism laws and a massive international effort was made, led by the United States, to coordinate a global campaign against non-state terrorism. Today, hundreds of new laws, agencies, and institutions have been established to fight against non-state terrorism, and thousands of new scholars have joined the effort to provide useful research in these efforts. In addition, the media have colluded with governments, rarely questioning the state's self-interested definition of terrorism or asking whether counter-terrorism measures taken in the 'war on terror' might themselves be a form of state terrorism. Some states, such as Israel, have engaged in sustained and coordinated efforts to influence the media and scholars into reserving the term for non-state groups like Palestinian militants, and have vehemently opposed the use of the term to describe their own actions.

In this context, the term 'state terrorism' appears inherently illogical and counter-intuitive to most people; it contradicts accepted common sense of what terrorism is and which actors can commit it. It also contradicts established public narratives of state sovereignty and the state's monopoly of legitimate violence. It is widely accepted that unlike non-state actors, states can legitimately use violence in pursuit of national interests, especially when their security is threatened. Within this widely accepted viewpoint, it is frequently forgotten that state violence

is highly circumscribed, and that in any case, it does not affect
the theoretical/definitional point that if states engage in acts
which have been defined as terrorism, then it cannot be the
case that these acts cease to be terrorism just because they are
committed by state agents.

A final reason relates to the broader place of scholars and
universities in society. As publicly funded institutions, there are
powerful expectations that scholars should produce research
that is useful to society, and norms of loyalty which dictate what
counts as appropriate research and activities, and what is taboo.
In this context, it is risky in career terms, and difficult in practical
terms of funding and support, for scholars to undertake studies
on state crimes, particularly if it involves their own governments
and societies. You could say that there is something of a taboo
in discussing state terrorism, especially if it involves Western
states or their allies.

**This taboo does not extend to state sponsorship of non-state
terrorism. But again the focus is firmly on the so-called 'rogue
states', most of which can be found on the US Department of
State's annual list of 'state sponsors of international terrorism'.
Very little is written about, say, US sponsorship of anti-Castro
or Contra terrorism. So would you not say that the taboo is
not state terrorism as such, but rather the crimes of one's own
state and its allies?**

RJ: On the face of it, this is true: there are annual lists published
of 'state sponsors of international terrorism' and they do usually
focus on states that are currently considered hostile to Western
interests. Interestingly, if you examine these lists over time,
you can see states move on and off them according to political
alliances and current strategic interests. This is an illustration of
the socially constructed nature of the terrorism discourse, where
meanings, facts and interpretations shift and evolve. From this
perspective, the taboo extends to avoiding any mention of 'our'
terrorism or its sponsorship at the state level.

On the other hand, it is curious that there is still only a fairly
small literature (within orthodox terrorism studies) on 'state

sponsorship' of terrorism, and even less media scrutiny or commentary. I think this is because states (and their publicists and intellectuals) know that if too much is made of it – if scholars or reporters go into too much detail in investigating which states sponsor which groups – it will quickly be revealed that our states also sponsor groups and actors who could easily be considered terrorists: the Contras, anti-Castro groups, loyalist paramilitaries, Lebanese militias, the Northern Alliance in Afghanistan, and so on. It is interesting and a little surprising that Daniel Byman's book on state sponsorship of terrorism, a mainstream analysis by a respected traditional terrorism scholar, discusses US sponsorship (admittedly at a low level) of IRA terrorist activities, in addition to the usual suspects of Iran, Syria and the like.[1] In this sense, the book illustrates how even when a traditional terrorism scholar opens up the Pandora's Box of state sponsorship, they cannot help but see Western examples. The central point is, if it still wasn't something of a taboo, we would probably see a lot more discussion and analysis of state sponsorship which would naturally reveal extensive Western involvement in sponsoring the terrorist activities of certain groups around the world. Nevertheless, in comparison to the volume of discussion and analysis of non-state terrorism, the state terrorism literature, including the literature on the issue of 'state sponsorship', is so small as to constitute a major lacuna – or, a taboo from an anthropological perspective.

Many of the leading terrorism scholars are affiliated with, for instance, the RAND Corporation, which has links with the US government. Would you say that this undermines their academic rigour and integrity? Or can academic independence be maintained when policymakers call upon the expertise of scholars in such matters?

RJ: It is perfectly reasonable for policymakers to call upon experts to advise them on how to deal with challenging social and political issues. The problem comes when the process and context in which this occurs creates a kind of echo chamber in which the advisers provide the policymakers with advice which simply legitimates what they had intended to do anyway, rather than offering objective, non-partisan advice. The context in which terrorism studies emerged historically as part of Cold War counter-insurgency has, in my view, contributed to producing exactly this situation. I don't believe this is some kind of conspiracy, or that scholars are acting in bad faith. Rather, socialised into conceptualising terrorism in a state-centric way, and institutionalised into orienting their research towards the priority of countering terrorism, real non-partisan, objective advice becomes difficult, if not impossible. In a way, Gramsci's notion of organic intellectuals becomes relevant as a description of this situation: terrorism scholars, through institutional, financial and ideational ties to the state, become part of the dominant ideological structures and processes of hegemony. It is not necessary that they are conscious of it to play this role.

A perfect example of how this broad structure functions relates to a little-known study by Ivan Eland of the CATO Institute in 1996 entitled 'Does US Intervention Overseas Breed Terrorism? The Historical Record'.[2] Eland wanted to examine the empirical basis of a Pentagon Science Board statement which had linked US foreign policy to acts of anti-American terrorism. After extensive research on the historical record, Eland concluded: 'The large number of terrorist attacks that occurred in retaliation for an interventionist American foreign policy implicitly demonstrates that terrorism against US targets could be significantly reduced if the United States adopted a policy of military restraint overseas.' What interests me is that leading terrorism scholars have never cited this research or followed it up with further research. Certainly, I have never seen US military intervention included as one of the possible explanatory variables in studies on the causes of anti-American terrorism. The reason for this is that the structures of intellectual production heavily militate against the inclusion of such a perspective. Only scholars outside of the operational structures of terrorism studies could follow this up, and even then, they would risk forms of exclusion.

What do you mean by 'exclusion'?

RJ: By 'exclusion', I mean being shut out of certain discussions and debates, and being ignored when it comes to contributing to policy advice or media coverage. In practical terms, it means being unable to get an op-ed in the national newspapers or into media outlets where key debates are taking place, and being overlooked when scholarly experts are called in to advise and testify to parliamentary committees and the like. There are also more subtle forms of exclusion, such as facing difficulties getting on panels at major conferences, having articles rejected from the mainstream journals, never being cited in major publications by your peers, having your expertise ignored by the media, or the failure to get a publishing contract with a prestigious mainstream publisher. Often, such exclusion is seen in the way certain 'outsider' scholars have a following among a certain activist community where they are free to debate and discuss certain issues, but are largely excluded from the debates and conversations going on in the academic mainstream.

In his seminal article *Social Forces, States and World Orders*, Robert W. Cox distinguishes between problem-solving theory and critical theory. He contends that problem-solving theory 'takes the world as it finds it, with the prevailing social and power relationships and the institutions into which they are organised, as the given framework for action'. Consequently, 'the aim of problem-solving theory is to make these institutions work smoothly by dealing effectively with particular sources of trouble'.[3] You consider this approach to be a factor in the limited way in which terrorism is theorised in conventional terrorism studies, with many terrorism scholars reduced to providing policy recommendations to governments.[4] Would you say that these scholars are conscious of the ideological support they provide to those in power?

RJ: I don't subscribe to the bad faith model of scholars who consciously choose to support hegemonic states regardless of their actions. The terrorism scholars I know are very sincere, scrupulously honest in their work, and many of them have openly criticised government policies they view as either ineffective or unethical. Many have also produced excellent research which challenges widely accepted attitudes and beliefs about terrorism. The problem is a broader structural one in which institutional arrangements, funding structures, scholarly training and widely held assumptions operate in a problem-solving mode, and serve to perpetuate rather than challenge dominant ideological structures.

In my view, a key problem relates to scholarly training in critical analysis. Too often, students are not taught to question basic assumptions and ideas, or the existing structures of society. Instead, they are encouraged to study terrorism within an existing state-centric, problem-solving framework, and to accept a lot of ideas about terrorism which are not actually proven, such as that terrorism is an exceptional form of violence, it poses a serious threat to national security, it is caused by religious extremism, it is practised by abnormal people, it is an irrational strategy, and so on. This serves to reproduce existing forms of knowledge and practice regarding terrorism, thereby perpetuating the intellectual systems that make policy advice the primary goal of research and stops state terrorism from being a major focus of research and teaching.

You have noted that a disproportionately large literature on 'Islamic terrorism' has developed in the past ten years.[5] Considering terrorism carried out by individuals who mostly come from Muslim countries or claim to act in the name of Islam has had the greatest impact in the West in that period, is this not to be expected?

RJ: There are several ways of approaching this question. First, we should consider the empirical record of state versus non-state terrorism. The curious fact is that most leading terrorism scholars admit that state terrorism – and they do almost all admit the existence of state terrorism – is a much greater problem than non-state terrorism, although these scholars always then go on to say that it is not something they are interested in studying.

The fact is that if we examine the historical record of terrorism (using widely accepted definitions), then the terrorism committed by so-called 'Islamic terrorists' pales in comparison to the past and present record of state terrorism. So, on this basis alone, the vast literature on 'Islamic terrorism' is disproportionate and a distortion of empirical reality. To better reflect the real-world experiences of terrorism in the world today, the literature should instead be dominated by studies of state terrorism.

We might also add that if one examines the empirical record worldwide, most terrorism occurs in the developing world. It is simply untrue that most non-state terrorism is either committed by Muslims, or is directed against Western states, or indeed, can seriously affect the stability of Western states. Western states are robust enough to deal with acts of terrorism, even destructive ones like 9/11; the destabilising effects of terrorism come from the response by the authorities who choose to disrupt society with intrusive counter-terrorism measures.

The point is, from this perspective, the literature should be dominated by studies of terrorism in the developing world. The fact that it focuses instead on anti-Western 'Islamic terrorism' is an indication of the Eurocentric character of the field, not the state of terrorism as it actually is. In addition, we might note that in recent years, any empirical analysis of the record of terrorist plots, arrests, and incidents would demonstrate that less than 10 per cent of terrorism reported to official agencies in the EU and US is related to Muslims. The vast majority is right-wing, nationalist or single-issue in nature. It is due to the ideological nature of the media, as well as that of terrorism scholars and officials, that this terrorism receives so little attention, while every 'Islamic' plot, no matter how ineffectual, receives undue attention.

I would also argue that distinguishing terrorism by virtue of the purported religion of the perpetrators is misleading, counter-productive, and a counter-terrorist strategy in itself. In an article I recently published with Jeroen Gunning entitled, 'How religious is "religious terrorism"?', we discuss how this notion misunderstands the causes of the terrorism, and the political motives and strategies of the terrorists.[6] More importantly, it serves to demonise and depoliticise their struggles. For example, the reason why there is terrorism related to the Middle East is not because the region is dominated by Muslims, but because the region is dominated by wars, interventions, and military occupations by numerous internal and external powers.

The point is, the notion of 'religious terrorism' is part of the broader structures of hegemony which seek to deny certain groups a real politics and legitimate grievances, and obscure the ways in which non-state actors are frequently resisting violent and oppressive forms of hegemony. Interestingly, the current obsession with 'Islamic terrorism' mirrors the disproportionate focus on left-wing terrorism during the Cold War by the same group of scholars. This illustrates how the field functions largely as the intellectual arm of state security and hegemony, which means that the field's focus tends to reflect the priorities of the state at any given moment in history. If the Middle East was not a priority for Western foreign policy at the present juncture, I expect we would see a lot less studies on Middle Eastern 'Islamic terrorism'.

You say that distinguishing terrorism by virtue of the religion of the perpetrators is misleading, and that it only serves to depoliticise their struggle. But it is also the terrorists themselves that articulate their political grievances in unmistakably religious terms. Is it not just the case that the terrorism scholars are taking them at their word?

RJ: It is true that terrorists articulate their grievances in religious terms, but to focus on the religion is to be distracted by the wrapping paper and to forget about what's inside the package. It is also slightly misleading to think that they only ever speak about religious issues. If you read bin Laden's 'Letter to America', for example, you'll find some references to Islam there, but the fact is that most of the letter discusses completely intelligible political issues such as support for Israel, oil politics, and the Kyoto Accord. This is true of virtually all his communications: mostly he opines about political issues and grievances that affect the Muslim world. In other words, if you look past the cultural packaging of the message – and all political communicators package their message in cultural terms which make sense to their audience – then you can see the concrete issues they are motivated by. From this perspective, terrorism scholars rarely take terrorists at their own words. Usually, they dismiss their real-world political grievances as merely propaganda for their real purposes – which are variously held to be nihilism or religious fundamentalism.

I would also argue that there is a degree of hypocrisy involved, in the sense that Western political leaders also use a great deal of religious rhetoric (they too are often appealing to a certain constituency for support), and Western militaries are inherently bound up with religious symbolism and practice (army chaplains, for example). But it is rarely suggested by terrorism scholars – or international relations scholars more generally – that we should classify US counter-terrorism policy as 'religious' or invasions as religious wars. Adopting such a focus would be misleading and would get us about as far as the notion of 'Islamic terrorism' has got us towards a real understanding of what's going on.

You have said that some scholars have over-exaggerated the terrorist threat against Western nations, and as a consequence contributed to the rise of 'politics of fear'.[7] It is perhaps easy to see how this 'politics of fear' can benefit, say, politicians and the military–industrial complex, but what does academia gain from it?

RJ: In recent years, academia has benefited tremendously from the politics of fear about terrorism. One key benefit is the increased funding for research on terrorism. There are now hundreds of millions of dollars allocated to research projects aimed at trying to understand the nature, causes, and solutions to terrorism, or into ever more sophisticated security measures, such as scanners and biometric surveillance technologies. Scholars who secure such funding also receive related benefits in terms of career advancement, prestige, publications, and the like. Within the university, the politics of terrorism fear has also fed the massive rise in the number of (fee-paying) students wanting to study courses on terrorism. Every major university in the world now has dozens of terrorism-related courses, which is beneficial to both the individual teachers (who may sell more copies of their books to eager students, for example), and the universities where the students come to study (who get more fees income).

However, the greatest benefit comes from the enhanced access to media and state power that comes from this broader fear. Whenever a terrorist event occurs, terrorism 'experts' are called upon to comment upon and discuss it in the media, thereby greatly increasing their exposure. In a media-obsessed society, such coverage can be incredibly seductive – not to mention lucrative. In addition, in the context of a national security emergency, scholars viewed as knowledgeable in the subject are often called upon to provide advice directly to policymakers. This direct access to power can also be incredibly seductive, but more likely, it simply reflects the existing social structures in which academics are required to demonstrate that they have an impact upon public policy and are playing a useful function in society. In other words, there are both material and prestige-based benefits that accrue to academics from the politics of fear.

You said earlier that you believed most terrorism scholars were 'sincere' and 'scrupulously honest in their work', and that the problem was a broader structural one. Does the idea that scholars also participate in the stoking of fear for material and prestige-based benefits not contradict this?

RJ: I would never imply that terrorism scholars participate *for* material and prestige-based benefits; this is most often simply a consequence of trying to be a good academic and following the structurally defined pathways to promotion and peer recognition. Once it happens, there are inbuilt incentives to keep the virtuous circle going. In other words, it is perfectly possible to accumulate material and prestige-based benefits without actively seeking them or engaging in certain behaviour for that specific end. In the post-9/11 period, given the level of political and media interest in the subject, if you write a book on terrorism, it will probably sell well and thus give you widespread recognition and prestige.

This is no different to any academic area: most scholars seek to do good research, disseminate their work widely, and make a contribution to policymaking and the betterment of society. The point is that at the current historical juncture this takes place in a context defined by moral panics and the politics of fear, which makes it likely that terrorism scholars will receive certain benefits from their work.

The real issue therefore, and challenge, is for scholars in a context which seeks to co-opt them and make them part of a broader operation of hegemonic power, to be self-reflexive and to try and ensure that they don't inadvertently function as organic intellectuals. This is not to say that there aren't state intellectuals who have fully bought into the hegemonic project. Rather, it's to say that I don't believe that most terrorism scholars operate on such a 'bad faith' model of actively pursuing benefits at the expense of truth. Unfortunately, it is mud-slinging of this nature – the labelling of whole groups of scholars as state lackeys or pro-state intellectual guardians – which has historically prevented a more productive kind of dialogue between the more traditional scholars and their 'critical' counterparts. If you go back and read some of the early literature, you can see that some of the traditional terrorism scholars acknowledged the kind of potentially unhealthy relationships between states and academics decades ago. However, the opprobrium they got, mostly from left-wing critics, and the language used, which called into question their motives and their morality, was so alienating that it closed off any possibility of a real conversation about this important issue. I think it is possible, and necessary, to discuss the issue in a way that doesn't blame individual scholars but looks at the structures of knowledge production which produce certain outcomes.

With the emergence of what is known as critical terrorism studies, which seek to challenge the way in which terrorism is studied in orthodox terrorism studies and advance a new approach to the subject, it is expected that more scholars will engage with state terrorism. With the structures of academic institutions as they are, is this set to remain a marginal sub-discipline with little impact on the debate?

RJ: I remain optimistic that no existing structure is so completely hegemonic that it cannot be successfully resisted and eventually changed, even one as entrenched as terrorism studies. People make history; they are not subject to it. The sustained and imaginative efforts of scholars, as well as artists, film makers, novelists, activists, and others, can bring about substantial change to the ideological and political–economic structures of society. This optimistic viewpoint, I believe, is borne out in the development of critical terrorism studies over the past few years, as well as related developments in a wide range of fields and areas of protest and resistance. In particular, I would point to the increasing number of undergraduate and graduate students who now study terrorism from an explicitly critical perspective at a great many universities around the world, including a large number of doctoral students. Trained in critical terrorism studies, they will form a major part of the next generation of scholars and thus help to establish the study of state terrorism more firmly in the wider field. I expect that a doctoral student, recognising the gap and seeing the opportunity of being the first to do it, will soon build a major database on state terrorism.

In addition, critical terrorism studies and its approach has been institutionalised in a fairly robust scholarly network (the Critical Studies on Terrorism Working Group (CSTWG) within the British International Studies Association) which regularly holds international conferences and participates through specially organised panels in major international conferences. It also has an established peer-reviewed journal (*Critical Studies on Terrorism*), and an academic book series (the Routledge Critical Terrorism Studies Series), both of which regularly publish high-quality studies on issues of state terrorism.

Related to this, the publication of several new studies on state terrorism in recent years, the establishment of a new journal on 'state crime', panels and papers at major international conferences, and the emergence of a new generation of scholars who are experts in state terrorism, indicate, to my mind, something of a revival of the study of state terrorism and the real possibility that it can start to influence public debates.

Of course, this is all contingent on the continuing production of courageous and rigorous scholarship on state terrorism, as well as the efforts of scholarly entrepreneurs who can institutionalise new research foci and practices, create broad networks of support, and link scholars, activists, artists, the media, and other influential actors in strategic campaigns to raise awareness. A key part of the process will involve working hard to change commonly accepted ideas and beliefs about terrorism, a difficult but not impossible task.

NOTES

1. Daniel Byman, *Deadly Connections: States that Sponsor Terrorism* (Cambridge: Cambridge University Press, 2005).
2. Ivan Eland, 'Does U.S. Intervention Overseas Breed Terrorism? The Historical Record', *CATO Foreign Policy Briefing*, No.50, 17 December 1998, <http://www.cato.org/pubs/fpbriefs/fpb-050es.html>.
3. Robert W. Cox, 'Social Forces, States and World Orders: Beyond International Relations Theory', *Millennium: Journal of Internal Studies*, Vol.10, Issue 2 (1981), pp.126–55 (p.128).
4. Richard Jackson, 'The Study of Terrorism after 11 September 2001: Problems, Challenges and Future Developments', *Political Studies Review*, Vol.7, Issue 2 (2009), pp.171–84 (p.181).
5. Jackson, 'Constructing Enemies: "Islamic Terrorism" in Political and Academic Discourse', *Government and Opposition*, Vol.42, Issue 3 (2007), pp.394–426.
6. Jeroen Gunning and Richard Jackson, 'What's so "religious" about "religious terrorism"?', *Critical Studies on Terrorism*, Vol.4, Issue 3 (2011), pp.369–88.
7. Jackson, 'The Study of Terrorism', pp.174–7.

9

Patrick Bond
International Financial Institutions
and the Economics of Terrorism

The slogan of the World Bank is 'Working for a World Free of Poverty', and the 'About Us' page of its website begins by saying, 'Our work is challenging, but our mission is simple: Help reduce poverty'.[1] The International Monetary Fund (IMF), meanwhile, explains its goals as 'working to foster global monetary cooperation, secure financial stability, facilitate international trade, promote high employment and sustainable economic growth, and reduce poverty around the world'.[2] According to some measurements, global poverty has decreased significantly in recent history, at least prior to the global financial crisis. How would you rate the efforts of these Bretton Woods Institutions (BWIs) in meeting their stated objectives?

Patrick Bond: The first point to make is that the abuse of language by Washington's multilateral financial crew is now totally out of control. To illustrate, after the Egyptian revolt in early 2011 and the emergence of young activists critical of the finance ministry in Cairo, the minister was pressured to reject the IMF's June 2011 loan offer of around $6 billion. Let's not forget that Washington mainly wants a pro-Israel Egypt but also $33 billion in Mubarak's foreign debt repaid by the new government, and repayment policing is one of the IMF's main jobs, after all. At that very point, some of the leading IMF staff in Washington and Cairo actually began referring to 'social justice' with a straight face, while imposing much the same menu on the Egyptian people that they were during Mubarak's reign.[3]

The World Bank's neoliberal orientation remains devastating for poor and working-class people. In considering growth and poverty trends, I mainly focus on Africa, where the misery is greatest and worsening, and where BWI bragging is most brazen. In debates I've had with the World Bank's chief Africa economist, Shanta Devarajan, one can sense the desperate lengths to which men like him must stretch the truth, to retain legitimacy as elites supposedly embarking on a poverty-reduction mission.[4] As a rare honest economist would admit, after a few beers at the end of the day, 'If you torture the data, they'll confess.'

There are typically three claims made. First, Africa is 'growing'. To simplify a complex argument, this claim requires us to ignore the vast outflow of not only flight capital by transnational corporations and Africa's unpatriotic bourgeoisie, but also what the Bank calls 'natural capital' in the form of non-renewable resources extraction. Bank staff and all other economists count extraction only as a positive event – not subtracting the country's diminished assets, which should logically be recorded as a debit in the national accounts.

Of course this is a profound flaw of the Gross Domestic Product indicator beloved of economists, and after making a variety of corrections to GDP we really should be referring to some sort of Genuine Progress Index, as does the group Redefining Progress. But if one makes even the most rudimentary corrections to GDP by subtracting non-renewable resources, considering pollution, adding in human capital investment in the form of education expenses, and better calculating machinery's wear and tear, then Africa is definitely not growing. In fact, the snapshot the World Bank took of African countries in the 2006 book *Where is the Wealth of Nations?*[5] shows most African countries recording a *negative* level of genuine savings, i.e. even after working a year, those debit factors push African wealth created over the 12 months of 2000 that were studied into a net deficit. The harder Africans worked to extract non-renewable resources, in other words, the poorer they became. During the 2002–08 and subsequent commodity boom, the situation grew even worse.

The second claim is that the African middle class is growing. It's an absurd claim that the African Development Bank has been making, backed by the BWIs. It works only by defining middle class as $2–20 in consumption each day, even though the cost of living in many African capital cities is way higher than in Western cities. And it works by not factoring in the problem of consumer indebtedness.

The third claim is that with African debt written down dramatically, globalisation is therefore working for Africa, responsible for Africa's 'resilience' to the recent and indeed ongoing world financial meltdown. In reality, according to the best research that unpacks the character of African growth, by John Weeks for the UN Conference on Trade and Development, the uptick comes thanks to once-off recovery from civil war in many countries (high short-term bounce-back growth) and to the commodities boom from 2002–08, and of course with the latter we get back to the first claim.

But even the sub-claim of dramatic African debt relief must be ridiculed, because the 2005 Gleneagles G8 agenda was to strip Africa's Low Income Countries (LICs) of their hard currency reserves – e.g. in the case of Nigeria, about $12 billion that year thanks to finance minister Ngozi Okonjo-Ikweala's generosity to the creditors – as a preliminary repayment, in exchange for writing off debt that was unrepayable and in dozens of cases technically 'odious' (i.e. borrowed by dictators and hence legally not liable to be repaid by democrats). The point – as even subsequent IMF data show – was to squeeze as much out as possible, and then ensure that Africa's annual interest payment flow continued rising (from 5 to 7 per cent of revenues), even at the same time that the debt stock was cut (from 35 to 18 per cent of GDP).

So if you ask whether 'stated objectives' – assuring genuine growth, world economic stability and the reduction of poverty – are being achieved, then certainly not. Nor would you expect them to be, if indeed the actual agenda of the BWIs is to deepen the commodification of all life in the interests of multinational capital, while assuring maximum repayment of odious debts to the financial markets, which are the ultimate arbiters of the BWIs' agenda.

The President of the World Bank, an institution located in the political heart of Washington, is always a US citizen, selected by the president of the United States. Also, in both the World Bank and the IMF, major decisions require an 85 per cent majority, and the method of apportioning votes means the United States is the only country that has a large enough share (over 16 per cent) to effectively veto decisions unilaterally. To what extent have the World Bank and IMF been designed to propagate US government policy?

PB: The BWIs were designed by the United States in 1944 at the Bretton Woods Hotel in New Hampshire, and two years later at their official launch in Savannah, Georgia, Washington dictated the devil in the details. The outcome was completely contrary to the need for international financial stability and balance, so the most far-sighted architect there, John Maynard Keynes, who favoured exchange controls and less uneven international trade, openly condemned the United States. The main website devoted to his memory recalls that Savannah was a 'difficult and ill-tempered' meeting. According to Keynes, 'Nations in debt to the Americans are voting with America, not because they want to but because, as a result of their dependence on American aid, they feel they have no other option.' On his way home from Savannah, the despondent Keynes suffered a heart attack, and died a few weeks later in England after another.[6]

Meantime, the World Bank president was set up to be a US citizen, apparently because Harry Dexter White would have moved from being Truman's Treasury secretary to becoming the first IMF managing director, a position that Truman realised would have been rejected by his own Congress as a result of allegations that White was a secret Soviet spy. So Truman reportedly let Europe have the IMF leadership because of this quirk of history.[7]

Things haven't changed, even in the twenty-first century, as reflected not only in the US president always picking the Bank president, but in George W. Bush making the most bizarre choices on behalf of the Petroleum–Military–Financial Complex, namely the incompetent neocons Paul Wolfowitz and Robert

Zoellick. The Bank continued its vast project loans in support of fossil fuel expansion, and along with the IMF also played the required geopolitical support role by financing the West's favourite dictators, e.g. the North Africans who were pushed out in 2011.

As the well-known neoliberal Massachusetts Institute of Technology economist Rudiger Dornsbusch admitted in 1998 when Larry Summers directed the BWIs from his US Treasury office three blocks away, 'The IMF is a toy of the United States to pursue its economic policy offshore.'[8]

And is there likely to be any change with Jim Yong Kim as World Bank president?

PB: It's a fascinating question. The situation for the many constituencies hopeful about Jim Yong Kim's 'election' as World Bank president is comparable to early 2009. Barack Obama entered a US presidency suffering institutional crisis and faced an immediate fork in the road: make the change he promised, or sell out his constituents' interests by bailing out Wall Street and legitimising a renewed neoliberal attack on society and ecology, replete with undemocratic, unconstitutional practices suffused with residual militarism. As president-elect, surrounding himself with the likes of Larry Summers, Tim Geithner, Paul Volcker, William Gates, Rahm Emmanuel, and Hillary Clinton, it was obvious which way he would go.

Unlike the corporate-oriented politician Obama, by all accounts Jim Kim is a genuine progressive, a wunderkind Harvard-trained physician and anthropologist with a terrific track record of public health management and advocacy, especially against AIDS and TB. Unlike predecessor Robert Zoellick, who in the service of power broke *everything* he touched since the late 1980s,[9] Kim spent the last quarter century building an extraordinary institution, the Boston NGO Partners in Health, and improving another, the ultra-bureaucratic World Health Organisation in Geneva, by working at its top level.

We will soon learn whether Kim's commitment to progressive change is as strong as his record suggests. We might learn most by watching what happens to the Bank's fossil fuel portfolio and culture of wanton climate change. The first test is a huge, irrational Kosovo coal-fired power plant loan he will probably sign off in his first few weeks in the job. His new underlings are, after all, the main financiers of coal-fired electricity, including their largest project loan ever ($3.75 billion), which was here in South Africa exactly two years ago.

The contradictions will be spectacular. The scholar who a decade ago co-edited the great anti-neoliberal book *Dying for Growth* will be compelled to actively ignore data (from Christian Aid) which suggest 185 million African deaths in the twenty-first century will be due to climate change, in addition to immediate coal-related health problems. Scientists working for the Environmental Defence Fund found that 'between roughly 6000 and 10,700 annual deaths from heart ailments, respiratory disease and lung cancer can be attributed to the 88 coal-fired power plants and companies receiving public international financing'.[10] Furthermore, writing in *Geotimes* on 'Health Impacts of Coal', three other scientists observe the rise in cancers, bone deformation, black lung and other respiratory diseases, sterilisation, and kidney disease associated with coal. And they point out, 'In the 13th century, the dense, sulfurous air in London attracted the attention of the British royalty, who issued proclamations banning the use of coal in London'.[11]

But it's easy to predict that for Kim to catch up to eight-centuries-old preventative health care is going to be impossible, given the balance of forces amongst Third World elites in sites like South Africa, within the fossil-addicted World Bank itself, and a few blocks away at the White House and Treasury, where mega-energy interests hold enormous sway. This is what multinational capital requires of Kim: a revitalised image for a crucial subsidised financier of coal-fired power plants and carbon markets when both are in extreme disrepute.

The sickening signs of Kim's retreat in the face of power were unmistakeable, beginning in early April, just after his nomination was announced by Obama. Kim's book *Dying for Growth* questioned neoliberalism in part because Washington's model didn't actually create broad-based growth, but instead austerity and parasitical finance-oriented GDP 'growth'. But Kim tried running away from that uncontroversial conclusion, telling an uncritical *New York Times* journalist:

> That book was written based on data from the early and mid-1990s. Our concern was that the vision was not inclusive enough, that it wasn't, in the bank's words, 'pro-poor'. The bank has shifted tremendously since that time, and now the notion of pro-poor development is at the core of the World Bank.[12]

This is nonsense, of course, as was the follow-up article in the *Washington Post* a few days later hyping his candidacy, by his co-editors Paul Farmer and John Gershman: 'In the 1990s, when the book was researched and written, too many of the world's poorest had been left behind by the growth of the global economy'; but '[t]hanks in part to Kim's trailblazing work, development approaches have changed'.[13] Farmer and Gershman provide no evidence of real change, only of rhetoric, using a throwaway line in a 2006 World Bank *World Development Report*: 'We now have considerable evidence that equity is also instrumental to the pursuit of long-term prosperity in aggregate terms for society as a whole.' But such banal phrasing can be found in Bank reports right through the neoliberal era, as Bank economists regularly wrote left (putting a 'human face' on structural adjustment) so they could walk right.

What might Kim do to change the Bank? As he told Bank directors who interviewed him in April 2012:

> The Bank is an unparalleled resource for its members, not only for financing but also knowledge and convening power. These strengths were apparent in the Bank's timely response to the recent financial crisis. The Bank must remain an effective partner in strengthening the foundations and fairness of the global economy, and in ensuring that the benefits of growth are widely shared.[14]

It is just too tempting to rearrange these words to get a more honest view, one Kim probably would have agreed with not long ago:

The Bank is an unparalleled force of social and ecological destruction, not only in its financing on behalf of multinational capital, but also its lack of real development knowledge and its overweening power. These flaws were apparent in the Bank's surprised response to the recent financial crisis, which it helped cause by increasing indebtedness, vulnerability, and financial deregulation through decades of loan conditionality and an ideology of financial liberalisation. The Bank has systematically weakened the foundations and fairness of the global economy, and ensured that the benefits of growth are enjoyed only by the top 1 per cent.

If Kim relegitimises the World Bank the way that Obama has done US imperialism, and if it is apparent that he and his otherwise trustworthy friends Farmer and Gershman stoop to fibbing in defence of his career, then we have a great step backwards to contemplate. In Obama's case it took 30 months before the Occupy Movement finally sprang up to contest his reactionary economic policies and ultra-rich beneficiaries. It had better not take so long to mount a struggle against Jim Kim's World Bank, for too many lives depend upon weakening that killer institution. The only constructive thing Kim can do at this stage, I suspect, is immediately tender his resignation and start a run on the Bank.[15]

In 1979, in what is now referred to as the 'Volcker Shock', the then chairman of the US Federal Reserve, Paul Volcker, began to raise interest rates sharply in an attempt to break free of stagflation using neoliberal measures. This became a major factor in the 'debt crisis' in the South that followed, as indebted nations could no longer pay back loans with such massively increased interest. But was the debt crisis merely an unintended side-effect of internal US policy? To what extent had there already been a deliberately aggressive lending policy in the IMF, World Bank and private banks (often lending to corrupt dictators), that had overburdened southern nations with debt?

PB: The lending to corrupt dictators occurred mainly through the commercial banks, which set up both lending offices in the major Third World capital cities, and then money-transfer systems to allow the dictators to move money to Cayman Islands or Panama accounts in the same banks. All of this has been well established and since the 1980s has generated campaigns devoted to compelling the cancellation of odious debt and the return of the dictators' flight capital. Amongst the most noteworthy were those of democracy movements, the Jubilee 2000 network, and even governments in Ecuador, the Philippines, Haiti, Nigeria, and South Africa. But by and large, the bankers who made those loans to dictators, such as to Mubarak and Ben Ali in Egypt and Tunisia until very recently, can still count on the IMF and the World Bank to ensure the debts are serviced. This still happens because by onlending, they are bailing out those banks when, as Jubilee put it, the 'dictators leave debt for the democrats', thus leaving the democrats to take orders from the BWIs. No reform of the BWIs has interrupted these relationships. So in that respect, the policy of terrorism visited upon so many people by US-aligned dictatorships is backed up by the multilateral financial system.

Was the 'Volcker Shock' – a rise in the real rate of interest on variable rate loans from –2 to positive 4 per cent – important in all of this? Without a doubt, it amplified the role Washington played, because after Mexico nearly defaulted in mid 1982 when the interest repayment became impossible, the responsibility for coordinating and funding bailouts went to the BWIs. What is perhaps most striking is that in previous eras when financial bankruptcy became the norm, affecting about a third of all borrowing countries during the 1830s, 1870s and 1930s, the clearing away of all that deadwood debt – what Marxists term the devalorisation of the overaccumulated financial capital – was a prerequisite for the system as a whole recovering from a long-term crisis. But instead, in the 1980s, the BWIs emerged on the scene to 'restructure' that debt, which meant – as we saw with Africa's debt relief – simply a degree of principal write-down so that interest repayments could be milked out of these wretched countries.

But let's not forget that this is the financial epiphenomenon that we might term a 'spatio-temporal fix' for all the liquid capital slushing around in the world after over-accumulation set in more generally, from the late 1960s. As you can sense even from a World Bank graph tracking declining rates of per capita GDP growth, there was a long stagnation that meant financiers desperately sought outlets elsewhere, including Third World dictatorships, because, as the head of Citicorp Walter Wriston infamously remarked, 'Countries don't go out of business'. The subsequent sloshing of funds from one investment outlet – one speculative bubble – to another is what characterised financial liberalisation and the huge global debt increase that began to burst in 2008, but that yet again was met by a bailout.

National debt has crippled some countries economically, forcing them to produce almost purely for export, just to service the interest. Debt relief programmes so far have been mere token gestures, and richer countries (especially the United States) rarely meet even the modest quotas of aid they commit to. Meanwhile, IMF emergency loans are conditional on the implementation of Structural Adjustment Programmes that demand state spending cuts in areas such as health, education, and infrastructure (but not defence), invariably making conditions worse for the majority. And yet, when banks want to cancel debt it is perfectly possible – for example, in the aftermath of the credit crisis of 2007, banks wrote off a larger amount of debt than the combined long-term debt of all developing countries.[16] Does all this not indicate a clear political project to hinder Southern development and self determination?

PB: Yes, but the most appropriate way to think about this, in my view, is if 'Southern' means the people and the environment of the 'Global South', in the sense Walden Bello uses it in the name of the Bangkok-based institute Focus on the Global South. And what that translates into, for a capitalist, is simple: move the problems of devalorising over accumulated capital into the societies, spaces, sectors, and scales where there is least resistance. That in turn means that during the kind of crisis that we're in, we witness the amplification of a typical process of uneven and combined development: more accumulation in some places than others, and in a manner that combines capitalist and non-capitalist spheres to the benefit of the former. This is how Rosa Luxemburg envisaged imperialism playing out, and she was very eloquent, a century ago in her great book *The Accumulation of Capital*, on the character of capitalist crisis mixed with financialisation and the worsening relations between colonial power and subjects. We would need to add much more on the gender and environmental dimensions of financial institutions' indirect and sometimes direct grabs of surpluses to fill out the picture, but the basic story has been understood since Marx's time.

If the policies of BWIs reflect US government dictates, to what extent are those dictates a reflection of corporate interests? Is the primary purpose of BWIs not debt as an end in itself, but opening new markets for multinational corporations?

PB: Yes, the expansion of debt typically follows a fairly clear pattern over time and space. The main researcher of this process, Christian Suter, explains the 'global debt cycle' by way of stages in a long wave of accumulation. It starts with technological innovations being introduced by corporations in a relatively more labour-intensive and unstandardised manner, with the demand for and supply of external financing typically low. As the innovation-led growth subsides, and as consumer markets of the advanced capitalist countries become saturated, corporate profit rates decline in the core. This pushes waves of financial capital out of the core investment sites of corporations, and into peripheral areas, where instead of achieving balanced accumulation and growth, low returns on investment plus a variety of other political and economic constraints inexorably lead to sovereign default. Suter sums up: 'first, intense core capital exports and corresponding booms in credit raising activity of peripheries; second, the occurrence of debt service incapacity among peripheral countries; and third, the negotiation of debt settlement agreements between debtors and creditors'.[17]

The Paris-based researchers Gérard Duménil and Dominique Lévy studied how US corporate profits were generated in the most recent wave and broke down the process into three lines: value-producing (non-financial) corporations earned about half their profits from production 50 years ago, steadily declining to around 10 per cent by 2000. The profits from what we can call 'globalisation' – or the 'spatial fix' – rose from 5 per cent to more than 20 per cent, and the 'financialisation' profits rose from 10 to 30 per cent of these corporations' total during the same period. The latter index went as high as 40 per cent at peak in 2007 before the financial meltdown. So this indicates something much more durable than mainstream descriptions of mere financial sector chaos: the problem is much worse from the standpoint of broader capitalist reproduction.

In his analysis of global poverty, Thomas Pogge describes the existence of a de facto 'international borrowing privilege' for any government, so that 'whoever succeeds in bringing the preponderance of the means of coercion under his control gets the borrowing privilege as an additional reward'.[18] According to this, such default recognition of regimes from creditors tacitly encourages coup attempts and civil wars. Is this an accurate portrayal of the relationship between BWIs and dictatorships? Is there not actually a politically motivated decision whether to lend or not, based on a regime's compliance with Western interests, with even private banks following the lead of BWIs in this respect?

PB: Pogge is correct, historically, insofar as seignorage – the ability of a country to print money – was correlated to imperial power, and others like Giovanni Arrighi and David Graeber have traced this historically. But what is most interesting is the correlation of financial power with dictatorship and the BWIs' attempt to preserve a civilised image. Recently, the mask slipped off in sites like Honduras in 2009 and the North African dictatorships in 2011, and it was no surprise to find close-knit relationships that included Dominique Strauss-Kahn being awarded Tunisia's highest honour by Ben Ali.

And on the other side of the coin, so to speak, is financial aid not also *withheld* for political reasons? For example, there is Nixon's reaction to the election of Allende in Chile – the infamous demand to 'make the economy scream' – and the subsequent removal of various forms of financial support, including from the World Bank, which did not lend or grant any funds to Chile under Allende – a policy that was completely reversed as soon as Pinochet took power. Does this not show that, in effect, there is no automatic 'borrowing privilege'?

PB: Yes, there are a few cases along these lines, in which a bias towards the imperialist geopolitical agenda was paramount, especially during the Cold War. In the case of South Africa, the World Bank was requested by the United Nations General Assembly to halt apartheid loans in 1966, after Martin Luther King and the South African Nobel Peace Prize laureate Albert Luthuli campaigned for early financial sanctions. The Bank's lawyer replied that 'the Bank's articles provide that the Bank and its officers shall not interfere in the political affairs of any member and that they shall not be influenced in their decisions by the political character of the member or members concerned'.[19] The Bank did halt shortly afterwards, as South Africa became ineligible due to a rising per capita income.

But conversely in a decision to starve a country of what is sometimes urgently needed hard currency, the political character of a borrowing government certainly plays a role. After 1998, when it had been lauded by the World Bank for imposing structural adjustment, with brutal results, the Zimbabwean government defaulted on several billion dollars of foreign debt. By 2012 the unpaid arrears and principle reached $9 billion. In making a down payment of $210 million to the IMF in 2005–06, Robert Mugabe thought this might open new credit lines, which were needed especially for trade finance and import of oil. But with the US explicit about vetoing any new credits, Mugabe's strategy failed, so the money was wasted. In that case, democrats and progressives generally supported a financial boycott of Mugabe, but it was only possible because the US State Department wanted to make Zimbabwe's economy scream.

In the case of 1980s Nicaragua, like Allende's Chile, the critical question to ask is whether there is any alternative hard-currency source of funding. If not, then like the case of

Argentina's default in 2002, the economic managers have to run a trade surplus to get the net positive hard-currency inflow that will support imports. But like Argentina or Ecuador more recently, it is terribly important for governments to retain the option of defaulting once a Debt Audit reveals that odious debt exists which should be cancelled. I wish that in South Africa we'd had that power, since this was one of the most obvious cases, but Nelson Mandela was too weak and agreed to repay the apartheid debt.

There was a continual connection between the BWIs and South African apartheid throughout its duration. You have written how the World Bank 'began developing business plans just two years after apartheid was formally introduced in 1948, and the World Bank's first loans ... were granted in 1951', and that a lot of this money went to supplying electricity to white households only, even though the debt was repayable by all South Africans. These loans, you say, continued until 1968, and then subsequently 'the World Bank still contributed to apartheid through the Lesotho Highlands Water Project, which dammed rivers and tunnelled through mountains to supply water to thirsty Johannesburg customers – mainly wealthy households, white-owned farms and white-owned mines – notwithstanding huge social and environmental costs'.[20] We could also mention that the IMF bought major quantities of gold from South Africa in 1970–71,[21] and in turn lent back $2 billion to Pretoria between the political crunch of 1976 and early 1980s gold boom.[22] How much did this economic support aid the apartheid regime?

PB: Apartheid was definitely powered by the BWIs, first through the huge World Bank project loans, for electricity and also for railroads which carried migrant workers to mines and factories at ultra-cheap costs due to apartheid restrictions, and after the 1976 Soweto uprising through IMF bailouts that in the early 1980s were vital to the Botha regime because the price of gold fell sharply after 1981. That's why the international anti-apartheid movement and US allies like Ralph Nader put such emphasis on cutting off IMF facilities in 1983, even during the Reagan era, and causing the run on the banks in mid-1985 when Botha could no longer get financing for short-term debt repayments. He defaulted on $13 billion in payments, imposed exchange controls and shut the stock market. These actions convinced white English-speaking capital to cut a deal with the Lusaka-based African National Congress leadership. This is a story told well in Connie Fields' remarkable movie series *Have You Heard from Johannesburg?*

In the transition from apartheid to universal democracy in South Africa, many facets of neoliberal economic policy were agreed upon before elections ever allowed the ANC to take office (contradicting the ideas of the ANC's 'Freedom Charter'). To what extent was this a matter of internal politics, with the de Klerk government (representing the interests of major South African corporations) simply taking advantage of factors such as inexperience and a focus on political negotiations among the ANC leadership, along with the compliance of certain influential ANC members such as Thabo Mbeki and Trevor Manuel? On the other hand, to what extent was it the result of external pressures – market volatility, BWIs and foreign governments?

PB: It's a both–and not either–or situation, of course. When observers asked of the ANC, 'Were they pushed or did they jump?', John Saul quips that the typical answer from the ruling party here is, 'Globalisation made me do it!' The process was most critical in the decisions to repay the $25 billion in inherited apartheid debt in 1993, to retain the apartheid finance minister and central banker in 1994 – which Mandela was ordered to do by the head of the IMF, Michel Camdessus – and to relax exchange controls in 1995. Then there were similar pressures by forces in Washington and Geneva who set up the World Trade Organisation in 1995 with South Africa in a very weak position. The ditching of the Reconstruction and Development Programme and its replacement with a supposed 'home-grown' structural adjustment programme – co-authored by two World Bank staff with a Bank model – were symbolic, in 1996, but already throughout the early 1990s the Bank had launched numerous 'reconnaissance missions' to subvert progressive ANC policymakers and empower the local neoliberal crew. Not a single major sector of social and infrastructural policy was untouched, and the 'Elite Transition' in every aspect of life was decisive.

Throughout the Cold War period, US military intervention and sponsorship of right-wing dictatorships largely kept out nationalist or social democratic rule that might limit the access of US corporations, nationalise industries, and increase social spending. But, as Joseph Stiglitz wrote in 2002, 'Today, the emerging markets are not forced open under the threat of the use of military might, but through economic power, through the threat of sanctions or the withholding of needed assistance in a time of crisis.'[23] Indeed, perhaps South Africa's transition serves as an example. But is this economic power and lack of need for force exaggerated, especially given, say, the invasion of Iraq? And is economic coercion any less terrifying than the brutality of the past anyway?

PB: The process of extracting surplus shifts according to local conditions. The idea of South Africa being a 'shock doctrine' victim was not immediately obvious, as critics of Naomi Klein here argued. But I think she was basically correct in that important book, insofar as our cadres were shocked into giddiness by how quickly the transition went from unbanning in early 1990 to power sharing in mid 1994. It turned out, simply, that in the desperate search for a spatio-temporal, globalised, and financialised way out of their economic crisis, white capitalists found Afrikaner politicians like de Klerk willing to cut a deal that ultimately just replaced racial apartheid with class apartheid. The policies adopted increased inequality to the world's leading rate, doubled unemployment, wiped out major local manufacturing sectors unable to compete, dramatically lowered the wage/profit share, temporarily restored corporate profits and assured that a small fraction of the new black ruling class gained enormous wealth.

It's a long and sorry story, but the upside is that we have resistance, not resignation, with amongst the world's highest rate of social protest. The economics of coercion definitely ran up against South Africa's Polanyi-style 'double movement', and about a dozen years ago we found progressive activists in diverse arenas such as labour demanding real wage increases, or the Treatment Action Campaign demanding free AIDS medicines (that cost $15,000/year before), or critics of water and electricity privatisation slowing services commodification and opening the door for free basic supplies, and the like. Many have won extraordinary victories. Yet by all accounts, it is terribly difficult to fight class apartheid when a neoliberal–nationalist regime retains such prestige and electoral popularity in spite of widespread corruption. This is certainly a less dangerous site than the Middle East and Central and South Asia, where so many people lose their lives in struggle, and the BWIs' role here will always be a source of great interest and conflict.

Economic coercion is now also witnessed through the transfer of power from residual democracies in southern Europe to Washington and Brussels, after Iceland and Ireland first went through hell. The April 2012 IMF–World Bank meetings made evident that the IMF will raise another $430 billion to address what appears to be another round of financial melting, when Spain cannot repay vast debts, requiring yet more bailouts. We learned a great deal about the contradictions between finance and democracy when the Greek people were denied a democratic right to vote on austerity in late 2011, as George Papandreou had initially promised. The break-up of the Euro may be the only solution, so as to re-decentralise power at national scale and get out from under the thumb of German capital and especially the European Central Bank.

Along with the growth and dispersion of the Occupy movement, that option is probably the strongest counter-terrorism strategy, if you will, that people have open to them. It means defending the welfare state as well as savings and pension funds, once more banks topple. The mistakes made by neoliberal governments in 2008–09, when trillions of dollars worth of bailouts went from taxpayers to banks, will continue until social and labour movements in more countries stand up and fight. This is inevitable, and may well result in a return to more brutal and open expressions of power by the 1 per cent, but this is the fight that appears inescapable for at least the next years ahead.

NOTES

1. World Bank, 'About Us', <http://tinyurl.com/8non9>.
2. International Monetary Fund, 'About the IMF', <http://www.imf.org/external/about.htm>.
3. See Patrick Bond, 'Chilling the Arab Spring: Neoliberal financiers in North Africa and Palestine', *Pambazuka News*, 9 June 2011, <http://www.pambazuka.org/en/category/features/73932>; and Patrick Bond, 'Beware "social justice" promises by international bankers', *Pambazuka News*, 13 October 2011, <http://pambazuka.org/en/category/features/77088>.
4. Patrick Bond, 'Is Africa still being looted? World Bank dodges its own research', *Links*, 15 August 2010, <http://links.org.au/node/1843>.
5. *Where is the Wealth of Nations? Measuring Capital for the 21st Century* (Washington: The World Bank, 2006), <http://tinyurl.com/2c8vby2>.
6. 'After the War: The World Bank, the IMF, and the End, 1945 to 1946', maynardkeynes.org, <http://tinyurl.com/bscw7ck>.
7. Benn Steil, 'Banker, Tailor, Soldier, Spy', *New York Times*, 8 April 2012, <http://tinyurl.com/c2hdjm5>.
8. 'Opinion: World Central Bank', *Journal of Commerce*, 7 January 1999.
9. Patrick Bond, 'What Will Robert Zoellick Break Next?', *Counterpunch*, 19–21 March 2010, <http://tinyurl.com/csbedko>.
10. Sarah Penney, Jacob Bell, and John Balbus, 'Estimating the Health Impacts of Coal-Fired Power Plants Receiving International Financing', *Environmental Defense Fund*, 2009, <http://tinyurl.com/bnh7vcl>.
11. Robert B. Finkelman, Harvey E. Belkin and Jose A. Centeno, 'Health Impacts of Coal: Should We Be Concerned?', *Geotimes*, September 2006, <http://www.geotimes.org/sept06/feature_HealthImpacts.html>.
12. Annie Lowrey, 'Obama Candidate Sketches Vision for World Bank', 9 April 2012, <http://tinyurl.com/ceue7qj>.
13. Paul Farmer and John Gershman, 'Jim Kim's humility would serve World Bank well', *Washington Post*, 11 April 2012, <http://tinyurl.com/cd8d6sa>.
14. 'Statement by US Nominee for the World Bank Presidency Dr Jim Yong Kim to the World Bank Board of Directors', *US Department of the Treasury*, 11 April 2012, <http://tinyurl.com/84wacea>.
15. Defunding through a World Bank bonds boycott is the argument in a decade-old book, and it still holds. See Patrick Bond, *Against Global Apartheid: South Africa Meets the World Bank, IMF and International Finance*, 2nd edn (London: Zed Books, 2003).

16. Éric Toussaint and Damien Millet, *Debt, the IMF, and the World Bank: Sixty Questions, Sixty Answers* (New York: Monthly Review Press, 2010), p.89.
17. Christian Suter, *Debt Cycles in the World Economy* (Boulder: Westview Press, 1992), p.41.
18. Thomas Pogge, *World Poverty and Human Rights* (Cambridge: Polity, 2002), p.115.
19. World Bank, 'Statement to Executive Directors', 29 March 1966. Cited in Mac Darrow, *Between Light and Shadow: The World Bank, International Monetary Fund and International Human Rights Law* (Oxford: Hart Publishing, 2003), p.151.
20. Bond, *Against Global Apartheid*, p.64.
21. International Monetary Fund, 'Factsheet: Gold in the IMF', 1 September 2011, <http://www.imf.org/external/np/exr/facts/gold.htm>.
22. Bond, *Against Global Apartheid*, p.68.
23. Joseph Stiglitz, *Globalization and Its Discontents* (New York: W.W. Norton, 2002), p.62.

10
Ismael Hossein-zadeh
The Guiding Force of US Militarism

Let's start with some official reasons for US wars, low intensity military operations, and sponsorship of state violence since the Cold War ended: homeland security, international drug trafficking, global terrorism, Islamic fundamentalism, human rights and democracy. To what extent have any of these genuinely been primary or secondary aims?

Ismael Hossein-zadeh: Official reasons such as 'global terrorism' or 'Islamic fundamentalism' for US military interventions abroad can easily be dispensed with as flimsy, hare-brained pretexts for war and militarism. US beneficiaries of war dividends have proven quite resourceful in frequently inventing (or manufacturing, if necessary) new 'external threats to our national interests', or 'the interests of our allies', in order to justify their imperial wars of choice. US military adventures since the Second World War, especially since the collapse of the Berlin Wall, are driven not so much by some general or abstract national interests, as they are by the special interests vested in the military–security capital, which need an atmosphere of war and militarism in order to justify their lion's share of the public purse. This helps explain why since the Second World War powerful beneficiaries of war dividends have almost always reacted negatively to discussions of international cooperation and tension reduction, or to détente.

When the collapse of the Soviet system and the subsequent discussions of 'peace dividends' in the United States threatened the interests of the military–industrial conglomerates, their representatives invented 'new external sources of danger to US national interests'. The 'new sources of threat' are said to originate in the 'unpredictable' and 'unreliable' regional powers of the so-called Third World. Instead of the Soviet Union, the 'menace' of China, Iran, Cuba, North Korea, drug lords, global terrorism, weapons of mass destruction, and so on would have to do as new enemies. This tendency of the beneficiaries of war dividends to foment international convulsions in order to justify continuous haemorrhaging of the Pentagon budget also helps explain why the United States viewed the 9/11 tragedy as an opportunity for further militarisation. The monstrous attacks of 9/11 were treated not as criminal acts but as war on America. Once it was thus established that the United States was 'at war', military build-up followed accordingly.

The pretexts or tactics for pursuing higher profits for the business of war may change, but the objective or strategy remains the same – continued war and military aggressions and, consequently, further escalation of the Pentagon budget and war dividends. Viewed in this light, militaristic tendencies to wars abroad can be seen largely as reflections of the metaphorical fight over allocation of public finance at home, of a subtle or insidious strategy to redistribute national resources in favour of the wealthy: to cut public spending on socio-economic infrastructure and to reverse the New Deal social safety-net programmes by expanding military spending.

But what of apparent 'humanitarian intervention', such as in Kosovo, or, more recently, Libya? Even if there are other motives too, do the positive results of such conflicts not make them worthwhile?

IH: In a moment of utter heartlessness, let us use the imperialist term 'collateral damage' to gloss over all the death and destruction wrought by the so-called 'humanitarian intervention', and focus exclusively on the alleged 'positive results' of such interventions. The most widely touted of such results is said to be 'replacement of dictatorship with democracy', as reflected by periodic voting and election rituals. Such elections are, however, often money-driven exercises to legitimise the dictatorship of capital. This is clearly evidenced by the experiences of Afghanistan, Iraq, Honduras, Haiti, former republics of Yugoslavia, and the like.

Along with the artificial presidential or parliamentary elections, the largely orchestrated or scripted voting results are used to justify the privatisation of state enterprises, the outsourcing or auctioning off of the public capital entities such as seaports, airports, bridges, water resources, sewer system facilities, major communication facilities, and more – including wholesale privatisation and outsourcing of health and education services. Thus, the 'positive' consequences of the 'humanitarian regime change' tend to benefit only a small minority of local elites and their foreign patrons and partners, while the overwhelming majority of citizens, who traditionally benefited from the state-sponsored social safety net programmes, lose their sources of livelihood and their means of benefiting from government-subsidised, affordable education and health care services.

The purported US/NATO support for human rights as grounds for 'humanitarian intervention' tends to be narrowly focused on purely cultural issues such as lifestyle and identity politics, that is, the politics of race, gender, and sexual orientation. As such, this concept of human rights is largely devoid of basic economic needs for survival. Even a cursory comparison with the Universal Declaration of Human Rights and Freedoms (UDHRF) reveals some fundamental shortcomings of the US-type human rights standards. Human rights according to UDHRF include basic economic or survival needs:

> Everyone has the right to work ... to protection against unemployment ... to just and favourable remuneration ensuring for himself and his family an existence worthy of human dignity, and supplemented, if necessary, by other means of social protection ... Everyone has the right to a standard of living adequate for the health and well-being of himself and of his family, including food, clothing, and housing and medical care and necessary social services, and the right to security in the event of unemployment, sickness, disability, widowhood, old age or other lack of livelihood in circumstances beyond his control ... Everyone has the right to education.[1]

Human rights à la USA does not include any of these basic human needs – all the nauseating propaganda of championing human rights notwithstanding. By contrast, the Libyan people under Gaddafi, for example, enjoyed many of these crucially important economic rights. Before it was devastated by the imperialist-orchestrated civil war and destruction, Libya had the highest living standard in Africa.[2] With the US–NATO-orchestrated regime change in Libya under the guise of 'humanitarian concerns', which is bound to replace the welfare-state policies of the Gaddafi era with the neoliberal policies of unbridled market mechanism, most of these social safety net programmes are destined to be eliminated, or drastically weakened.

Of course, the inauspicious changes that result from intervention for 'humanitarian' (or other similarly duplicitous) reasons are not limited to Libya; they are, indeed, part of an ominous pattern that includes Allende's Chile, Mossadeq's Iran, Arbenz's Guatemala, Sukarno's Indonesia, Aristide's Haiti, Sandinista's Nicaragua, and Zelaya's Honduras, among many others. This pattern of imperialist-orchestrated change also explains why the United States and other Western powers are now targeting Cuba, Venezuela, Iran, Ecuador, Bolivia, Syria, and other 'unfriendly, rogue nations'. The pattern further shows that the alleged defence of human rights as the basis for regime change is patently hypocritical: what is defended is not human rights, but the right to establish the neoliberal model of capitalism worldwide.

And what about the Cold War? You say that

> there is strong evidence that the US–USSR hostilities of the Cold War years were provoked not so much by the alleged Soviet plans to attack the United States, or its allies, but by the fact that US guardians of world capitalism simply could not tolerate the presence of a planned economy anywhere in the world.[3]

In your view, were there *any* points in the Cold War where a Communist attack on the United States was likely, necessitating a huge defensive military build-up? Or, is there validity in the claim that the United States, as superpower, effectively *had to* block the spread of the Soviet Empire (exemplified, say, in their post-war control of Poland or Romania, or the invasion of Afghanistan in 1979), even if it required extreme measures?

IH: There is convincing evidence not only that Joseph Stalin and his successors in the Soviet Union had no plans to wage war against the United States, but that, in fact, they played a restraining role in containing independent revolutionary movements worldwide. There are clear indications that in the aftermath of the Second World War, Stalin

> assumed an exceedingly moderate posture ... His nation had lost 25 million people in the war, was desperately in need of aid for rebuilding, and continued for a long time to nurture hopes of coexistence. Far from being revolutionary, Stalin in those years put the damper on revolution wherever he could.[4]

To accommodate the United States and other Western powers in the hope of peaceful coexistence, Stalin often advised, and sometimes ordered, the pro-Moscow communist or leftist parties in Europe and elsewhere in the world to refrain from revolutionary policies that might jeopardise the hoped-for chances of coexistence.

A number of leading political figures and statesmen in the United States also acknowledged Stalin's live-and-let-live policy in the years following the war. Here is a sample:

> It was perfectly clear to anyone with even a rudimentary knowledge of the Russia of that day that the Soviet leaders had no intention of attempting to advance their cause by launching military attacks with their own armed forces across frontiers. (George Kennan, May 1965)

> [The Soviet government] does not contemplate the use of war as an instrument of its national policy. I do not know any responsible official, military or civilian, in this [US] government, who believes that the Soviet government now plans conquest by open military aggression'. (John Foster Dulles, March 1949)[5]

Evidence thus clearly suggests that the US policy makers built the gigantic military–industrial complex not out of any genuine fear of Soviet military attack but for other motives. Top among those motives was to establish a US-led world capitalist order in which unhindered market forces would flourish, a world no part of which would be excluded from the free flow of trade and investment. Here is how President Truman explained it: 'Regimented economies' were the enemy of free enterprise, and 'unless we act, and act decisively', those regimented economies would become 'the pattern of the next century'. To fend off that danger, Truman urged that 'the whole world should adopt the American system'. The system of free enterprise, he went on, 'could survive in America only if it becomes a world system'.[6]

You argue that, in the present situation,

> under the sway of military imperialism, instigation of international conflicts and military adventures abroad are often prompted not so much by territorial or economic gains for the empire or the nation as a whole ... but by a desire to appropriate the lion's share of the existing wealth and treasure for the military establishment.[7]

However, is it not the case that recent conflicts have also been a means to open up new markets and expand the wealth of the empire? Surely it is no coincidence that recent and current US 'enemies' – Afghanistan, Iraq, Libya, and Iran – all offer potentially lucrative trade opportunities, especially in oil?

IH: US military transgressions have in fact become economic burdens because they devour a disproportionately large share of national resources, and because such adventurous operations tend to create instability in international markets, subvert long-term global investment, and increase energy or fuel costs. In addition, the resentment and hostilities that unprovoked aggressions generate in foreign lands are bound to create backlash at the consumer level. A leading Middle East business journal, *AME Info*, reported in its 8 April 2004 issue that

[i]n 2002, a cluster of Arab organisations asked Muslims to shun goods from America, seen as an enemy of Islam and a supporter of Israel. In Bahrain, the Al-Montazah supermarket chain, for example, boosted sales by pulling about 1,000 US products off its shelves, and other grocers followed suit.

The report further pointed out that 'Coca-Cola and Pepsi ... took the brunt of the blow. Coca-Cola admitted that the boycott trimmed some $40 million off profits in the [Persian] Gulf in 2002.' In addition, the report noted that 'US exports to the Middle East dropped $31 billion from 1998–2002'.[8]

Concerns of this nature have prompted a broad spectrum of non-military US business interests to form coalitions of trade associations that are designed to lobby foreign-policy makers against unprovoked military aggressions abroad. One such anti-militarist alliance of American businesses is USA*Engage. It is a coalition of nearly 700 small and large businesses, agriculture groups, and trade associations working to seek alternatives to militaristic US foreign policy actions and to promote the benefits of non-military US engagement abroad. The coalition's statement of principles points out that 'American values are best advanced by engagement of American business and agriculture in the world, not by ceding markets to foreign competition' through unilateral foreign policies and military aggressions.[9]

In regards to oil, it is true that the United States has used military force in the past for energy purposes. But this precedent fails to explain the current US military aggressions abroad. It is also true that once an 'insubordinate' regime like that of Saddam Hussein or Muammar al-Gaddafi is overthrown, oil companies (along with other transnational corporations) will swoop over the vanquished country to divvy up the booty of war and conquest. However, such vulture-like behaviour fails to prove that oil companies instigated, *ab ovo*, the war against those countries. Indeed, evidence shows that major oil companies, along with many other non-military transnational corporations, lobbied both the Clinton and Bush administrations in support of changing the aggressive, militaristic US policy towards countries like Iran, Iraq, and Libya in favour of establishing normal, non-confrontational business and diplomatic relations.

A large part of the perception that big oil is behind military operations in oil-rich countries stems from the fact that oil companies do benefit from oil price hikes that result from war and political turbulence. Certainly oil companies welcome the spoils of war in the form of oil price hikes. Such benefits are, however, largely incidental. Evidence shows that for the last quarter century or so oil interests have not favoured war and turbulence in the oil-rich Middle East; they have come to prefer stability and predictability to the periodic oil spikes that follow war and political convulsion.

It is true that for a long time, from the beginning of Middle Eastern oil exploration and discovery in the early twentieth century until the mid 1970s, colonial or imperial powers controlled oil either directly, or through control of oil-producing countries – at times, even by military force. But the pattern of imperialist exploitation of global markets and resources has changed now. Today, even militarily occupying a country like Iraq does not guarantee exclusive benefits or contracting rights to US oil companies. The following report by *TIME* magazine on an important auction of the Iraqi oil contracts clearly supports this point:

> Those who claim that the US invaded Iraq in 2003 to get control of the country's giant oil reserves will be left scratching their heads by the results of last weekend's auction of Iraqi oil contracts: Not a single US company secured a deal in the auction of contracts that will shape the Iraqi oil industry for the next couple of decades. Two of the most lucrative of the multi-billion-dollar oil contracts went to two countries which bitterly opposed the US invasion – Russia and China ... The distribution of [Iraqi] oil contracts certainly answers the theory that the war was for the benefit of big US oil interests ... That has not been demonstrated by what has happened this week.[10]

Big oil seems to have known this would happen, and perhaps that's why, as Fareed Mohamedi of PFC Energy, an energy consultancy firm based in Washington, D.C., that advises petroleum firms, pointed out: 'The big oil companies were not enthusiastic about the Iraqi war ... Corporations like Exxon–Mobil and Chevron–Texaco want stability, and this is not what Bush is providing in Iraq and the Gulf region.'[11]

The big oil companies were not enthusiastic about the NATO military strike and regime change in Libya either. It is true that after the overthrow of the Gaddafi regime every major oil company from every major industrialised country is scrambling to carve out a bigger slice of the pie of the Libyan oil. There is no evidence, however, that these companies instigated the civil war and NATO's military strike against Libya: for one thing, they were already enjoying lucrative deals with the Gaddafi regime; for another, they tend to be averse to political turbulence and an unpredictable business atmosphere. Furthermore, the big oil companies are not alone in the imperialist looting of Libya; many non-oil transnational corporations (such as construction, transportation, communication, banking, and armaments firms) are also partaking in the loot.

While the purported evidence of big oil as the driving force behind the wars on Iraq, Afghanistan and Libya is dubious, the evidence of the powerful interests vested in the military–security capital having played such a role is undeniable. It is no secret that most of the post-Cold War US military aggressions have been instigated by the corporate-backed militaristic think tanks, such as Project for the New American Century, the American Enterprise Institute, Center for Security Policy, Middle East Media Research Institute, Middle East Forum, Washington Institute for Near East Policy, Jewish Institute for National Security Affairs, and National Institute for Public Policy. Major components of the US foreign policy, especially its military strategy, in the post-Cold War era are designed at the drawing boards of these think thanks, often in collaboration, directly or indirectly, with the Pentagon and the arms lobby.

Even a cursory look at the records of these belligerent think tanks – their memberships, their financial sources, their institutional structures, and the like – shows that they have (since the demise of the Soviet Union) been set up essentially to serve as institutional fronts to camouflage the incestuous relationships between the Pentagon, its major contractors, and the Israeli lobby. There are strong indications that the leading warmongering politicians (whether the blatantly jingoistic neo-conservative figures of the Bush era, or the more subtle but no less militaristic liberal hawks of the Obama era) have been long-time political activists who have worked through a network of militaristic think tanks that are set up to serve either as the armaments lobby or the Israeli lobby or both.

To follow up on a couple of points there, first, US (and UK) companies were not completely shut out of Iraq oil deals. Exxon and Occidental won bids in the West Qurna 1 and Zubair oil fields, respectively, and UK companies Shell and BP also won bids. It also seems that they would have hoped for more had the conditions been made more favourable by the expected passing of the proposed Iraq Oil Law. Indeed, Antonia Juhasz points out that in the bidding of June 2009, 'only one consortium – BP and the Chinese National Petroleum Corp. – agreed to the terms. The rest of the companies balked, saying the terms just simply were not generous enough.' All this came after the National Energy Policy Development Group, set up by the Bush regime at the beginning of 2001 and chaired by Dick Cheney, had among other things discussed Iraqi oil with major US and UK energy corporations. The problem was that, 'were Saddam to remain in power and the sanctions to be removed, ... contracts [with other countries, especially France, Russia and China] would take effect, and the US and its closest ally would be shut out of Iraq's great oil bonanza'.[12]

IH: The point here is not whether US and UK companies were shut out of Iraq oil deals or not; they certainly were not. It is rather whether they were granted exclusive rights or preferential deals. And the answer is no; they had (and have) to participate in bidding just as did (or do) oil companies from many other countries. Major oil companies insisted in the immediate aftermath of the overthrow of Saddam Hussein's regime that oil contracts be signed only after the passage of the Iraq Oil Law, since that law, as initially crafted, would grant more lucrative contracts to these companies. The fact that, due to resistance by Iraqis, seven years after it was initially drafted the law has not yet passed, and US/UK oil companies have not (so far) received any no-bid, preferential deals, is an indication that the role of oil in recent US military aggressions in the Middle East is highly exaggerated.

Antonia Juhasz's argument that 'were Saddam to remain in power and the sanctions to be removed ... the US and its closest ally would be shut out of Iraq's great oil bonanza' borders on speculation; it is based on precedence, not hard evidence. It is true that, as Juhasz points out, from the mid 1990s through the end of Saddam Hussein's rule in 2003 major US and UK oil companies were prevented from doing business with Iraq. But that had to do as much, if not more, with the US-sponsored sanctions against Iraq, which prohibited US companies from doing business with that country, than with Iraq's oil policies. In fact, major US and UK oil companies were not happy with the sanctions, as the sanctions shut them out of oil deals with Iraq.

As I have pointed out,

> No matter how crucial oil is to the world economy, the fact remains that it is, after all, a commodity. As such, international trade in oil is as important to its importers as it is to its exporters. There is absolutely no reason that, in a world free of the influence of the powerful beneficiaries of war and militarism, the flow of oil could not be guaranteed by international trade conventions and commercial treaties.[13]

Oil companies are, of course, aware of this. And that's why (for the last three decades or so) they have come to prefer peace and predictably, which are more conducive to long-term investments and contracts, to short-term oil price hikes that follow from war and geopolitical turbulence.

The Iran–Libya Sanction Act (ILSA) of 1996 is a strong testament to the fact that oil companies nowadays view wars, economic sanctions, and international political tensions as harmful to their long-term business interests and, accordingly, strive for peace, not war, in international relations. In May 1997 (and in reaction to ILSA) major US oil companies such as

Conoco, Exxon, Atlantic Richfield, and Occidental Petroleum joined other non-military US transnational corporations to create an anti-sanction coalition. Earlier that same year, Conoco's chief executive Archie Dunham publicly took a stance against unilateral US sanctions by stating that 'US companies, not rogue regimes, are the ones that suffer when the United States imposes economic sanctions'.[14] Texaco officials have also argued that the United States can be more effective in bringing about change in other countries by allowing US companies to do business with those countries instead of imposing economic sanctions that tend to be counterproductive.

As you say, the Israeli lobby is often deemed an important influence on US policy in the Middle East. How closely tied are the goals of this and the military–industrial complex?

IH: Although the unconditional support for Israel's geopolitical designs in the Middle East is detrimental to the overall national interests of the United States, the interests of the military–industrial complex tend to converge with those of expansionist Zionism over war and military adventures in the region. Just as the military–industrial–security complex views international peace and stability as inimical to its interests, so too the militant Zionist proponents of 'greater Israel' perceive peace between Israel and its Palestinian neighbours as perilous to their goal of gaining control over the 'promised land'. The reason for this fear of peace is that, according to a number of United Nations resolutions, peace would mean Israel's return to its pre-1967 borders. Since this is not acceptable to Israel, it systematically sabotages all efforts at peace negotiations.

Not surprisingly, partisans of 'greater Israel', stretching from Jordan to the Mediterranean, view war and geopolitical convulsion as opportunities that are conducive to the expulsion of Palestinians and the expansion of Israel's territory. But because waging war and applying force in the name of territorial expansion would be politically unpalatable, instigation of diversionary or proxy wars in the region is deemed necessary in order to avail the expansionist Zionist forces of the needed pretext for the projected expulsions. David Ben-Gurion, one of the key founders of the state of Israel, explained the importance of the convulsive or 'revolutionary' social circumstances to the goal of expelling Palestinians and expanding the Jewish territory in these words: 'What is inconceivable in normal times is possible in revolutionary times; and if at this time the opportunity is missed and what is possible in such great hours is not carried out – a whole world is lost.'[15]

While (based on a convergence of interests on war and military aggression in the Middle East) there is an unspoken, de facto alliance between the military–industrial complex and expansionist Zionism, the alliance is primarily tactical, opportunistic, or utilitarian. Each side takes advantage of the needs of the other side for its own nefarious interests. It is necessary to note in this context that, despite its immense political influence, the Zionist lobby in the United States is ultimately a junior, not equal, partner of the military–industrial complex. Without discounting the extremely important role of the Zionist lobby in the configuration of the US foreign policy in the Middle East, I would caution against exaggerations of its power and influence over the US policy in the region.

Regarding the presidency of George W. Bush, you say that 'the powerful military establishment ... manipulated the unseasoned president', and claim that 'the socio-historical role of militarism and/or military imperialism ... is much grander and more powerful than the power or authority of a president'.[16] However, in the 1990s, the Bush senior and Clinton administrations did manage to reduce military spending, suggesting that the elected government still has power to resist Pentagon demands. How much influence does the military–industrial complex have over the democratic process? Has this grown significantly even since the Clinton era?

IH: To say that the military–industrial complex plays a bigger role over issues of war and peace than the president is not to say that all presidents are equally powerless vis-à-vis the military machine. An assertive or less trigger-happy president may minimally or temporarily slowdown the pace or the growth of the war juggernaut, but he will not be able to deter the military machine from pursuing its long-term strategies. For example, both Presidents Carter and Clinton initially resisted the unbridled demands of the military establishment in an effort to curtail military spending and contain US military operations abroad. Both were decisively defeated.

Jimmy Carter ran for president as a dove and a champion of détente, or tension reduction with the Soviet Union. But partisans of war and militarism turned him into a Cold War hawk by the time he left the White House. Powerful beneficiaries of war and military spending sounded false alarms that the Soviet Union was outspending the United States on armaments and would soon surpass the US in overall military power. Organising around opposition to tension-reducing talks with the Soviet Union, they reconstituted the brazenly militaristic Committee on the Present Danger (CPD), which had been instrumental to President Truman's militarisation policies of the early 1950s.

As a major brain trust of the military–industrial complex, the CPD set out to derail the Carter administration's initial tendencies toward détente, global interdependence, and human rights concerns. Arguing that the CIA's estimate of Soviet arms outlays was too low, the CPD succeeded in presenting the policymakers with an alternative estimate that came to be known as the 'Team B Report'. Not surprisingly, the report validated CPD's 'fears of the Soviet threat'; it discovered a 'significant error' in previous CIA/NIE (National Intelligence Estimate) estimates of Soviet military spending. It reported that the USSR was spending 11–13 per cent of its GNP on arms, not 8 per cent, which 'called for bigger increases in the US military spending in order to catch up with the Soviets'. Effectively outmanoeuvred by the beneficiaries of war dividends, by the late 1977 or early 1978 President Carter had moved 'from his campaign pledge to reduce military spending every year to increasing it'. Furthermore,

[p]ressured by the CPD ... Carter began a sustained buildup in military expenditures in July of 1979. Thus long before the Soviet invasion of Afghanistan, Carter had moved considerably over to the CPD's position.

By December 1979 ... Carter revealed comprehensive long-term plans for a major military buildup to the influential Business Council at the White House.[17]

It is sometimes argued that the fact presidents Bush senior and Bill Clinton managed to slow down the rise in military spending shows that the power of the military–industrial complex is exaggerated. I think this is a false argument. The power and influence of the military establishment should be judged not by the slowdown in the growth of the Pentagon budget following the collapse of the Soviet Union, but by its extraordinary success in averting a major downsizing of the military apparatus in the immediate aftermath of the Cold War. In the days and months following the collapse of the Berlin Wall there were widespread expectations and vigorous demands by the American people for a drastic downsizing of the military colossus, and an unprecedented reallocation of a significant portion of the Pentagon budget to 'peace dividends'. Under the presidency of Bush senior and the stewardship of Richard Cheney as secretary of defense, the Pentagon moved swiftly to avert such a widely expected overhaul by successfully inventing all kinds of 'new threats' (rogue states, global terrorism, and Islamic fundamentalism) and effectively substituting them for the 'communist threat' of the Cold War era.

Most of the post-Cold War strategies to fend off demands for 'peace dividends' following the collapse of the Berlin Wall were crafted by Pentagon officials soon after the demise of the Soviet Union. Here is how James Mann of the Center for Strategic and International Studies explains those strategies:

The Berlin Wall came down in November 1989, effectively ending the Cold War and prompting the Pentagon to undertake a search for a new set of principles, in part to prevent Congress, then controlled by the Democrats, from slashing the defense budget. The key participants were Cheney, Wolfowitz and Colin L. Powell, then chairman of the Joint Chiefs of Staff [and] the three men worked closely together on forestalling cutbacks. The Soviet Union's collapse added new urgency to their task. 'What we were afraid of was people who would say, 'Let's bring all of

the troops home, and let's abandon our position in Europe,' recalled
Wolfowitz in an interview.[18]

Most of what the Pentagon team (Richard Cheney, Colin Powell,
Paul Wolfowitz, Lewis Libby, Zalmay Khalilzad, and others)
crafted in the immediate aftermath of the collapse of the Soviet
Union was published as a government document under Cheney's
name (defense secretary at the time) as America's 'Defense Strategy
for the 1990s', also called the Defense Planning Guidance.
Almost all of the Pentagon's post-Cold War aggressive military
strategies, such as regime change, humanitarian intervention,
pre-emptive strike, and the expansion of NATO, can be traced
back to the notorious Defense Planning Guidance.

President Clinton's modest increases of the Pentagon budget
are often taken as indications that he was somewhat averse to
aggressive military operations. Yet the Federation of American
Scientists has recorded a list of US foreign military engagements,
which shows that in the first decade after the collapse of the
Berlin Wall, that is, under Presidents Bush senior and Bill Clinton,
the United States engaged in 134 such operations. Here is a
sample: Operation Eagle Eye (Kosovo), Operation Determined
Effort (Bosnia–Herzegovina), Operation Quick Lift (Croatia),
Operation Nomad Vigil (Albania), Operation Desert Thunder
(Iraq), Operation Seva Verde (Colombia), Operation Constant
Vigil (Bolivia), Operation Fundamental Response (Venezuela),
Operation Infinite Reach (Sudan, Afghanistan), Operation Safe
Border (Peru, Ecuador), Operation United Shield (Somalia),
Operation Safe Haven/Safe Passage (Cuba), Operation Sea Signal
(Haiti), Operation Safe Harbor (Haiti), Operation Desert Storm
(south-west Asia), and many more.[19]

As noted earlier, presidents might slightly modify military
plans, or offer different justifications for those plans, but they
cannot drastically change or put a stop on them. The US military–
industrial complex is an amazingly sophisticated institution; it is,
indeed, an empire in its own right. Beneficiaries of its expansion
are extremely sophisticated, cunning, and calculating. They do
not directly confront or challenge a president. Instead, they
subtly and artfully invent or manufacture 'external threats to

the national interests or security of the Unites States', or of 'its allies', in order to compel reluctant presidents or other policy makers to go along with their nefarious plans of aggression.

Historically, greater military spending in times of recession has helped reinvigorate the US economy. But in the current economic climate, following the banking crisis of 2008 and the Bush presidency, military spending is already at its highest level since the Second World War, and faces minor cuts (excluding interest on defence-related debt). Has the United States always relied on military spending to get out of economic difficulties, and what are the repercussions if this is no longer possible?

IH: Let me make three points regarding the long-standing misperception that war and military spending help stimulate a relatively advanced market economy. First, to the extent that (under certain circumstances) war and military expenditures create jobs and stimulate the economy, it is not war or military spending per se that leads to such positive economic results; it is, rather, government spending as such that brings about such desirable outcomes. Indeed, evidence shows that, dollar for dollar, non-military public spending would lead to a much bigger economic impact than military spending. For example, a 2002 Congressional Budget Office report found that every $10 billion spent on weapons generates 40,000 fewer jobs than $10 billion spent on civilian programmes.[20] Nonetheless, the ruling class prefers military to non-military spending as a fiscal stimulus measure because, while the economic benefits of non-military public spending are more widely spread throughout society, the benefits of military spending are funnelled largely into the deep pockets of the military–industrial–security complex. In addition to directly benefiting from military expenditures, the rich and powerful also prefer military to non-military public spending for yet another, more subtle and insidious reason: to keep the working class in check by systematically cutting social spending while steadily adding to military expenditures.

Second, while military spending may have a positive economic impact in the short term, it is bound to undermine the economy in the long run, for continued allocation of a disproportionately large share of public resources to war and militarism steadily undermines the critically important national objective of building and maintaining public capital or infrastructure. This includes both physical infrastructure (such as roads, bridges, mass transit, dams, levees, and the like) and human capital such as health, education, nutrition, and so on. This explains why not only are the continued escalation of war and military spending in recent years failing to stimulate the dormant US economy, but they are indeed aggravating the recession.

Third, let us assume for a moment that the argument that military spending creates jobs and stimulates economic growth is valid. Still, people of good conscience would find it difficult to support such an argument because it would mean that economic stimulation and job creation would be dependent on permanent war and destruction!

Now, a well-meaning sceptic could reasonably argue: 'OK, granted; war and military spending may be immoral, they may be less efficient in terms of economic stimulation and job creation than non-military public spending, and they may be detrimental to long-term growth and prosperity.' Nonetheless, the sceptic could further reason, 'As things stand, many jobs, businesses and communities in the United States depend on military spending; which means that cutting military spending would lead to loss of jobs, businesses, and sources of livelihood for millions. So, doesn't this mean that we are stuck with continued increases in military spending in order to save the millions of jobs, businesses, and source of livelihood that have become dependent on it?'

This is obviously a fair question. It explains why some policy makers who may be opposed to war and militarism on philosophical grounds, may nonetheless find it difficult to oppose constant increases in military spending. On the face of it, this seems an inexplicable or unsolvable dilemma. But there is, in fact, a reasonable solution to it: to slash the Pentagon budget while protecting jobs and livelihoods that have become dependent on military spending, the overall public spending should not be cut, but a significant portion of it should be redirected from military to non-military spending. As the old cliché goes: *If there is a will, there is a way.* It is all a matter of priorities, of who would benefit most from public spending.

Some economists predict that China will surpass the United States economically by 2016.[21] Given this scenario, the main remaining advantage of the US as a global power would likely be its massive military might. Does it seem likely that the United States will have to rely even more on military coercion to maintain its dominance in the future?

IH: Further reliance on military might to contain China's economic advances in global markets does seem to be an important element in the geopolitical and economic calculations of US foreign-policy makers. Whether the strategy of trying to use military advantage will succeed in making up for economic disadvantages remains to be seen. While further strengthening of US military power may limit China's access to certain global markets and resources, continued escalation of military spending that this imperial strategy of policing global markets requires may also drain the empire's own financial resources and undermine its long-term economic expansion and competitiveness – that is, the costly means may defeat the desired end. Furthermore, by narrowing China's global markets for sales of manufactured products and purchases of raw materials, especially sources of energy, the US militarists may end up further enhancing that country's economic advantages by forcing it to become even more cost-efficient and more competitive in the global market – once again, a case of misguided means subverting the end.

The problem is that for the powerful interests that are vested in the military–security capital, the 'end' has a different meaning: continued escalation of military spending, not protection or advancement of broader national interests. To further their nefarious interests at the expense of long-term national interests, and to justify the parasitic role of the military–industrial complex, these powerful militarists have managed successfully to redefine and expand the role of the Pentagon (and its handmaiden accomplice NATO) beyond the traditional 'responsibility to guard against potential military or terrorist attacks', to include all kinds of new 'missions' and responsibilities worldwide. The Pentagon's and/or NATO's new areas of 'global responsibility', as reflected, for example, in both the notorious Project for the New American Century and NATO's latest Strategic Concept, include human rights; sources of energy; 'vital communication [including the internet], transport and transit routes on which international trade, energy security and prosperity depend'; 'threat of extremism, terrorism and trans-national illegal activities such as trafficking in arms, narcotics and people'; and the 'ability to prevent, detect, defend against and recover from cyber-attacks'.[22] The expanded Pentagon/NATO 'respon-sibilities' are neither theoretical nor by definition. The recent expansion of NATO to include a number of new members in Eastern Europe and the formation of at least ten other global joint military commands (such as CENTCOM, AFRICOM, EUCOM, NORTHCOM, PACOM, SOUTHCOM, and more) are all designed to carry out these 'global responsibilities'.

US preaching of laissez-faire economics on an international level is altogether hypocritical. It self-righteously promotes this sacred principle of capitalism where or when it enjoys an international competitive advantage. As soon as it loses that advantage, however, it does not hesitate to switch from economic to military means (or 'extra-economic' means, as the late Ernest Mandel put it) in pursuit of regaining advantage against its economic rivals. This explains why the United States is methodically using its military machine and other types of geopolitical alliances to contain China's economic activities in places like Africa, Central Asia, South America and the Middle East.

While this is conveniently providing the beneficiaries of war dividends with additional justifications for ever more usurpation of taxpayers' money, it is unlikely to reach its purported goal of restoring US economic competitiveness in global markets. On the contrary, the policy of relying on the colossal military machine in the hope of restoring economic supremacy may turn out to be the wrong medicine for the anaemic US economy: as a dis-proportionately large allocation of resources to further enlarge the military machine sucks the financial blood out of the US economy, the parasitically growing military–industrial complex may turn out to be the Frankenstein that could destroy the US economy instead of protecting it, as alleged by its creators, the beneficiaries of war and militarism.

NOTES

1. 'The Universal Declaration of Human Rights', Articles 23–6, <http://tinyurl.com/n68aou>.
2. Joachim Guilliard, 'Libya: The Price of Freedom', *Global Research*, 27 April 2011, <http://globalresearch.ca/index.php?context=va&aid=24518>.
3. Ismael Hossein-zadeh, *The Political Economy of U.S. Militarism* (New York: Palgrave Macmillan, 2006), p.77.
4. Sidney Lens, *The Military–Industrial Complex* (Kansas City: Pilgrim Press, 1970), p.19.
5. As quoted in Lens, *The Military–Industrial Complex*, p.21; and in David Horowitz, *The Free World Colossus* (New York: Hill & Wang, 1965), p.85.
6. D.F. Fleming, *The Cold War and Its Origins* (New York: Doubleday, 1961), p.436.
7. Hossein-zadeh, *The Political Economy*, p.28.
8. 'Coke and Pepsi battle it out', *AME Info*, 8 April 2004, <http://www.ameinfo.com/news/Detailed/37492.html>.
9. USA*Engage, 'What USA*Engage Stands For', <http://usaengage.org/About/Our-Principles/Our-Vision/>.
10. Vivianne Walt, 'US Companies Shut Out as Iraq Auctions Its Oil Fields', *TIME*, 19 December 2009, <http://tinyurl.com/yhzo8xe>.
11. As cited by Roger Burbach, 'Bush Ideologues vs. Big Oil: The Iraq Game Gets Even Stranger', *Counterpunch*, 3 October 2003, <http://www.counterpunch.org/burbach10032003.html>.
12. Antonia Juhasz, 'Did Big Oil Win the War in Iraq?', Black Tide, 14 November 2009, <http://www.black-tide.org/article.php?id=799>.
13. Hossein-zadeh, *The Political Economy*, p.142.
14. David Ivanovich, 'Conoco's Chief Blasts Sanctions', *Houston Chronicle*, 12 February 1997.
15. Quoted in Norman Finkelstein, *Image and Reality of the Israel–Palestine Conflict*, 2nd edn (London: Verso, 2003), p.xii.
16. Hossein-zadeh, *The Political Economy*, p.127–8.
17. James Cypher, 'The Basic Economics of Rearming America', *Monthly Review*, Vol.33, No.6 (1981), pp.20–2.
18. James Mann, 'The True Rationale? It's a Decade Old', *Washington Post*, 7 March 2004.

19. Federation of American Scientists, as cited by Gore Vidal, *Perpetual War for Perpetual Peace: How We Got to Be So Hated* (New York: Thunder's Mouth Press/Nation Books, 2002), pp.22–41.

20. Cited in David Gold, 'Fewer Jobs, Slower Growth: Military Spending Drains the Economy', *Dollars and Sense*, July–August 2002, <http://tinyurl.com/3cpuev>.

21. Alex Newman, 'IMF: Chinese Economy to Surpass U.S. by 2016', *The New American*, 26 April 2011, <http://tinyurl.com/6psqkvm>.

22. NATO, 'Active Engagement, Modern Defence', 19 November 2010, <http://tinyurl.com/29p5767>.

11

Gilbert Achcar
The United States in the Middle East

How did the US intervention in the First World War impact its relationship with the Middle East?

Gilbert Achcar: The First World War was the first real projection of US force beyond the Americas and the Pacific area. It was the first time the United States assumed the status of a global power. It became interested in the Middle East for the very same reasons that had led France and Britain to take an interest there. The Sykes–Picot agreement, through which France and Britain carved up the Arab domain of the Ottoman Empire between themselves, was concluded before US involvement. That happened in 1916, and the United States got involved in the war in 1917, the year after. So of course it had no colonial position there, but it wasn't its intention to get one anyway.

The United States took an interest in the oil concessions, especially as it itself was an oil-producing country, and the oil issue was becoming more important. The Second World War would be an even more important turning point with regard to oil, with the generalisation of its use by the transport industry and so on. Therefore the United States, as a latecomer to the Middle East oil race, tried to get concessions, and in fact got the best prize by pure chance. It got involved with the House of Saud in the 1920s when their kingdom was being established. The Saudis conquered most of the Arabian Peninsula, which was not part of the division of spoils between the French and the British, or other interests looking to exploit the oil of the Arab–Iranian Gulf Area. There was no knowledge at that point of the existence of exploitable oil resources in the vast stretch of desert land that fell under Saudi control. American companies got deals with the Saudis to prospect for oil, and they hit the jackpot in 1938, when it was established that there was plenty of commercially exploitable oil there. It turned out that the new kingdom had the most important oil reserves in the whole area, and the whole world actually, with one quarter of the global oil reserves beneath its soil. Of course, this oil wealth became the centre of gravity of US interests in the Middle East. Before the end of the Second World War, the United States started building one of its largest US military bases abroad in the heart of the Saudi kingdom's Eastern province.

After the war, of course, the Middle East became a crucial theatre in the Cold War – a major stage for the rivalry between Washington and Moscow. This new conflict superseded the competition between France and Britain as colonial powers. The United States gradually replaced Britain as overlord of the region's monarchies.

Indeed, Eisenhower went against Britain and France in the Suez Crisis, for example, or didn't support it at least.

GA: Yes indeed, Washington saw this late colonial war as a blunder. It opposed the 'tripartite aggression' of Britain, France, and Israel as politically clumsy. It saw the popular reaction around the Arab world, which was very much in favour of Egypt. That's definitely one of the key reasons why Washington demanded the immediate cessation and withdrawal of the tripartite allies. This is also an important episode in US–Israeli relations, confirming that, contrary to common perception, the United States was not dealing with Israel as an untouchable strategic asset until the 1960s. It had been observing an arms embargo on the whole region, including Israel, for several years after 1948.

Israel was relying more on France, wasn't it?

GA: Israel was definitely relying more on France, as well as Germany, until the shift in the 1960s. Again this was connected to the US relationship with the Saudi kingdom. Until the 1970s, when it was nationalised, there was a state within the state of the Saudi kingdom called Aramco, the Arabian American Oil Company, which was run by American oil majors and was the main focus of US policy in the region, geared towards the interests of the oil lobby. The military base was there to protect the US enclave. Such 'expatriate' enclaves still exist, incidentally, but they are much more under Saudi control than they used to be. Anyway, at that time the United States was facing a rise of Arab nationalism. The year 1956 was an important watershed, with the United States itself acted clumsily in its relations with Egypt, attaching strings to the latter's requests for aid, thus contributing to a radicalisation that accelerated in the early 1960s. With this radicalisation of Arab nationalism, turning to the left, proclaiming socialism, and building closer ties with the Soviet Union, the pressure on the United States became increasingly stronger. They reached a low point in their presence in the area in the 1960s, to the extent that they had to evacuate their base from the Saudi Kingdom in 1962. This was strategically a big problem, because at that time, unlike now, they could not project huge forces to such faraway places in a matter of weeks. That's when Israel became a major asset, and a turning point occurred in the US–Israeli relationship. The United States started exporting tanks, aircraft, and various other sophisticated weaponry to Israel just before the 1967 war. This was the first of Israel's wars which the United States backed; they had condemned the previous one, and had not backed the first one in any form. Indeed, the war was perceived in the Arab world as an Israeli war supported by the United States. And, because of the shift in alliances, France changed its attitude under de Gaulle, from being a pretty close ally of Israel to trying to cosy up to Arab nationalism.

Israel proved in the Six-Day War that it was a fantastic military asset for the United States, which led to the development of a very close strategic relationship. In fact, Israel became the primary recipient of American public aid, not to mention non-public aid. Egypt has become second since the 1970s, when it shifted towards the United States under Sadat, but it gets less than half the amount Israel receives. If we compare the amount of aid to the size of the recipient's population, Israel stands very far

above all other countries. The Israeli left used to say that Israel
has become a giant aircraft carrier for the United States in the
region. Israel is actually much more than an aircraft carrier,
because after all there are real US aircraft carriers in the region.
It has a 400,000 strong army, and is a politically reliable ally. Of
course, Israel's image has been affected in recent years, especially
with the Lebanese fiasco, in the same way that US 'credibility'
has been affected by the Iraq fiasco.

So, from a low point in the early 1960s, the United States
started regaining lost territory in the Middle East because of its
influence after 1967, benefiting from the Israeli victory. The most
dramatic consequence of that was the political shift of Egypt
after the death of Nasser in 1970. Two years later, under Sadat,
Egypt expelled Soviet military advisers and shifted to the US
camp. That's when the United States really started increasing its
influence again. This would peak in 1990–91, when it intervened
with massive military force in the region after Iraq's invasion
of Kuwait, and re-established its direct military presence in the
Saudi Kingdom for the first time since the 1960s.

**You mention there how crucial oil has been to the US presence
in the Middle East. Indeed, in *Eastern Cauldron*, your opening
sentence is 'In the beginning was the "open door" to oil', and
you end your introductory chapter with the same line.[1] To what
extent is oil the main driving force of US policy in the region,
and where do you rate other factors, such as the military–
industrial complex, or even ideology and culture, in terms of
their importance for US military expansionism?**

GA: The importance of the military–industrial complex in US
politics in general was heavily reduced over the last decades, first
after Vietnam and then again at the end of the Cold War, for
various reasons, including changes in the business practices of the
Pentagon. The state-monopoly character of the complex faded
away, military supplies to the US government becoming more
competitive. The relative importance of military expenditure for
the US economy as a whole was also greatly reduced. To believe
that the United States is waging wars for the sake of wars is

certainly wrong. Indeed I don't think that at any point in time the US did wage war purely for the sake of war. It can increase arms production without necessarily using those arms – through the arms race, creating tensions, exporting weapons to their clients, and so on. Of course every now and then the Pentagon likes to have a live test of their weaponry, but they wouldn't just 'invent' an opportunity for no other reason, especially if it is harmful to economic interests. Why would the United States harm its overall economic interests for the sake of the military–industrial complex alone?

But what if there is an influential elite who profit greatly from war, and don't necessarily concern themselves with wider economic interests?

GA: Well, the interface between civilian and military industry is nowadays much bigger than it used to be. The kind of separation you had between the two doesn't exist any longer in the electronic age. And of course, although the arms industry is an important one, the oil corporations in the United States rank much higher than any of those that specialise in arms. Actually for the largest companies that produce arms, military hardware is but a small piece of their overall production.

Furthermore, one would have to explain how any of the wars in the Middle East could be separated from the oil factor. It is absolutely clear that oil is of greatest importance in that area: this is clearly laid out even in US strategic documents. Of all parts of the global South, the area where the United States has been investing most of its military effort since the end of the Cold War is the Middle East. How can one separate the two wars in Iraq from wider US economic interest? The thesis that the Israel lobby is the reason for these wars, as put forward by John Mearsheimer and Stephen Walt, is unconvincing.[2] They are members of the establishment who, discovering that the 2003 occupation of Iraq turned out to be a disaster for the United States, came to the conclusion that it wasn't waged with US interests in mind from the start (even though the overwhelming majority of the ruling elite in the United States thought it served US interests), and therefore attributed it to the Israel lobby. This is counterfactual. Israel actually tried to convince the United States to strike at Iran rather than Iraq, because, with the 1991 war, followed by a harsh embargo, Iraq had been completely crippled. We saw how easily the United States invaded it in 2003. Militarily the invasion was a cakewalk, to use Rumsfeld's expression, even if the aftermath was definitely not a cakewalk.

It is absolutely clear to my mind that the United States invaded Iraq because it believed that it would consolidate, and substantially increase, its control of this most important oil-exporting region. The oil factor is of huge economic and strategic importance. Its economic dimension is obvious and can only increase in the decades to come, unless a renewable and economically competitive alternative energy source is found. Up to now there hasn't been anything suitable. Since oil is a non-renewable resource, with a supply on its way to inevitable depletion, and an ever increasing demand with the rise of new gigantic economies, the structural tendency is towards a rise in its real price. Economically it is becoming increasingly important, until the point when its price will match the cost of alternative energy sources. At the same time, the strategic value of oil will also increase tremendously. By controlling access to oil resources, the US holds a huge strategic leverage over its major rival country, China, as well as its allies in western Europe and Japan, who will be even more dependent on US power. The strategic and economic importance of oil cannot be overstated, and I really can't understand why anyone would feel a need to outsmart everybody and claim it's not about oil. Alan Greenspan himself said in his memoir that he didn't know why people were so reluctant in Washington to say the plain truth: that the Iraq war was about oil.[3]

But when we look at the increase in the military budget, especially during the second Bush presidency – not just the spending on Iraq and Afghanistan, but the overall increase – does it not become so costly to secure oil that it detracts from other areas of the budget, undermining domestic facilities?

GA: That's a choice at the heart of the neoliberal turn. The truth is that the United States combined warfare and welfare during the 1960s, at a level that proved unsustainable. The neoliberal turn emerged from that, of course, and the choice was made in favour of warfare against welfare. In the Reagan years this became very clear – they cut welfare dramatically and increased arms expenditure tremendously. That represented a peak in the direct use of the arms industry as an economic tool, and a key point in reversing the decline of the United States technologically. Since then the importance of this factor has declined, as I already explained.

As for the Bush administration, the truth is simply that they were not expecting what happened in Iraq. They expected that it would be a cakewalk from beginning to end, that they could control the country with 125,000 troops, and that this would happen at a very limited cost. They couldn't imagine in their wildest nightmares that it would turn out a disaster as it did. The thought that they wanted this to happen is like saying they wanted to lose the war in Vietnam. The Vietnam War cost them a lot. It contributed to the crisis of the American and the global economy. In 1968, the massive expenditure for the Vietnam War led to big problems in the balance of payments of the United States. Here again, in Iraq, they went into gradual escalation which they didn't plan for initially. They got into this vicious circle where they couldn't cut and run because they would have lost everything they had gained, but by staying they sunk even deeper into disaster. So, as I said, claiming that since the war didn't serve their interests, it was therefore a war waged in spite of their interests, doesn't make sense. What is crucial in this regard is how they conceived it at the start. Ruling classes do make errors and blunders, but they make them believing they are acting in what they perceive to be their interest.

You mentioned how the major threat to the United States during the Cold War became radical Arab nationalism, and in their attempts to destroy it successive US administrations became bedfellows with Islamic fundamentalists. Should they have foreseen that this would then mutate into the chief form of anti-Americanism in the region? You do say in *Eastern Cauldron* that the United States mistakenly perceived that 'violent hostility to the United States among Islamic fundamentalists was a peculiarity of Shiite Islam, and that Sunni and particularly Wahhabi variants ... were inherently inclined to ally with the West'.[4] Does this explain their willingness to collaborate with the Wahhabis, and the Taliban in Afghanistan?

GA: US collaboration with Islamic fundamentalism is as old as US collaboration with the Saudi kingdom, which is by far the main embodiment of Islamic fundamentalism in the world. The kingdom's ruling family governs in alliance with the religious establishment, and uses it as an ideological apparatus to keep control of the country, with the United States as the military protector. Indeed, in the 1960s the Saudi–American alliance became the central aspect of the US fight against radicalising Arab nationalism, and Soviet influence in the Middle East, especially after Washington was compelled to abandon its base in the kingdom under the regional pressure of Arab nationalism led by Gamal Abdel-Nasser's Egypt. The United States closely collaborated with Islamic fundamentalism through the Saudi Kingdom, and built an alliance with the Muslim Brotherhood, the bitter enemies of Nasser, who had become the United States's public enemy number one in the Middle East. In this period, US collaboration with, or instrumentalisation of, Islamic fundamentalism through the Saudis greatly expanded.

Of course, at that point they did not expect it to turn against them, and indeed it didn't until many years later. In the 1970s, a combination of factors enhanced the clout of the Saudis and Islamic fundamentalism. On one hand, there was the defeat of Arab nationalism in the 1967 war and an ideological backlash against it, and on the other there was the oil boycott at the time of the 1973 Arab–Israeli War, which led to a sudden increase in oil revenues, making the Saudis much richer. Consequently, Saudi influence in the Middle East became much greater, while movements following their religious ideology expanded. Islamic fundamentalism was on the rise, but at that point it was still in step with the expansion of US hegemony. That lasted until the Iranian Revolution, which was the turning point that saw the emergence of a bitterly anti-Western brand of Islamic fundamentalism. It took the United States by surprise, and for a while Washington tried to reassure itself, counterposing Iran's Shia bad Muslims to Sunni good Muslims. Indeed, Washington continued to bet on Sunni Islamic fundamentalism throughout the 1980s, supporting the Mujahedeen in Afghanistan against Soviet occupation.

A second turning point, however, would come with the first war on Iraq. There was a powerful popular rejection of the US intervention in Arab countries, and whole sections of Sunni Islamic fundamentalism, especially the Muslim Brotherhood, stood against it. Their relations with the Saudis collapsed consequently as did the relation of the Saudis with other brands of Sunni fundamentalism. Al-Qaeda turned its weapons against the United States and the Saudi monarchy. In the 1990s, the Saudis kept funding the expansion of a specific brand of Sunni fundamentalism, called the Salafi movement, who are the most conservative. But at the same time there was a surge in anti-American discourse among Islamic fundamentalist currents – some violent, some, like the Muslim Brotherhood, mostly non-violent. The emirate of Qatar replaced the Saudis as the main source of funding for the Muslim Brotherhood. Indeed, the Qatari–Saudi rivalry is also part of the picture in the region. From the 1990s onwards the United States tended to look at Islamic fundamentalism as a threat.

Now, however, we are witnessing a new shift in that regard. With the collapse of several of their allies in the region and the apparently irresistible sweep of democratisation, the United States has realised that it doesn't have any allies enjoying real popular support. It thus needed to establish a new relationship with forces enjoying real popularity, the Muslim Brotherhood being the obvious candidate. The United States is now attempting to co-opt again Islamic fundamentalism into collaboration. However, in this relationship it is no longer in a position of power and suzerainty: it has to negotiate and offer a partnership. It is willing to help the Muslim Brotherhood get a piece of the pie on the understanding that it would respect US interests, and control the most radical fundamentalist fringes. This is what the United States has been doing since the beginning of the Arab uprising in 2011, because the Muslim Brotherhood was by far the strongest organised political force in the opposition everywhere. In the initial stage of democratisation and elections, it's no surprise that the Muslim Brotherhood stood to gain the most. But I don't think it will last very long. Things might change quite rapidly when the Muslim Brothers will be confronted with the experience of trying to rule, because they lack adequate response to the huge social and economic problems of the region's countries. But in the meantime, this is the best possible bet the United States can make.

You mentioned the Iranian Revolution as the turning point in the US relationship with Islamic fundamentalism. To what extent do you think post-Second World War US policy towards Iran, through Operation Ajax and the overthrow of Mossadegh, and the 25 years of support for the Shah's repressive dictatorship, contributed to the anti-Western and Islamic fundamentalist nature of the Iranian Revolution? Is it reasonable to assume, as Stephen Kinzer says, that 'if the United States had not sent agents to depose Prime Minister Mohammad Mossadegh in 1953, Iran would probably have continued along its path toward full democracy'?[5]

GA: Such a conclusion belongs to counterfactual history and is therefore very speculative, to be sure, but one thing that can be clearly stated is that the United States contributed greatly to making Islamic fundamentalism become the dominant expression of popular discontent in most of the Muslim world. This happened due to Washington's systematic fight against every brand of progressive nationalism, not to mention leftist or communist forces. Indeed, what you mentioned about Iran is part of the story – the way the US toppled Mossadegh, followed by its support for the very harsh repression by the Shah regime against the left in Iran. At the same time, however, the Shah regime did not repress the religious establishment, for the reason that it regarded it as an ally against communism, and even progressive nationalism. This paved the way for what would happen later.

The same story unfolded in Egypt, where the United States fought bitterly against Nasser, supporting the Muslim Brotherhood against him in alliance with the Saudi kingdom, until Nasser died and Sadat came to power. When he shifted to the Western camp, Sadat released the Muslim Brotherhood from jail and gave them a lot of leeway for their activities, especially in the universities. He allowed them to rebuild their social network, and regarded them as allies in his fight against the remnants of Nasserism and the left. As you know, he ended up being killed by a radical fringe of the same Islamic movement that he had unleashed. So this is a repeating pattern in the history of the region. I described some time ago, in my *Clash of Barbarisms*, how allegories like the Sorcerer's Apprentice, or Frankenstein, fit this story well – people unleashing forces that they cannot control afterwards, and which end up turning against them.

Is Iranian influence growing in the Middle East, perhaps even partly *because of* the regime changes in Iraq and Afghanistan? Does this really create 'destabilisation' in terms of nuclear threat, danger to Israel, spread of Shiite fundamentalism, and sponsorship of terrorism, or is it merely that it undermines the ability of the United States to shape the region according to its dictates?

GA: Destabilisation is of course the way the United States sees the situation – it is destabilisation of its own interests. Indeed, any challenge to US interests is seen as destabilisation, because stability is synonymous with US hegemony, or the dominance of US interests in Washington's conception of the world. Iran has been confronted with many threats from the United States over the years since 1979, and more recently from Israel. Thus, it has been developing its network of friendly forces in the region, which include Hezbollah, Shia forces in Iraq, and for a long time the Palestinian Hamas, in addition to its alliance with the Syrian regime. Overall, however, if one looks at the situation in terms of stability and destabilisation, Hezbollah has had a rather stabilising effect in Lebanon. They have even contributed to the neoliberal order imposed there. As for Iraq, Iran has actually been cooperating with Washington in supporting the Maliki government, and therefore they are playing the role of a stabilising force there. So stability is not a goal in itself unless it serves US interests. Clearly, Iran is a challenger to these interests: it seeks stability only where it has achieved an important position of force, as is the case in both Iraq and Lebanon, but this is at the expense of US hegemony.

Regarding Afghanistan, you wrote in 2003 that there was 'a low level of interest in Washington in controlling the Afghan interior or in building the promised "modern" state, to be led by its loyal vassal, Hamid Karzai'; and also that 'the stakes are too small in Afghanistan to justify the enormous financial and military investment that would be needed to try and control this country in reality'.[6] Are you surprised by what happened afterwards – on one hand the continued commitment of American troops in the area, and the military presence they maintained, and on the other the way the country started to develop in some ways, such as health and education, under the Karzai government?

GA: The United States is doing its best to try to give the Afghanistan occupation an air of success, but it is definitely not a success story. Everyone knows that the Karzai government is completely rotten. Afghan elections are rigged and the 'model democracy' there is completely fake. It is actually a disaster. It is obvious that if foreign troops were removed from Afghanistan the Karzai puppet regime wouldn't be able to hold on for long. In the Pashtun area certainly, at the very least, the Taliban would completely overwhelm them. Incidentally, just as a complement to what I said earlier, Afghanistan is one case in which I never claimed that war was motivated by oil. I don't see the oil factor playing everywhere, but was only referring to US wars in the Gulf area. I even dismiss explanations of the Afghan war that attribute it to a gas pipeline project. To explain wars by such small hypotheses is rather unconvincing.

But that was a factor, wasn't it?

GA: I don't think that oil was and is a factor in the Afghan war. That's why I said that the Bush administration were not interested in really controlling the country. They were more interested in setting a military foot in the region, four bases in Afghanistan then other bases in former Soviet Central Asia. The reason for seeking bases in Central Asia is partly for oil and gas, to be sure, because the Caspian Basin and Central Asia are very important gas producing areas, but I would say nevertheless that this is secondary to the more important strategic dimension here. For the United States, building a military presence in the region located between the European heart of Russia and China has enormous strategic value.

But Afghanistan turned into a quagmire, as did Iraq. The Obama administration tried to replicate in Afghanistan the 'surge', which had been used as an exit strategy in Iraq. If you recall, starting in 2006, the United States increased its troops in Iraq, and changed its policies, starting to buy Sunni tribes, and started preparing for an exit. Washington would certainly have not wanted it to be a complete exit; it wished to be able to keep bases and troops in the country, but it couldn't even achieve that. Iraq will remain in the history of the US Empire as a major disaster and in certain ways a more serious one than Vietnam, the previous major disaster. This bodes ill for the replica of the 'surge' in Afghanistan. Whatever they claim in Washington, it's a failure in the same way that Iraq was a failure.

All these setbacks are occurring in a time of global decline for US power. This decline has been forecast many times since the 1970s, but wrongly until now. US power rebounded with Reagan, and even reached a peak in the 1990s in the aftermath of the collapse of the Soviet Union, but for the last few years, with the combination of major economic crisis at the heart of the US and global capitalist economies, and the disasters in Iraq and Afghanistan, it has become very clear that the United

States has entered a period of decline. And right now I can't see how it could redress the situation. Indeed, we can see how much even the image of the United States has been affected. Just think of its image after 2001, or after the first Iraq War in 1991, and compare it to its image today. US hegemony reached such a peak in the early 1990s that the strategic value of Israel decreased, and Washington even allowed itself to exert pressure on Israel to cut deals with the Palestinians and Arabs, although the Israeli–Palestinian 'peace process' reached a stalemate soon after the 1993 Oslo agreement. After 2001, however, the choices made by the Bush administration were so disastrous that by 2011 the United States was actually quite weak in facing the so-called Arab Spring, which marked a very low point in its influence in the region. I'm not burying US power, it's still mighty, but it's definitely not *almighty*, and it's definitely on the decline.

As you say, in the Arab Spring, the United States had to follow rather than lead. In Egypt in particular they tried to support Mubarak as long as possible, then welcomed the short-lived idea of regime stalwart Omar Suleiman taking control, and finally were very happy with the interim military regime, run by Mohamed Tantawi, Mubarak's defence minister. They started to talk about democracy eventually, for example when Obama finally said, 'Egyptians have made it clear that nothing less than genuine democracy will carry the day';[7] but doesn't that quote itself imply the acceptance of democracy only as last resort?

GA: Oh definitely, this is pure hypocrisy. Of course, US politicians have to speak like this because democracy has been part of their ideological baggage for so long. The United States claims to be the beacon of democracy, and this has been its main ideological weapon since the Cold War and a major aspect of its imperial legitimation. When there is a popular uprising for democracy and freedom, how could the United States condemn it? They can't, officially at least, so they have to pretend to be happy with what's happening. But it's very hypocritical, because as you mentioned they were actually very much relieved with the outcome that the Egyptian military engineered. In truth, it was a kind of coup. Mubarak was pushed aside, but the military took direct power. Of course, the army had always been the backbone of power in Egypt, but they took over directly. The United States immediately contemplated the scenario seen in Turkey in the 1980s, of transition under military control – what they called 'orderly transition'.

In the same way, if you look at Yemen, the United States hailed the Saudi-sponsored agreement even though it was rejected by the democrats of the mass movement, the young people. If you look at Morocco, the United States hailed the democratic elections there although there was an important boycott of the election due to its undemocratic character. Official figures are that 45 per cent of registered voters, a minority, took part in the election, and this in a very peculiar situation where the number of registered voters has been reduced from what it was previously. This came after a massive campaign for boycott by the left opposition and the protest movement in Morocco. You see therefore where the United States stands, on the side of regimes which are definitely not democratic, whether the Gulf monarchies or other regimes. They may be liberal in some cases like Morocco, but not democratic. The range is one of absolute to liberal autocracies.

In fact, the United States cannot wish for real democracy in this part of the world for two related reasons. The first is that due to its involvement in the region in recent decades, and the connection with Israel, the United States is incredibly unpopular. It's very different from eastern Europe, where it was on the safe side, and could advocate free elections because it was clear that no parties other than those supported by it were poised to win. In the Arab world it's the contrary. The second reason is that there is so much at stake in the region, economically and strategically. This explains why the United States is still following the same policy that it implemented during the Cold War, when it supported authoritarian regimes in the name of anti-communism.

On the other hand, the Iranian Revolution was an example of the United States allowing one of its favoured dictators to

be overthrown by an uprising that did not entirely appeal to Western rhetoric. Certainly, the Carter administration considered continuing to back its long-term ally, the Shah, but eventually did not. According to David Schmitz, this was because Carter, with his commitment to human rights policies, 'refused to be swayed by the old rationales for supporting right-wing dictatorships that had led to the original backing of the Shah, even if his fall from power was the result'.[8] To what extent was Carter's concern for human rights a factor in this case?

GA: I would not want to comment on Carter's intimate thoughts, all the more since his subsequent evolution has been rather better than the average US president's. However, the United States is not an autocratic system, and when a president is not willing to do something that is necessary according to 'the system', it finds ways to compel him to do so. So, the fact is that the US did not intervene militarily at the time of the Iranian Revolution for practical reasons: not because of any respect for human rights, but simply because the United States did not have the means to intervene. On one hand, in 1979 the United States was still fully affected by the so-called Vietnam syndrome, and was not actually able to send troops anywhere. Even Reagan, who came after Carter, wrote in his autobiography following his presidency that his major regret was his inability to overcome this 'syndrome'. In fact it is only in 1990–91, with Iraq's invasion of Kuwait and the changing global conditions in which the Soviet Union was on the verge of completely vanishing, that Washington recovered its ability to militarily intervene abroad in a massive way. On the other hand, Iran is a big country and it would have been very difficult for the United States to occupy and control it. For these reasons, it was just out of the question for the United States to intervene. The only attempt Carter made, which again was not motivated by human rights, was the operation to try to rescue the American hostages, and that was a total fiasco. It gives you an idea of how weak the United States was at that point.

Carter's National Security Adviser at the time, Zbigniew Brzezinski, reportedly recommended that something be done to

save the Shah in Iran, but Carter did not listen. Would Brzezinski
not have been aware of the Vietnam syndrome?

GA: Well, 'something' is one thing and a major intervention is
another thing. And it is not just Brzezinski, or even any American
president, that decides such things alone. They have to take into
consideration how the Pentagon brass sees things and what they
want. I am quite sure that the US military would not have been
enthused about any idea of massive military action in the region
at that point.

**At the time, Reagan was campaigning for the presidency, and
part of his campaign involved criticising Carter for allowing the
Shah, as well as Somoza in Nicaragua, to fall, and following the
Jeanne Kirkpatrick doctrine that the US should have supported
its allies there. Are you saying then that even Reagan could not
have done anything in those cases?**

GA: As I say, Reagan himself experienced the inability to
massively use military means during his own presidency.
Throughout his two mandates, over eight years, he couldn't
conduct any invasion, except that of the tiny Grenada. Against
Nicaragua, or Iran, he had to resort to violations of US law –
which led to the Iran–Contra scandal – playing petty politics, and
sending weapons to Iran through the Israelis. In fact, this is the
best proof that intervention is not a matter of what the president
of the United States has in his mind, whether human rights or
hawkish views. It's basically down to the objective ability to
take action, which is ultimately decided by the Pentagon. If the
military are very much opposed or extremely reluctant to do
something, it's very hard for a president to impose it on them.

**And do you think short of actual military intervention the Shah
could not have been saved?**

GA: I don't think he could have been saved in any other manner,
and any intervention by the United States would have led to a
situation like Vietnam, or at the very least like Iraq. Given that

the United States proved unable to control Iraq in these recent years, how could it have controlled Iran, which is much larger with a much bigger population? Again, this is counterfactual history, but in this case it's rather clear that the United States would not have been able to crack such a big and tough nut.

Is this something they should bear in mind with Iran today?

GA: I think they do. They are not contemplating an invasion of Iran, only military strikes from a distance. This is the new, almost risk-free, kind of intervention – another level of what has been aptly called the post-heroic war. They have already used that tactic in Libya, where anyway the insurgent population did not want them to send ground troops. Operations from thousands of feet away are not a problem for the United States today, and that is what they are contemplating for Iran, under Israeli pressure.

In your view, what were the motives of the United States and Europe in Libya, in aiding the removal of Gaddafi? Obviously there was quite a lot of debate about whether they should have been involved or not.

GA: The uprising was basically a movement for democracy, rights, and political freedoms, and in that sense I can't see how any progressive person could not support the uprising of the Libyan people against a 42-year old dictatorship. As for why the United States and its allies intervened in the way they did, on the one hand it was because the Gaddafi regime was so isolated that it was not a big problem, politically, to do so. But also, they saw the possibility of regaining what they thought they had lost to a great extent in the events in Egypt and the rest of the area, that is, the credentials of appearing to side with a mass democratic movement. But they did so still with a view to exerting control on the political process. They knew that there weren't any major organised forces that represented a direct threat to the United States in Libya, so they thought there was a chance that through their intervention they could get the political scene in that country to turn pro-West. And, given that it's a rich oil country, it was worth doing that in their view, because it represents important economic and strategic interests.

However, they were delusional in thinking they could control the process there. They thought they would have a major say in what would happen in the post-Gaddafi era, but the truth is no one controls anything in Libya. It is now a country without a state, if we define a state by the monopoly of legitimate armed force. There are militias and various sorts of armed groups, and no one can tell which political forces will ultimately prevail. The United States plays the same game in Libya as it plays in Egypt and elsewhere. It tries to make a deal with the Muslim Brotherhood, and to create some kind of broad coalition of allies, from liberal to Islamic. Of course, in a sense, Western intervention in Libya diminished or defused anti-Western resentment in that country, preventing the development of stridently anti-Western currents in the short term; but the future is unclear. In the short term it doesn't look like there will be an especially anti-Western government, but it doesn't mean either that the Libyan people have become pro-Western, and that's an important distinction. Indeed, the attitude towards Israel can be seen as a kind of touchstone. The Libyans are very anti-Israel, and this is one key reason why they look at the West with suspicion and mistrust. Also, they know that Western countries are coming to Libya to secure contracts. They can see all these visits by Western rulers coming along with businessmen trying to get contracts – to get oil, to sell weapons, to secure reconstruction contracts, and so on. In fact, that's exactly the spirit in which the Libyans dealt with the Western intervention in the first place. They saw the Western powers as mercenaries that they were hiring to help them fight Gaddafi, and which they would reward with contracts. Obviously they had to conclude contracts anyway; they need Western input in rebuilding and developing their country. But they have the money for that and are not dependent on foreign funding.

After the liberation of Tripoli, the Syrian movement saw in the Western intervention in Libya a factor of success in the fight against their own dictatorship, and started requesting the same – disregarding the huge differences between the situations in the two countries. So in that regard you could say that the Western intervention in Libya achieved some success in changing the image of Western powers in the region. But even in Syria, the demands are addressed to the United Nations, as were those of the Libyans, and the Syrian uprising sees that it is the United Nations and the Arab League, rather than the United States, that have a duty to prevent the regime from perpetrating mass murder against the people. This said, there is no consensus among the opposition in Syria for the request of foreign direct military intervention. Actually, there are probably more people opposed to that idea than in favour of it, contrary to the demand for weapons deliveries, which is popular indeed and a very different matter. The Syrian people are aware that Western countries are more on Israel's side than theirs, and they don't trust them.

NOTES

1. Gilbert Achcar, *Eastern Cauldron: Islam, Afghanistan, Palestine and Iraq in a Marxist Mirror* (London: Pluto Press, 2004), p.9 and p.45.
2. John J. Mearsheimer and Stephen M. Walt, *The Israel Lobby and US Foreign Policy* (London: Allen Lane, 2007).
3. See Alan Greenspan, *The Age of Turbulence: Adventures in a New World* (New York: Penguin, 2007).
4. Achcar, *Eastern Cauldron*, p.28.
5. Stephen Kinzer, *All the Shah's Men: An American Coup and the Roots of Middle East Terror*, 2nd edn (Hoboken, N.J.: John Wiley & Sons, 2008), p.ix.
6. Achcar, *Eastern Cauldron*, p.40.
7. See '"Egypt's transition begins" – Barack Obama', *BBC News*, 11 February 2011, <http://www.bbc.co.uk/news/world-us-canada-12437116>.
8. David F. Schmitz, *The United States and Right-Wing Dictatorships, 1965–1989* (New York: Cambridge University Press, 2006), p.181.

12

Norman G. Finkelstein
US Support for Israeli State Terror

Prior to the 1960s, and in particular the Six-Day War in 1967, the US attitude to Israel was one of cautious support, or even pressure. Was the shift in policy, and substantial military funding, merely a matter of strategy, perhaps due to perceived Soviet influence in Arab countries at the time?

Norman Finkelstein: US policy in the Arab world during the 1950s was more cautious than hitherto, and the United States kept Israel at arm's length, because the Egyptian president, Nasser, and the brand of 'radical Arab nationalism' he championed, appeared to be potent political forces. The United States also held out hope that via various inducements – wheat subsidies, support for the Aswan Dam, etc. – it could wean Nasser away from 'radical Arab nationalism'. By the early 1960s it became clear, however, that Nasser could not be neutered. The United States then grew closer to Israel. The turning point came in 1967 when Israel inflicted a historic defeat on the Arab world by cutting Nasser down to size and in effect hammering the last nail in the coffin of Nasserism. The confluence of interests between Washington and Tel Aviv had much less to do with fear of 'perceived Soviet influence' than a common desire to maintain control of the Arab world.

So to what extent did US support around 1967, a time when previous supporter France had placed an arms embargo on Israel, effectively bring legitimacy to Israeli actions that might otherwise have been missing?

NF: The United States became much less critical of Israeli belligerence after the June 1967 war, in part because Israel was now an American 'strategic asset', so 'You scratch my back, I scratch yours', in part because the Arab world was now quiescent, and in part because of the Israel lobby. Washington had no real stake in the Israeli occupation of Palestinian lands and would have probably exerted a lot more pressure on Israel were it not for the lobby.

Had the Israel lobby in the United States always been a substantial force, even prior to 1967, albeit one that the US government largely resisted? Was there a sudden ideological shift after the 1967 victory, which changed US government attitudes towards the lobby?

NF: The American Jewish lobby played a critical role in getting President Truman to support the 1947 Partition Resolution (dividing Palestine into Arab and Jewish states) and to recognise Israel. But it is also true that no fundamental American interests were at stake. The major US regional investment was in Saudi oil, and King Saud had already signalled to Truman that he would not react if Washington supported Israel diplomatically. The King did however add that if Washington supported Israel *militarily*, he would be forced to act. So the United States imposed an arms embargo on the whole Middle East.

How do you see the role of the US government, and especially Henry Kissinger, around the Yom Kippur War of 1973? You say that a UN Security Council resolution was in place demanding Israeli withdrawal from the territories occupied in 1967, but that 'Kissinger aligned himself completely with the Israeli position' and the United States vetoed the resolution. Because of this, no negotiations were possible, and 'the last hope of averting a war [with Egypt] was dashed'.[1] At the same time, however, it seems that the United States wanted to see Israel hurt, as despite the subsequent Egyptian attack being expected, it advised Israel against a pre-emptive strike. Also, even after the United States finally sent arms to support Israel, helping it gain the upper hand, the United States pressured Israel not to push forward and destroy the Egyptian army. According to Kissinger, the aim was

to let Israel 'bleed just enough to soften it up for the post-war diplomacy he was planning'.[2] What does this say about the US attitude towards Israel at the time, and towards the United Nations?

NF: Kissinger's version of events is mostly self-serving fiction. Neither Israel nor the United States expected an Egyptian attack in 1973. The received wisdom after Israel's lightning victory in June 1967 was that 'war was not an Arab game'. The nickname among Israelis for Egyptian soldiers was 'monkeys'. It is true that Israel had some hours' forewarning of the Egyptian attack, but (1) after international criticism of it for launching a preventive attack in 1967, Israel didn't want to risk international outrage after launching a second such attack, and (2) Israel was confident that even in the event of an Egyptian attack, the Israeli armed forces would quickly be able to seize the offensive because of the Arabs' genetic incompetence. I very much doubt that Kissinger was thinking in terms of 'post-war diplomacy' at the time of the attack. He was not so prescient; in the case of the Middle East he was a monument to stupidity and incompetence.

You wouldn't say then that there was a calculated US plan around this time to push Israel and Egypt deliberately into war, whether or not in order to manufacture better conditions for peace?

NF: This is an invention of Kissinger and his acolytes in order to cover up for his disastrous underestimation of Egypt's ability and willingness to wage war in order to recover the Sinai. There isn't a scratch of evidence to support this self-serving 'theory'.

The killings of Palestinian refugees in the Sabra and Shatila camps in Lebanon in September 1982 is recognised as a massacre even by Israel, although they claim 'indirect responsibility'. Apparently, the United States tried to stop the possibility of the attack, albeit unsuccessfully. It seems clear, first, that the United States did not want Israeli forces to advance into West Beirut, and then were 'horrified' at the Israeli idea of sending anti-PLO Lebanese militia forces into the camps, because it was apparent that a massacre would result.[3] But did the United States subsequently take any punitive measures because Israel broke these agreements? For example, did it distance relations in any way? Did it seek prosecutions through international law? Did it subsequently have problems dealing with Ariel Sharon, who was judged to bear personal responsibility for allowing the massacre, as Israeli prime minister?

NF: The fear was palpable at the time among Palestinians that the Lebanese Christian forces would commit a massacre. In an agreement negotiated by US envoy Philip Habib, the United States promised the Palestinian leadership before it departed Lebanon that it would watch over the safety of the Palestinians left behind. But Israel almost immediately breached the American-brokered agreement, moved into West Beirut, and then ordered the Christian militias under its command to 'clean out' the camps. Everyone understood what would happen. It was also clear that the Lebanese militias did not expect to encounter any resistance in the camps; that it was going to be a straight-out massacre. The Christian militias were not known for their bravery, yet only 200 of them entered the camp, where many thousands of Palestinians lived, because they knew that the armed Palestinians had gone. The United States was not pleased with what happened, but it did not substantively affect the US–Israeli relationship. 'Accidents happen …'

In both the 1982 and the 2006 Lebanon Wars, Israel was accused of using cluster bombs in civilian areas, which, among other things, broke the 1952 Mutual Defense Assistance Agreement with the United States. In 1982, after 'the Reagan Administration determined that Israel "may" have violated' the agreement, it 'prohibited U.S. export of cluster bombs to Israel for six years'. However, in the latter case, although 'the State Department issued a preliminary report to Congress concluding that Israel may have violated the terms of classified US–Israeli procurement agreements on the use of cluster bombs in populated areas', it was left to an Israel Defense Forces investigation to determine whether violations had occurred and it decided they had not.[4]

Does this demonstrate a change in the relationship between the two countries since 1982, or perhaps a lapsed US attitude to international law in the absence of a rival superpower?

NF: It is hard to make exact political comparisons between the two Israeli aggressions because of so many variables. It's useful to recall, however, exactly what happened in 2006. A Human Rights Watch report found that Israel dropped as many as 4.6 million cluster munitions on south Lebanon during the attack. It was the 'most extensive use of cluster munitions anywhere in the world since the 1991 Gulf War',[5] while relative to the size of the targeted area the density of the attack was historically unprecedented. (Apparently the only reason Israel did not drop yet more cluster munitions was that its stocks had been totally depleted.) Some 90 per cent of these cluster munitions were dropped 'over the final three days when Israel knew a settlement was imminent',[6] the UN ceasefire resolution having already been passed but not yet gone into effect. Entire villages in South Lebanon were saturated with cluster munitions. In this respect the 2006 crime was of an entirely different order of magnitude than what occurred in 1982. On the other hand, Israel killed somewhere between 15,000 and 20,000 Lebanese and Palestinian civilians in the 1982 invasion, whereas in the 2006 invasion it killed 1,200 Lebanese, of whom approximately 1,000 were civilians. In this regard the order of magnitude of the crime was incomparably greater in 1982 as compared to 2006.

Overall, it seems that the 1982 example represents an exception to the norm, in that the United States actually penalised Israel in some way for breaking their agreements. Is it fair to say then that such agreements have largely been for show, and substantially meaningless in the post-1967 relationship? Why might the United States have deemed it necessary to ban sales of cluster bombs to Israel in 1982, when the breaking of agreements had been ignored at other times?

NF: When Israel starts carrying on publicly in a barbaric fashion, the United States pays a price in terms of restiveness in the Arab world. When the pressure from below exposes the collaboration of Arab leaders with US–Israeli policy, the Arab leaders call on Washington to give them cover. There's also international public opinion, which was outraged at the devastation and carnage Israel visited on Lebanon in 1982. Robert Fisk makes the point in *Pity the Nation*, a phenomenal book, that for the first time reporters were able to move freely in an Arab country and present what the receiving end looks like during one of Israel's 'purity of arms' wars. It wasn't a pretty picture.

So which of these criteria didn't apply in 2006, that the United States didn't feel the need to penalise Israel?

NF: The Bush administration wanted Israel to deal a crippling blow to Hezbollah in order to pressure or pave the way for an attack on Iran. In her memoir, Condoleezza Rice remarks in passing that even when international pressure on the United States to stop Israel's rampage peaked, Vice-President Cheney was insisting that Israel must be allowed to finish the job.

You say that the aim of the December 2008 Gaza invasion by Israel was to restore Israel's 'deterrence capacity',[7] effectively a tactic of intimidating and terrorising the population through such a display of force, abandon, and destruction that its enemies would not dare oppose Israel again. The Goldstone Report and other independent studies back up theories that the result of the attack was a massacre, and an act of state terrorism which deliberately targeted homes and infrastructure with no clear military purpose. To what extent did this attack utilise US supplied weaponry? Has the United States in any way condemned the attack or threatened withdrawal of any support for Israel as a result?

NF: In its post-invasion report *Fuelling Conflict*, Amnesty International inventoried the foreign-manufactured weapons used by Israel during the Gaza invasion, such as the US-made white phosphorus shells, tank ammunition, and guided missiles, as well as the scheduled US arms deliveries to Israel just before and during the invasion. It reported that 'the USA has been by far the major supplier of conventional arms to Israel'; that 'the USA has provided large funding each year for Israel to procure arms despite US legislation that restricts such aid to consistently gross human rights violators'; and that *'Israel's military intervention in the Gaza Strip has been equipped to a large extent by US-supplied weapons, munitions and military equipment paid for with US taxpayers' money'*.[8] The United States blocked any condemnation of the Israeli massacre in Gaza and was quick to condemn the Goldstone Report after its publication.

What did you make of Richard Goldstone's 'reconsideration' of the Goldstone Report, published in April 2011? He claims that subsequent Israeli investigations 'indicate that civilians were not intentionally targeted as a matter of policy'.[9] However, you stated prior to this that 'the Goldstone Report never said or implied that the principal objective of Israel's attack was to murder Palestinians'.[10] Does this reconsideration, in which Goldstone also says, 'If I had known then what I know now, the Goldstone Report would have been a different document', have any substance?

NF: I wrote a booklet on Goldstone's so-called recantation. Every word in his recantation rings false. He claims that he recanted because of 'new information'. In fact, there wasn't any new information, just more of the usual Israeli denials, without a scratch of evidence to support them. For two years Israel and its minions hounded him. They finally got to him. Exactly how, we'll probably never know. But the fact that Israel invested so much in discrediting him and the report testifies to the power of the original report and how much Israel fears the exposure of its crimes by credible sources.

The relationship between Barack Obama and Benjamin Netanyahu has been strained, especially regarding 'freezing' the building of Israeli settlements in occupied territories as a precondition for peace talks. Reportedly, ex-Secretary of

Defense Robert Gates complained to Netanyahu that after supporting Israel with arms, intelligence, and diplomacy, 'the US has received nothing in return, particularly with regard to the peace process'.[11] Is the Obama administration unable, or rather unwilling, to force Israel on this matter?

NF: On a regional level – whether it be Iran or Iraq – there is a broad confluence of interests between the United States and Israel. But on the 'local' question of the Israel–Palestine conflict the interests of the United States and Israel diverge. The United States has no stake in the Israeli occupation or in the expansion of Israeli settlements. The only rational explanation for US support of *these* Israeli policies is the financial and electoral pressure exerted by the Israel lobby. On the other hand, after the Arab Spring, the Palestine conflict ceased to be a 'local' one and began to have regional ramifications as the newly awakened Arab–Muslim people rallied around the cause of Palestine. Now that fundamental US interests might be at stake, it's quite possible that, lobby or no lobby, the United States will begin to exert more pressure on Israel to withdraw.

You mention the role of the Israel lobby, which is often thought of as having a major influence on US political decision making. How important, in your view, is the Israel lobby in terms of political funding, vote winning and pressure? What are its limits?

NF: In my opinion, it makes no sense to underplay the efficacy of the Israel lobby. Lobbies have clout in our political system, and the Israel lobby is very well organised and funded. Why shouldn't it have an impact in Congress? There's just too much anecdotal evidence of Congress people feeling threatened and intimidated by the lobby to pretend it's a figment of the imagination of Israel's critics. On the other hand, it's also naive to believe that a lobby, however powerful, can decide on fundamental American interests. When the United States went to war in Iraq in 2003, it wasn't because of the lobby. It's because Cheney and Rumsfeld believed such a war would serve American interests (as they construed these interests), and Bush's advisors thought it would help his re-election bid. The war is easily explicable without invoking the lobby, which was a cheerleader, for sure, but not the prime mover.

Does Israel still rely on US financial support to the extent that it must respond to US pressures, or does it have enough economic autonomy to resist? For example, one possible punitive measure available to the United States if Israel refuses to comply with peace-process demands is to withhold loan guarantees, but Israel has not drawn on these in recent years anyway. Also, Israel is now itself a major global arms supplier, and a US stipulation that 75 per cent of military aid to Israel must be spent on US-manufactured arms appears to benefit the United States more than Israel. Is the pressure available to the United States only political now, and how crucial is that to Israel?

NF: It's impossible to separate out Israel's financial dependency on the United States from its political dependency. They are integral to each other. The simple fact is, if Israel lost the US veto in the Security Council, it would suffer the same sanctions as many other countries that have broken international law. It couldn't endure these sanctions for a single day, not for economic reasons, but because Israelis would be hysterical at the prospect of their total isolation, and the popular pressure on Israeli leaders to mend relations with Washington would be overwhelming. Israel talks big, but it is terrified at the prospect of having to stand alone.

Would Israel ever be able to forge a strong enough alliance with, say, China, with which it has been developing close economic and military ties in recent years, to the point that it could secure similar veto support? Does the United States stand to lose out if this relationship becomes closer?

NF: I very much doubt this. The foundations of the US–Israeli relationship – historical, cultural, military, political, familial – are so deeply entrenched that I don't believe Israel can replicate them anywhere else.

The United States has not been prosecuted or forced to disarm for civilian casualties it is directly responsible for in various wars, most recently in Iraq, Afghanistan, and Pakistan. The same goes for other NATO countries, such as, say, Turkey in its war against the Kurds.[12] Speaking about the use of cluster bombs, Israel Foreign Ministry spokesman Mark Regev reportedly said, 'If NATO countries stock these weapons and have used them in recent conflicts – in Yugoslavia, Afghanistan and Iraq – the world has no reason to point a finger at Israel'.[13] Indeed, is it the case that even if Israel's actions have been contemptible, it is merely following existing standards established by other (Western) powers?

NF: I see no reason to quarrel with this statement. Take Israel's Operation Defensive Shield in March–April 2002. Israel committed many atrocities in the course of its attack, notably in Jenin and Nablus. But the total number of deaths came to three digits. At roughly the same time the United States committed massacres in Fallujah and al-Najah where the total number of deaths came to *five* digits.

So with this and the veto issue, could we conclude that current international law is not much of a deterrent, and its principles are not taken seriously by the United States or any state that has its support?

NF: Speaking as a resolute atheist, *God helps those who help themselves*. International law is an ideological weapon to reach a broad public, to say, 'Look, this is what the law says. All we want to do is enforce the law.' But if we don't build a popular movement behind it, the law in and of itself is ineffectual unless a powerful state gets behind it. The United States uses international law selectively to promote its agenda. The deaths on the Mavi Marmara (the vessel headed towards Gaza to break the blockade) captured international attention and stayed in the news for a few weeks because the Turkish state stood behind international law (if only briefly).

You talked in your most recent book in 2010 about the possibility of Israel gearing up for another war, probably again in Lebanon, which would aim to 'devastate Lebanese civilian infrastructure'.[14] Do you think this has become any more or less likely given the changing face of Israel's regional ties, such as with Turkey, and even Egypt? Does this strain US loyalties and complicate its role in the region more than before?

NF: The Arab Spring has shaken the chessboard. No one quite knows what it will look like after the dust settles. The US-backed dictatorships suffered a big setback, but so did the 'Resistance Front'. Prime Minister Erdoğan's stock sharply rose as he championed democracy in the Arab world, but Hezbollah leader Sayyed Nasrallah's stock dropped precipitously as he championed resistance over democracy in Syria. It seems no one will make a move now, but everyone will patiently wait to see where things stand when the situation stabilises.

NOTES

1. Norman Finkelstein, *Image and Reality of the Palestinian Conflict*, 2nd edn (London: Verso, 2003), p.164.
2. *New York Times*, 17 March 1976.
3. 'The Accused', *Panorama*, broadcast by the BBC, 17 June 2001, <http://tinyurl.com/dfao>.
4. Jeremy M. Sharp, 'U.S. Foreign Aid to Israel', *Congressional Research Service*, 16 September 2010, pp.16–17, <http://www.fas.org/sgp/crs/mideast/RL33222.pdf>.
5. *Flooding South Lebanon: Israel's Use of Cluster Munitions in Lebanon in July and August 2006*, 17 February 2008, Human Rights Watch, Vol.20, No.2(E), <http://www.unhcr.org/refworld/docid/47b943b12.html>.
6. Ibid.
7. Norman Finkelstein, *This Time We Went Too Far* (New York: OR Books, 2010), p.29.
8. Amnesty International, *Fuelling Conflict: Foreign Arms Supplies to Israel/Gaza*, 23 February 2009, < http://tinyurl.com/ajeq8f> (emphasis added).
9. Richard Goldstone, 'Reconsidering the Goldstone Report on Israel and war crimes', *Washington Post*, 2 April 2011, <http://tinyurl.com/3bemx37>.
10. Finkelstein, *This Time We Went Too Far*, p.141.

11. Jeffrey Goldberg, 'Robert Gates Says Israel Is an Ungrateful Ally', *Bloomberg*, 6 September 2011, <http://tinyurl.com/3d7k98n>.

12. See, for example, John Pilger, 'The "secret" war which has seen a 300 per cent increase in bombing raids on Iraq', johnpilger.com, 20 December 2002, <http://tinyurl.com/7v35xxc>.

13. Quoted in Ina Friedman, 'Deadly Remnants', *Jerusalem Report*, 13 November 2006.

14. Finkelstein, *This Time We Went Too Far*, p.192.

13
Greg Grandin
The United States in Latin America

By the end of the Second World War, Latin America was experiencing what some commentators have called 'a democratic spring'. What inspired this 'democratic spring?' And how did the United States initially respond to it?

Greg Grandin: Yes, social scientists like to talk a lot about the post-Cold War 'transition to democracy', by which they mean a transition to neoliberal democracy, with democracy defined nearly exclusively as a return to the rule of law after the anti-communist repression and civil wars of the 1970s and 1980s. But what they often overlook is that the region underwent a previous, although short-lived transition, a 'transition to social democracy'. In 1944, only five Latin American countries – Mexico, Uruguay, Chile, Costa Rica, and Colombia – could nominally call themselves democracies. By 1946, only five – Paraguay, El Salvador, Honduras, Nicaragua, and the Dominican Republic – could not. Dictators toppled throughout Latin America and governments extended the franchise and legalised unions. To varying degrees in different countries, urbanisation, industrialisation, and population growth had created an emerging middle class and urban working class that joined with students, intellectuals, and, in some cases, a militant peasantry. Such coalitions generated both the demands for democratic restructuring and the social power needed to achieve it. Following the Second World War, revitalised labour unions in Mexico, Brazil, Peru, Guatemala, Colombia, Argentina, and Chile led strike waves of unparalleled belligerence. In a number of countries, populist reform parties, many of them organised in the 1920s, came to power, impelled by this increased mobilisation. The more democratic elements of liberalism which since the mid-nineteenth century had functioned primarily as an elite justification of domination and economic modernisation, came to the fore, now advanced not just by urban political elites, but by mass movements. One country after another not only embraced democracy, but passed sweeping legislation that put into place or extended government-run education, health care, social welfare, pensions, and so on.

But starting in 1947, shortly after the establishment of branch CIA offices in many countries, and continuing through 1948, a series of coups and anti-communist legislation rolled back this democratic spring. By 1952, with a coup in Cuba, dictators once again ruled much of Latin America. It's not so much that the United States engineered any of these coups (though there is little scholarship on them), as that the dawning Cold War signalled a shift in the political and class alliances of the region. An emerging international political and economic regime greatly shortened the life expectancy of post-war democracies, throwing momentum to those groups – the landed class, the Catholic Church, and sectors of the military – that were threatened by the post-war spring. Following the Second World War the world divided into contending camps represented by the United States and the USSR, with Latin America clearly falling under the sway of the former. As this global order took shape with the establishment of the United Nations, a series of military, cultural, political, and economic treaties, along with the formation of the Organization of American States, bound the Americas together, creating a 'closed hemisphere' in an increasingly open and interdependent world. Desperate to attract capital investment, domestic elites, many of them committed reformers, offered little resistance to or dissent from the twin goals of US Cold War foreign policy: to halt the spread of communism and not only advance capitalism but ensure US dominance within that system.

The first post-Second World War direct US intervention in Latin America was in Guatemala in 1954, which led to the overthrow of the democratically elected president, Jacobo Arbenz. It is well documented that the United Fruit Company (UFCo), which lost land under Arbenz's Agrarian Reform Law, exerted

a huge influence on the Eisenhower administration; but some historians still argue that it was Arbenz's close ties with the Guatemalan Communist Party that eventually led to the US intervention. How do you evaluate the different factors that led to the downfall of Arbenz?

GG: Well in many ways, Guatemala both exemplified and was exempt, for a short period, from the history I just described above. Having suffered decades of dictatorship, in 1944 an urban revolution of students, city unionists, and an urban middle class led a revolution that implemented one of the most social democratic governments in all of Latin America. But because it didn't have a Communist party in 1947, there was nothing that could serve as a lightning rod to attract and unite diverse conservative forces, so therefore it survived the 1947–48 continental crackdown. Where other 'democratic springs' turned quickly into a Cold War winter, reforms in Guatemala, including an ambitious land reform, continued through the early 1950s. A Communist party, known as the Workers' Party (Partido Guatemalteco del Trabajo), or PGT, wasn't formed until later, and when it was, it still operated largely within a popular front/ anti-fascist world view. That is, it worked ceaselessly to bring about basic democratic rights, working with all sectors of society that were considered democratic. The land reform, which did expropriate UFCo land, was largely a PGT-designed policy, and the idea was to be able to bring basic political liberties into private realms of power which previous political reforms hadn't yet reached.

Often, historians ask either-or questions concerning the coup: Was it fear of communism or economic interests that moved Eisenhower and the CIA to act? It's as though, if it can be proved that Washington was motivated by fear of communists rather than acting on the interests of the UFCo, then somehow the overthrow of Arbenz – however lamentable its long term effects (i.e. genocide) – could be pardoned, since US actors worked not to derail democracy but to contain communism. It is true that until recently, scholars attempting to answer why the United States intervened in Guatemala in 1954 have focused on the threat the

Agrarian Reform posed to US economic interests, particularly to the United Fruit Company. Lately however, historians have stressed the growing influence of the Communist Party over Guatemalan society and over Jacobo Arbenz, the quietly serious army colonel picked by the revolutionary coalition to succeed Arévalo. While United Fruit complained incessantly first about the labour code and then about the Agrarian Reform, the company played only a peripheral role in Eisenhower's decision to act against Arbenz. According to this perspective, the United States was neither contemptuous of the kind of third-world nationalism represented by Arbenz, fearful of a more democratic distribution of political power, nor mobilised in the defence of private economic interests. Rather, Cold War anti-communism and an accurate evaluation of the PGT's strength drove US agents. Yet interpretations that highlight the political culture of the Cold War in order to counter less sanguine accounts of US motivation often miss a key point: there would not have been a significant expansion of democracy in Guatemala were it not for the communists.

You have called Guatemala 'a staging ground of the continental Cold War'.[1] What did you mean by that?

GG: Yes, for a small nation, Guatemala has had an outsized history, both paralleling and driving many broader Latin American conflicts. As I mentioned, in October 1944, Guatemalans overthrew a 13-year dictatorship. For one full decade, two democratically elected presidents – Juan José Arévalo and Jacobo Arbenz – presided over a series of impressive political and social reforms, including an expansion of the franchise, abolition of forced labour, ratification of a social democratic constitution, adoption of a labour code, creation of a national health system and social security, extension of public education, and the ambitious Agrarian Reform. As the rest of Latin America fell to coups or clampdowns, Guatemala became a refuge. Pablo Neruda, a Communist Party senator fleeing Chile, showed up in the early 1950s after a popular front president elected with

Socialist and Communist votes cracked down on labour unions. He gave a beautiful speech:

> Chile has joined the sombre age of America, where treason and imprisonment cast their shade over the white southern sunlight ... Today, with every audacious assault intended to swath your territory in shadow, once again, the same faith causes me to think that you will not shrink from the task, that you will fight for your country and for your liberty, that you will fight against the privileges that must end, and for the people who must be born; that you will fight and you will defend your independence. And to the poets, to the writers, to the painters, to the musicians, I say: This is your path ... We have other work to be done. We must light every snuffed-out lantern. We must bring light to all the dark corners. We must clean all the rooms of our heartbroken America. We must spark the invincible stability of liberty. We must build schools in which our painters will paint the walls, in which our musicians will give their song, in which our writers will find the new seed of new Americas.[2]

And in turn, the CIA's June 1954 overthrow of Arbenz was one of the most consequential events in Latin American history. It was a full-spectrum coup, distinguished from previous US interventions in Latin America and elsewhere in that it drew on every aspect of US power, using politics, economics, diplomacy, psychology, and mass media to destabilise Arbenz's government. It too was a vanguard, not of democracy but of three decades of continental political polarisation and escalating government terror. Well before the Cuban Revolution, the event radicalised a generation of Latin American reformers (the coup also radicalised the then 'Tory' Gore Vidal, living in Antigua at the time and friend to many of the pro-Arbenz politicians and artists). A young Argentine doctor, for instance, after having completed a motorcycle trip through Chile and the Andes, found himself in Guatemala and watched the CIA's destabilisation campaign unfold. 'This is a country in which one can open up one's lungs and fill them with democracy', Ernesto Guevara wrote to his aunt in Argentina;

> there are newspapers supported by United Fruit that, if I were Arbenz, I would have closed down in five minutes, because they are shameful and yet they say what they like and contribute to the atmosphere that the USA likes.

And then after the coup, about to seek asylum in the Argentine embassy, he wrote that the effort to build a more just society 'has all gone by like a beautiful dream that one is bent upon continuing after one has woken up'.[3] Increasingly after 1954, Latin American reformers and nationalists viewed the United States not as a model to emulate, as they did during the 1930s and 1940s, but a threat to be confronted. 'Cuba will not be Guatemala', was how Guevara, after fleeing to Mexico and joining Fidel Castro's revolutionary movement, would explain the radicalisation of the Cuban Revolution. For its part, the United States would model its disastrous 1961 Bay of Pigs invasion on its 1954 Guatemalan operation, a serious miscalculation that not only failed to topple Castro but further polarised hemispheric politics.

The political terror that was later unleashed in Guatemala led to the deaths of over 200,000 people, most of whom were Mayan Indians. In 1999, the UN-administered Commission for Historical Clarification (CEH) ruled that Guatemalan state agents committed acts of genocide against the Mayan people between 1981 and 1983. Crucially, the CEH also criticised the United States for providing military assistance to Guatemala, which 'was directed towards reinforcing the national intelligence apparatus and for training the officer corps in counterinsurgency techniques, key factors which had significant bearing on human rights violations'.[4] Why did the political terror in Guatemala peak between 1981 and 1983? And to what extent did President Reagan's Central America policies contribute to the genocide?

GG: 1981–83 was the climax of the insurgency. By 1981, the opposition movement in Guatemala was at its strongest. Extreme economic immiseration and political repression had pushed large swaths of Guatemalans to see the government as illegitimate. The guerrillas, who had been operating in the country in different forms since at least 1960, had grown in number and were now operating in 18 of the country's 22 departments. Peasant unions in the countryside and trade unions in the city were joining, as were Mayans and non-Mayan Ladinos. It seemed as if the government was about to fall, just as Nicaragua had fallen to the Sandinistas in 1979. But a coup in 1982 brought a new cohort of military officers with a long-range counter-insurgent vision to power. They had a plan to stabilise and re-legitimate the government over the long haul, but the first task was to defeat the insurgency. And the way to do it was to separate the insurgency from their rural support base. They did this through genocide, fanning out into the rural highlands and committing one massacre after another. This is when the bulk of the killing, torture, and disappearing took place, most of it directed at Mayans. The war would drag out until 1996, and both guerrilla operations and political repression directed at anyone considered a threat would continue. But the tide of war turned in 1983. The guerrillas were effectively defeated and the social movement shattered. The task after 1983 would no longer be to topple the government and create a more just, equitable society, but to return to the rule of law, such as it is in a place like Guatemala.

As to Ronald Reagan's role in the genocide, it was both tangential and critical. Tangential in the sense that the United States had encouraged and supported this kind of murderous behaviour long before Reagan showed up on the scene, and the Guatemalan state and military – given what they saw happen in Nicaragua – probably would have regrouped whether he was elected or not. Episodes of extreme racial violence directed at mobilised indigenous groups have a long history in Guatemala. But I'd say it was also critical in the moral support Reagan gave to the Guatemalan military, and to the general who staged that 1982 coup; José Efraín Ríos Montt was by that time an evangelical Christian, well enmeshed in the kind of conservative networks that helped bring Reagan to power in 1980. In late 1982, just a few months after Ríos Montt seized power and well into the genocide, Reagan infamously said he was getting a 'bum rap' and that he was 'totally committed to democracy'. Reagan largely focused on Nicaragua and El Salvador, but the grassroots conservative movement I just mentioned, of which Reagan stood at the centre, provided much 'humanitarian' aid to Guatemala in the post-genocide phase of the counter-insurgency, the period when the state worked to win the hearts and minds of those not killed through the distribution of food and medical aid. And even before that, with Reagan's election in November 1980, there was just a sense among the Central American right – including in Guatemala – that the game had changed. We look back now at Carter and can judge, with the coolness of hindsight, that he put into place many of the things that we would associate with the rearming of the Cold War. But at the time, Central America's transnational 'death squad' right celebrated Reagan's election with fireworks and dancing in the street. All bets were off.

You have said that Ernesto Che Guevara wanted to ensure that 'Cuba will not be Guatemala'. Indeed, he often used the Guatemalan example to reiterate the ineffectiveness of reformism, arguing instead that a comprehensive and revolutionary change in the whole of society was required if the new social order was to be lasting. Was Che right that reformism couldn't work in Latin America? Would Cuba have become another Guatemala if it had not chosen a revolutionary path?

GG: I think Che was right that the strength of the landed oligarchy, conservative sectors of the Catholic Church, and military within the framework of the Cold War provided a formidable obstacle to the kind of social democratic reform that had briefly advanced in the mid 1940s. The scholars Leslie Bethell and Ian Roxborough have argued that to understand the mainspring of Latin American polarisation – the kind in which Che was caught up in Guatemala – during these years one needs to consider the region in relation to western Europe and Japan.[5] In those areas, public reconstruction aid and capital, in the form of the Marshall Plan, provided more space for an independent, non-Soviet-allied left – mainly in the form of Social Democratic parties and strong trade unionism – to operate, since investment was not based on ensuring absolute labour quiescence and political stability. In Latin America, in contrast, despite Truman's talk about development and equity, most of the desperately needed capital was, as Latin Americans at the founding of the Organization of American States in Bogotá in 1948 were told it would be, in the form of loans or private investment. So the twinned promises of democracy and development, which in the early 1940s had seemed mutually dependent, were by 1948 revealed to be mutually exclusive. In order to create a stable investment climate, and short of a Marshall Plan, governments, now fortified with the polarising rhetoric of the Cold War, cracked down on labour unrest and persecuted not just communists – who in many countries were indispensable to democratic advances – but, eventually, all reformers. Washington would continue to talk about the need to work with a 'democratic left' (as it apparently had done in Japan and West Germany) up until at least the Reagan administration – but those democratic leftists were just as likely targeted for execution by Washington-funded death squads as were Soviet- or Cuba-aligned activists.

Why could the 'democratic left' be tolerated in western Europe and Japan, and not in Latin America?

GG: Because public capital to finance reconstruction, via at first the Marshall Plan, didn't necessitate a crackdown on all forms of labour organising. And the lack of a crackdown made the European left more willing to accommodate itself to the confines of the Cold War, whereas in Latin America, ongoing repression tended to radicalise even the anti-communist left.

How did the 1959 Cuban Revolution impact the US Latin America policy?

GG: JFK responded to the Cuban Revolution by embracing counter-insurgency as a solution to the crisis of the third world. In particular, the Kennedy administration, through people like Walt Whitman Rostow, linked counter-insurgency to developmentalism through the 1961 Alliance for Progress. On the one hand, the Alliance for Progress pushed Latin American countries to modernise through tax and land reform, which in many places gave a boost to social movements. On the other hand, it provided an arsenal of weapons and a school of instructions to the revanchists who would target members of those movements for execution. It was in effect an intensification of the dynamic I just described. Beyond its moment, and beyond Latin America, much of the rhetoric of the Alliance for Progress continues to this day in the global counter-insurgency operations in the 'war on terror' – the idea that counter-insurgency needs to be paired with winning hearts and minds through development work and nation building. Of course in the early 1960s, 'nation building' meant building Keynesian welfare states, at least in theory. That was Rostow's goal in his 'stages of economic development'. Even many corporations imagined putting into place a mild version of reform capitalism, in order to create consumer markets – that is, not just treat Latin America as a source of raw materials. In actuality, of course, the limits of reform were extremely narrow, as the overthrow, for example, of João Goulart in Brazil in 1964 or Arbenz in Guatemala indicate. But Washington did nonetheless continue at least to tolerate a form of economic nationalism, including import substitution and some forms of nationalisation. All that ended though with Reagan. El Salvador in the 1980s was probably the first country where the United States really pushed simultaneously a hard counter-insurgency and a hard programme of neoliberal structural adjustment. And today, 'nation building' means neoliberal nation building, which is like throwing petrol on the fire.

Just a few days before Osama bin Laden was assassinated in Pakistan, Orlando Bosch died peacefully in Florida, USA. Clearly Bosch was no less a terrorist than bin Laden: the CIA-backed Cuban exile had been implicated in numerous terrorist crimes, including the Cubana airliner bombing in 1976, but had later been pardoned by President George H.W. Bush after intense lobbying from Jeb Bush and Cuban-American leaders in Miami.

How close was the relationship between the CIA and militant Cuban exiles?

GG: Extremely close, in that many militant Cuban exiles joined the CIA. After the Cuban Revolution, there was an alignment of interests, and a weaving together of the networks, of anti-communists, drug runners, organised crime, counter-insurgents, and intelligence ops. It's hard to describe without sounding like a conspiracist, but what was Iran–Contra other than one of the rare conspiracies that was forced into the light of day? Many a journalist and scholar has fallen down the rabbit hole trying to trace the linkages, and has never come up again. Think Gary Webb, who was driven out of journalism for exposing the links between the CIA's Contra war and the importation of cocaine into urban areas in the United States. And often the best portrayal of what was at stake after the Cuban Revolution is in fiction, including James Ellroy's *The Cold Six Thousand*, which captures the pulse of hate and fear that coursed through the United States in the early 1960s like no other – the way the combination of the Cuban Revolution abroad and the rise of the Civil Rights movement at home fused white supremacy, misogyny, and elite interest – or in the conspiracy networks drawings of the conceptual artist Mark Lombardi.

In 1976, the former Chilean ambassador to the United States Orlando Letelier published an article in *The Nation* in which he criticised Milton Friedman for failing to grasp the connection between the free-market economic policies and the brutal state repression in General Augusto Pinochet's Chile. Friedman, the superstar economist at the University of Chicago and unofficial adviser to General Pinochet, had claimed that 'in spite of my profound disagreement with the authoritarian political system of Chile, I do not consider it as evil for an economist to render technical economic advice to the Chilean Government'.[6] For Letelier it was clearly nonsensical to think that an economic plan so against the interests of the majority of Chilean people could be implemented through non-violent means. Do you think

academics like Friedman should be held accountable for their
dealings with dictators?

GG: They should at least be exposed. But the condemnation
should never lose its politics. That is, the condemnation shouldn't
lapse into a simple moralism, since simple moralism is more
often than not used to justify US intervention. Friedman's crime
wasn't simply that he was 'dealing with dictators' but that he
was advocating an economic regime that was profoundly unjust.

A month after writing the above-mentioned article, Orlando
Letelier was assassinated by Chilean secret agents in Washington,
D.C. This cast a long shadow on US–Chilean relations, and
when the Chilean Supreme Court later rejected the US petition
to extradite the three high-level Chilean officials implicated in
the assassination, President Carter was forced to act. By 1979,
the size of the American mission in Santiago was reduced
by one-fourth, foreign military sales were terminated, and
Export-Import Bank credits were suspended until positive steps
were taken. But Carter could not ignore a State Department
memo warning that a ban on private bank loans 'would be
more costly to the US than to Chile',[7] and the United States
continued to bankroll the Chilean regime through its bankers
and businessmen. Based on this evidence, can it be said that
Carter's Latin America policy was ever driven by the much
lauded human rights objectives?

GG: I think the question is a bit narrow. I take it as a starting
point that the motives that drive US policy, whoever is president,
are more complicated than altruism (and that even if there is an
element of 'idealism' involved, that idealism has many different
sources and undoubtedly reflects certain interests). In retrospect,
Carter is an interesting transitional figure, someone who came
into office charged with figuring out a solution to the crisis of
Keynesianism, and more broadly, to the multidimensional crisis
of the 1970s – which went well beyond economics. He tried
to disinvest the United States from the disastrous Cold War
framework which viewed all third world nationalism as cat's

paws for the USSR. I don't think the reason why he wanted to do this was altruistic or idealist (though that might have been his self-understanding) but reflected a new framework of foreign-policy thinking. His efforts failed (for a number of reasons), and by the end of his term he had largely laid the groundwork for Ronald Reagan's jump-starting the Cold War.

During the Cold War, Colombia was one of the largest Latin American recipients of US military aid, primarily for anti-communist counter-insurgency. In the post-Cold War period, US funding of the Colombian military has continued, although new reasons, such as the 'war on drugs' and the 'war on terror', have replaced the 'red scare'. Crucially, in both the Cold War and post-Cold War periods, the Colombian military and its right-wing paramilitary allies have targeted progressive groups that make political demands for reform and seek a more egalitarian distribution of Colombia's abundant natural resources, thus subjecting students, teachers, journalists, trade union members, human rights activists, and indigenous leaders to a campaign of terror. Does this not illustrate that the orthodox interpretation of the Cold War as merely the containment of Soviet communism is deeply flawed? Is it not rather the case that the interests of US capital have always been the main motivating factor?

GG: Colombia is an interesting outlier in the history of the Latin American Cold War, a region where, for a number of reasons, the post-war dynamics of reform–reaction–polarisation–repression didn't play out as it did in other countries. There was no effective 'resolution' of the conflict – that is, a right-wing military regime that effectively destroys the left, insurgent or not, and then paves the way for a guided return to a democracy now understood as neoliberal. For many reasons, the guerrilla movement in Colombia, led by the FARC and the ELN, did not come to an end with the Cold War, producing a unique situation, a situation which did in fact allow an almost seamless segue from the Cold War to the 'war on drugs' (and now to the 'war on terror'). This segue started under George H.W. Bush, intensified under Bill

Clinton with Plan Colombia, and then continued with George W. Bush and now Barack Obama. And as it did, the dynamic of repression outlined above – where security forces are armed, trained, and enflamed by Washington – interprets its mission in the broadest possible way. People like to talk about the 'war on terror' (into which the Pentagon has folded the 'war on drugs') as a 'long war'. I prefer to think of it as a 'wide war', since, as you say, target range is quite ample. It's not just in Colombia: activists in Mexico and Central America have long identified the 'criminalisation of protest' that has taken place under the drug war and the 'war on terror'.

NOTES

1. Greg Grandin, *The Last Colonial Massacre: Latin America in the Cold War* (Chicago: University of Chicago Press, 2004), p.4.
2. Pablo Neruda, *Neruda en Guatemala* (Guatemala City: Ediciones Saker-Ti, 1950).
3. Ernesto Guevara Lynch, *Young Che: Memories of Che Guevara by His Father*, trans. Lucía Álvarez de Toledo (London: Vintage, 2007).
4. 'Guatemala: Memory of Silence', Report of the Commission for Historical Clarification, Conclusions and Recommendations, <http://shr.aaas.org/guatemala/ceh/report/english/toc.html>.
5. Leslie Bethell and Ian Roxborough (eds), *Latin America Between the Second World War and the Cold War: Crisis and Containment, 1944–1948* (Cambridge: Cambridge University Press, 1992).
6. Orlando Letelier, 'The Chicago Boys in Chile: Freedom's Awful Truth', *The Nation*, 28 August 1976.
7. Cited in Vanessa Walker, 'At the End of Influence: The Letelier Assassination, Human Rights, and Rethinking Intervention in US–Latin American Relations', *Journal of Contemporary History*, Vol.46, No.1 (2011), pp.109–35 (pp.129–39).

14

Daniele Ganser
NATO's Secret Armies in Europe

In August 1990, the Italian prime minister, Giulio Andreotti, confirmed that NATO-linked secret armies existed in Italy and other western European countries. What was the purpose of these secret armies? And why was their cover finally blown in 1990?

Daniele Ganser: The purpose of the stay-behind network, as the secret armies were called, was to fight behind enemy lines in case of a Soviet invasion. The original idea, which was developed after the Second World War, was to have an underground network ready in case the Soviet Union occupied western Europe. That was the main purpose, confirmed later by many different documents, and also by members of the secret armies who took part in the training and meetings. But that was not the only purpose. The second purpose, which some are very reluctant to talk about, was to influence politics even in the absence of a Soviet invasion. That is a very delicate aspect of the secret armies, and therefore Andreotti, when he confirmed in 1990 that the secret armies existed, claimed they had never engaged in domestic operations, they had only waited for a Soviet invasion. But that is not true. In fact, the secret armies were discovered because a domestic terrorist operation was investigated in detail.

The context of the secret armies' discovery was one in which an Italian magistrate by the name of Felice Casson investigated a terrorist attack that had occurred in 1972 in the small village of Peteano in the north of Italy, and he found out that this terrorist attack had been manipulated. In the attack a few policemen were lured to a car, which then exploded, killing three people.

At the time there was a telephone call claiming responsibility for the attack and claiming to be the Red Brigades, which was a left-wing terrorist group in Cold War Italy. For many years people thought this was the correct narrative for the attack, until Felice Casson re-opened the case in the 1980s and realised it was necessary to research terrorism more closely, because it seemed the truth had not been uncovered. He looked at the data again and found that witnesses had given false testimony, and he found out that the terrorist attack had been carried out by Vincenzo Vinciguerra, a right-wing extremist. This changed the picture completely; not left-wing terrorists but right-wing terrorists had committed the crime. So Vincenzo Vinciguerra was arrested and he admitted carrying out this terrorist attack, but also claimed he had been protected by the military secret service in Italy and that in all NATO countries there existed a secret army that protected right-wing terrorist groups. Everybody said he was just mad, that such a thing was ridiculous, that NATO cannot be in any way linked to terrorism, and it was not possible that there were secret armies. But this Italian magistrate was then allowed to go into the archives of the Italian military secret service, which incidentally is very strange; we don't know why he was allowed. In the archives he found documentation that the secret army existed. In Italy, the code name of the secret army was Gladio, and the network was used to influence domestic politics. So it started with the investigation into terrorism in Italy and led to the discovery of secret armies in all NATO countries.

It's interesting that this happened in 1990 at the end of the Cold War. Was that also the reason why it came to light when it did?

DG: That's unclear, because the terrorist attack that initially blew the thing open had occurred in 1972, and then Felice Casson had started his investigation in the mid 1980s. Already by 1984 he had the testimonies of right-wing extremists who claimed they were being protected by NATO and the military secret service. But at that time it was probably more difficult to speak about something as secret as that. Of course in 1990 everything changed – there was the fall of the Berlin Wall in 1989 and also the invasion of Kuwait by Saddam Hussein in 1990 – so people were interested in different things. Maybe that helped, but it's unclear because NATO didn't want to talk about it at all.

And they still don't.

DG: No, they still don't. It's very strange. I've had contacts with NATO and some even still claim that Gladio never existed. That's absolute nonsense. We have the documents of the Italian military secret service that confirm they set up this secret army for both a post-invasion task as well as what they call a domestic-control task.

These secret armies were also set up in officially neutral countries, such as Austria and Switzerland. Why?

DG: That's true. In Switzerland the name of the secret army was P26, and its members were trained by the British secret service, MI6. We had a parliamentary investigation more than ten years ago which was very critical of the P26. And more recently there was a new book published on the subject.[1] The Swiss had witnessed how quickly Germany had occupied the countries of western Europe during the Second World War. They feared that in a new war the Red Army could defeat the Swiss army and occupy the country, so they thought they would need secret armies with underground arms caches, explosives, and training to make it more difficult for the occupiers to stay in the country for good. So the idea of resistance in the Cold War sense was important. Many people in the stay-behind networks say they had no intention of killing civilians in their countries with terrorist attacks. In fact in Switzerland we didn't have any terrorist attacks. But the problem is that in some countries, like Italy, Belgium, Germany and France, there was terrorism, and the most sensitive question, as far as the stay-behind armies are concerned, is whether in these countries the secret networks were involved in these attacks. Indeed that seems to be the case.

You explain how in post-war Italy, the United States funded the Christian Democracy Party (DCI) and recruited known fascists to be part of it. Why was it so important for the United States to deal with the extreme right faction of the party, rather than a more moderate one? Could they not have achieved their aims, such as bringing Italy into NATO and keeping the Communist and Socialist parties out of power, through more legitimate means?

DG: It's very hard to say. The main strategic thinking had already been developed during the Second World War. At the time the fascists, under Mussolini, were fighting against Washington and London, and so the Americans, the British, and also the Soviets cooperated very closely in Italy with the resistance movement against Mussolini. And all these people were on the left. Indeed, there was a very strong anti-fascist movement in Italy: some were communists, others were socialists and some were anarchists. It's hard to classify all these people, but they certainly didn't want Mussolini. So during the Second World War they received a lot of weapons and training from the American and British special forces. Then at the end of the war, when it became clear that Mussolini was going to lose, Washington and London became worried that these well-armed communists would seize power in Italy, and that's something they certainly didn't want. So, in the first elections in 1948, the CIA, which at the time was just a year old, decided that Italy was not ready to have free and fair elections. They didn't trust the Italians to make the right choice, so they rigged the elections. They started a smear campaign to discredit everybody who was on the socialist or communist side, despite the fact that these people had fought against Mussolini. Next, as you correctly said, they created this new party, the Christian Democrats. The idea behind it was just to take two words that sound good: Christian, because in Italy practically everybody is Catholic, and Democrat just sounds good to everybody concerned. They installed conservatives in the party to protect the established distribution of power, with the firm intention of keeping the communists out of the Italian government. The strategic thinking behind it was that if the communists in Italy had entered the executive, then there could be a communist Italian defence minister in NATO meetings who could betray all the NATO secrets to Moscow. This sort of thinking made NATO generals and British and American strategists very nervous and made them go to extreme lengths to keep the Italian communists out of power. And it worked. They never had Italian communists in the executive during the Cold War.

Doesn't this show that it wasn't just a fear of communist invasion, but a fear of any communist party coming into power, even democratically?

DG: That's true. If you look at the stay-behind network, some people on the lower levels were only interested in opposing an invasion. In Norway, for instance, they had suffered the German invasion, and felt it necessary to protect themselves from a feared Soviet invasion. Also in Sweden, a neutral country which was not a member of NATO, they established these networks. When they set up a network they always said they couldn't have communists in it. So they recruited from the centre or, as in Italy and Germany, from the extreme right. I am not saying that everybody in NATO's secret armies was a right-wing terrorist, that's not the case and it would be unfair to many people in the network. But some people in the German secret army, for instance, were former SS operatives, who had survived the Second World War and then directly entered the secret warfare group of NATO.

You have mentioned that there were many terrorist attacks in Italy, particularly during the Nixon administration in the United States, but also later, including the Bologna massacre of 2 August 1980. Do you believe these were incidents of state terrorism? What explicitly connects these incidents to right-wing factions of government? And what connects these factions to the United States or to NATO?

DG: Giandelio Maletti, a general in the Italian military secret service, said during the trial on the 1969 Piazza Fontana terrorist attack that the Italian military secret service was involved in such operations. He went on to claim that they didn't want to do it, and it was actually the Americans who told them to do it. He just passed the blame across the Atlantic and said that Nixon, who had been in charge at the time, had supported very strange activities. He couldn't say, of course, that President Nixon signed an order to carry out terrorism in Italy which was then executed by right-wing extremists in contact with Italian military secret service officers and the CIA. You will never find such a document in the archives, and Maletti's statement is about the closest we get.

In the research that we, the people involved in the peace movement, are doing, there is absolute proof that there were secret armies in Italy and other European countries. We also have 100 per cent proof that the secret armies were operated by the military and the civilian secret services, and that there were quite a few terrorist attacks in Italy, Belgium, Germany, and other countries. But we cannot prove in many of the terrorist attacks that the secret services and the Gladio secret army were involved. There is no solid evidence for the Bologna massacre so that I can say it was clearly Gladio that carried it out. We mostly have circumstantial evidence, or testimony such as that of Vincenzo Vinciguerra, who carried out one of the terrorist attacks in Peteano. And although he confessed in front of the courts that he had carried out the attack and that a secret structure existed in NATO, that was a relatively small attack. We'd rather have somebody confess that Bologna was carried out by Gladio, but so far we don't have that.

When Aldo Moro, the former Italian prime minister, was kidnapped and later killed in 1978, the crime was attributed to the left-wing Red Brigades. Indeed, a Red Brigade member, Mario Moretti, was convicted of the murder and confessed to killing Moro. You say, however, that 'Moro himself understood that he was the victim of a political crime in which the political right and the United States were instrumentalising the Red

Brigades'.[2] Is there convincing evidence of a wider conspiracy, and the involvement of Gladio in either the kidnap or the murder?

DG: The evidence is circumstantial. Aldo Moro was a member of the Christian Democrats, the party that the United States installed in 1948 and which was in power throughout the Cold War years. Shortly before his death he went to Washington, where he spoke with Kissinger and others in the Nixon administration, and told them he wanted to include the communists in the Italian government. He believed that Italy was a grown-up country and it was important that everybody with a powerful voice in parliament be part of the executive. When he returned, he talked to his wife, and indeed the information we have is from Moro's wife, who made it public after he was killed. She says that when Moro came back from the United States he was really depressed and wanted to leave politics altogether. He also confessed to her that Kissinger had warned him not to include the communists in the Italian government.

In the end, he decided to stay in politics and to go to parliament to ask for what they call in Italy a 'historical compromise', the inclusion of the communists in the Italian government. On the very day he was on his way to make this announcement, he was kidnapped and then killed. There's a lot of speculation about who killed Aldo Moro. It could very well be that the Red Brigades played a role in it, but also the Red Brigades could have been infiltrated by right-wing extremists, who then used them as a convenient cover. Certainly, the crucial players in the Red Brigades were already in prison at the time of the Moro murder. It remains one of the mysteries of Italian politics whether there was really an infiltration or whether it was originally a Red Brigade idea to kill Aldo Moro. Ultimately, however, there have been high-ranking politicians who wanted to break out of this very narrow path which insisted on keeping the communists out of government. But those who tried to escape this doctrine were killed.

You have said that 'the history of the secret army in Turkey is more violent than that of any other stay-behind in Western

Europe'.[3] In order to integrate Turkey (whose geostrategic position made it invaluable to the United States in the Cold War) firmly within NATO, the CIA established close ties with the ultra-fascist and ultra-violent Pan-Turkism movement, thus plunging the country into what many consider to be a full-blown civil war. What was the modus operandi of this movement? Did it operate under the full control of the CIA?

DG: I don't think that there is anything under the full control of the CIA anywhere in the world. So I don't think that in Turkey the CIA was in full control of the Grey Wolves (the armed wing of the extreme right Nationalist Action Party) during the Cold War. But at the time there was a mutual strategic interest. The United States wanted Turkey in NATO. If you look at Turkey's position on the map, you can see how easy it is from there to move spy systems very close to the Soviet border. Just remember that in the Cold War it was impossible for the Americans to enter Soviet territory. All the spies who entered Soviet territory were found and hanged, so they tried to get as close as possible to the Warsaw Pact countries, and Turkey was ideal because Romania and Bulgaria were directly to the north and the Soviet Union was directly to the east.

In order to keep Turkey in the NATO camp, the Americans had to make sure that within Turkey the distribution of power would not shift in an anti-NATO direction. So the Pan-Turkism movement, and especially the Grey Wolves, were promoted because the Americans knew that they were very strong nationalists. It was a completely different situation to Italy, where the Americans had decided to work with the Catholics, who are very anti-communist, but from a religious perspective. In Turkey they worked with the Grey Wolves because they were a group that was convinced that Turkey should go back to the glory days of the Ottoman Empire and become a superpower. The Americans also had close ties with the Turkish military, which at the time was a powerful anti-communist force wary of giving too much power to civilian government. It's all very complicated, but ultimately this led to a situation where the Turkish military carried out a coup d'état, then another coup d'état, and then another coup d'état. We can't say that NATO's secret armies or the CIA carried them out, but we know that NATO's secret armies and the CIA were always very close to these coups d'état.

The Turkish Secret service, MIT (Milli Istihbarat Teşkilati), also had very close ties with the CIA.

DG: Yes, that's absolutely confirmed.

But MIT also had ties with Israeli Mossad and Iranian SAVAK. Were these non-NATO countries ever informed about the secret armies?

DG: This I frankly don't know. It's very hard to say, because the secret army usually operates on a strict need-to-know principle, where they limit the information available to the smallest possible group of people. But we know that in East Germany, for instance, the Stasi were aware that NATO had set up stay-behind networks in West Germany. So my guess is that Mossad knew it too, but it's only a guess.

You mentioned that Turkey experienced three military coups (1960, 1971 and 1980) during the Cold War. You also mentioned that there was some involvement by the United States. What level of involvement are we talking about here?

DG: It's very difficult to say, because even today the official narrative in the United States, which most Europeans have fully bought, is that America would never support a military coup d'état. Instead, they support human rights and democracy everywhere. Now that is obviously nonsense, and it's not backed by historical evidence. The clearest example of this is of course the Pinochet coup d'état in Chile in 1973, which was supported by the CIA. But if you look at Europe, it's more complicated. It's not the case that I can prove the CIA was behind the military coups in Turkey in the same way that they were behind the military coup in Chile. However, I do have data to support the idea that the CIA was in contact with the people who carried out the coups. The difficult question for a historian then is: Where did these coups start from? Did they start from the Turkish military or from Washington? It's very difficult, and I am not sure what the correct narrative is. But we do know that the military coups d'état in Turkey were carried out, and we do know that the CIA supported them.

The 1980 coup happened while Jimmy Carter was in the White House. The Turkish Air Force commander Tahsin Şahinkaya visited Washington just before the tanks rolled into Ankara. And Carter was also in close contact with CIA station chief in Turkey, Paul Henze, who famously celebrated the military takeover by saying 'Our boys in Ankara have done it!' So it can't be said that Carter was caught unawares by the coup. Indeed, later he supported the Turkish junta with economic and military assistance, even though it was widely known that serious human rights violations were taking place in Turkey. So can it really be said that US involvement in Europe was worse under more aggressive presidents, such as Nixon?

DG: Yes, that is an old game that the Americans play, where they set the Republicans against the Democrats and the Democrats against Republicans. We have it now again with Obama. But really if you look at the foreign policy of the United States in the last 60 years there is just one very consistent principle: to maximise strategic and economic interests. So if you can gain territory you gain territory, if you can gain resources you gain resources, if you can make money you make money, and it's absolutely independent of whether Republicans or Democrats are in the White House.

Everybody says that Carter was a dove, that he supported peace, and I can see a difference when I look at domestic politics. But I am personally interested in US foreign policy, and on Carter's watch a number of things happened. One is the military coup in Turkey. Now I am not sure whether Carter was well informed or whether it was in fact the CIA who ran the coup together with the Turkish generals. I don't actually know because the problem is that in all coups d'état the president uses 'plausible denial'. That means that he does not sign a letter in which he writes, say, 'Please overthrow Allende'. We just don't have that kind of document. It is therefore very difficult for historians to prove that coups d'état, which, incidentally, are crimes, are being supported by the White House. This makes it possible for American citizens to be fooled into thinking that the United States always supports democracies.

Some people in the US military hierarchy and also in the intelligence services have explained this need-to-know principle, and they say there are two possible interpretations. We can either assume that the CIA and the Pentagon are completely out of control and the White House has no idea what's going on, which is not very comforting and not very plausible. Or the CIA and the Pentagon are under the direct control of the White House, which means that whatever the CIA or the Pentagon do is on the orders of the president. I wish I could show exactly what Carter wanted with respect to the Turkish coup d'état, but for that to happen we would need to look at the National Security Council records, most of which are classified.

On 22 November 1990, the EU parliament passed a resolution which criticised NATO and US intelligence services for setting up clandestine networks that interfered in the internal political affairs of many European countries and requested that parliamentary inquiries take place to investigate its activities. How did the United States and NATO respond to this EU resolution? Were they hostile towards the countries which eventually undertook parliamentary inquiries?

DG: The US president at the time was Bush senior, and he was preparing for the war in the Gulf after Saddam Hussein had invaded Kuwait. So he completely ignored the resolution. He never made a statement. A few people from the CIA admitted that secret armies had been set up but only in case of Soviet invasion and occupation of Europe. That is half true. There is a good side of the story, and the Americans highlight this good side. William Colby, the former director of the CIA, confirmed in his memoirs that they set up these secret armies, and that's on the record. But the European parliament came forward and criticised these secret armies, claiming that some of them had deviated from a resistance network into a terror network and had been active despite the fact that there was no Soviet invasion. The European parliament came to the conclusion that some of the right-wing terrorists who were active in these networks had actually carried out terrorist attacks in Europe.

NATO followed the example of Bush and completely ignored the question. So did the British. The prime minister, John Major, declined to comment. That's very bad because it was actually London and Washington who had set up the secret networks. It was MI6 and the CIA who were operating the stay-behind armies. When NATO ambassadors became aware of the European parliament's resolution they called for a meeting because even they had no clue about these secret armies. And then the supreme allied commander Europe, the SACEUR, which is the highest ranking military officer in NATO – who incidentally is always an American general, thereby showing that NATO is essentially US controlled – said that there were stay-behind armies but again only offered the narrative of post-invasion function. That is contradicted by original documents we have from the Italian defence ministry, which say that the secret armies have two tasks: one, in case of invasion, and two, in emergency cases of domestic control. So the European parliament was very frustrated because it had passed a good resolution, but it was just ignored.

The countries that later carried out investigations were Belgium, Italy, and Switzerland, so only three countries on the European continent followed up on the resolution. They confirmed the existence of stay-behind armies in all countries, and that they had an anti-communist function, and that operatives had undergone training with British and US special forces (the SAS and the green berets), or secret services (MI6 and the CIA). In Belgium they tried to find out whether there was a link to, for instance, the Brabant massacre in the 1980s. But that proved very difficult.

You mentioned that George H.W. Bush refused to comment when the secret armies were discovered in 1990. Indeed, it was left to his son George W. Bush's administration more than 15 years later to acknowledge the secret armies, although it was denied that they were engaged in terrorism in Europe. A statement released by the State Department focused on *US Field Manual*, FM 30–31B, which instructs US agents to infiltrate the enemy and carry out false-flag terrorist operations, and claimed that it was a Soviet forgery.[4] Do you think FM 30–31B is authentic?

DG: Yes, I think so, but I can't prove it. The thing is if you have a good forgery it is very hard to identify. That is the case with bank notes as well as paper documents. What we can do with such a document is look at when it first surfaced and who had it in their possession. In Italy it was Licio Gelli and in Turkey it was people who were rather critical of the military, so it always showed up in circumstances that I judge interesting and trustworthy. Overall, the best sources available confirm that there were secret armies, there were terrorist attacks, and there were right-wing terrorists who spoke out claiming that there were protected by NATO. In Italy, there were right-wing terrorists who were surprised at all the fuss, and claimed they had been flown directly to Franco's Spain so nobody could prosecute them and that it was the military secret service that had done this. Basically it means that these secret service people didn't want to carry out the dirty work of bombing supermarkets and train stations, killing babies, women, and civilians. They left it to the extreme right and then protected them from prosecution according to the law.

Returning to FM 30–31B, I think it is genuine and indeed I quote a few people from the US administration and the CIA, Ray Cline and a few others, who claim that it is an authentic document. Also, Allan Francovich, who was an investigative documentary film maker, got a few people to comment on FM 30–31 B. Unfortunately he's now dead, so we can't ask him how he managed that, but he did a brilliant job. What I am trying to say is that it is extremely difficult to research US terrorism in Europe. You tell people what you are researching and they think you have the title wrong. They ask why it should be US terrorism in Europe. I tell them that I have data indicating that during the Cold War the United States supported groups that carried out terrorist attacks, but people do not believe it is possible. I tell them to look at the data, but they completely shut their minds and say they don't want to hear about it. Interestingly though, the US government did react to my book. It was published in 2005 when Bush junior was in power and he had the State Department of Condoleezza Rice write a public reply. It was somewhat flattering because usually if a Swiss historian publishes a book, nobody reacts. But this book drew a response, which was that this Swiss historian has got it completely wrong, he's saying that the secret armies were linked to terrorism and he's quoting a document FM 30–31B which is just a Soviet forgery. And to this very day that is their position, but I think *they're* wrong. It's a debate that will continue.

Do you think all these secret armies are dismantled now?

DG: It's very hard to say. The data of the secret armies show that they were set up to fight the Soviet Union, so they were anti-communist networks. Still, the idea lives on that there are people undercover outside the secret services who can carry out covert action operations. Obviously we still have terrorist attacks, but the big elephant in the room is the question: Can it be that some of these terrorist attacks are being sponsored and supported by secret services, thus taxpayers' money? There again most people's minds just shut down. They say that terrorism as such is already something dreadful and it would be too dreadful to think that secret services carry out terrorist attacks. People basically refuse to talk about these things, because it's too dark. But I don't think this phenomenon that was taking place in the Cold War stopped in 1990, and that today we don't have the problem anymore. Felice Casson, who discovered the secret Gladio army, called it the 'strategy of tension', thus to create fear and tension in the population through false-flag terrorism in order to discredit a political enemy or start wars.

NOTES

1. Martin Matter, *P-26 – Die Geheimarmee, die keine war: Wie Politik und Medien die Vorbereitung des Widerstandes skandalisierten* (Baden: Hier & Jetzt, 2012).
2. Daniele Ganser, *NATO's Secret Armies: Operation Gladio and Terrorism in Western Europe* (London and New York: Frank Cass, 2005), p.80.
3. Ibid., p.224.
4. Cited in Daniele Ganser, 'The CIA in Western Europe and the Abuse of Human Rights', *Intelligence and National Security*, Vol.21, No.5 (2006), pp.760–81 (p.775).

Notes on Contributors

Gilbert Achcar is professor of development studies and international relations at the School of Oriental and African Studies, University of London. His authored books include *Eastern Cauldron: Islam, Afghanistan, Palestine and Iraq in a Marxist Mirror*; *The Clash of Barbarisms: The Making of the New World Disorder*; and *The Arabs and the Holocaust: The Arab-Israeli War of Narratives*.

Patrick Bond is professor and director of the Centre for Civil Society at the University of KwaZulu-Natal, Durban, South Africa. His many books include *Looting Africa: The Economics of Exploitation*; *Against Global Apartheid: South Africa Meets the World Bank, IMF and International Finance*; and *Politics of Climate Justice: Paralysis Above, Movement Below*.

Judith Butler is Maxine Elliot professor in the Departments of Rhetoric and Comparative Literature and the co-director of the Program of Critical Theory at the University of California, Berkeley. Her many books include *Gender Trouble: Feminism and the Subversion of Identity; Bodies That Matter: On the Discursive Limits of 'Sex'; Precarious Life: Powers of Violence and Mourning*; and *Frames of War: When Is Life Grievable?*

Noam Chomsky is an institute professor and professor of linguistics emeritus at MIT, widely credited with revolutionising modern linguistics, and a globally renowned political writer and activist. He has written over 100 books, including *Deterring Democracy*; *Failed States: The Abuse of Power and the Assault on Democracy*; and *Hegemony or Survival: America's Quest for Global Dominance*.

Marjorie Cohn is a professor at Thomas Jefferson School of Law and past president of the National Lawyers Guild. She is the author of *Cowboy Republic: Six Ways the Bush Gang Has Defied* *the Law*; co-author of *Cameras in the Courtroom: Television and the Pursuit of Justice*, and *Rules of Disengagement: The Politics and Honor of Military Dissent*; and editor of *The United States and Torture: Interrogation, Incarceration, and Abuse*.

Richard A. Falk is professor emeritus of international law at Princeton University and an appointee to two United Nations positions on the Palestinian territories. He has authored, edited or contributed to 40 books, including *The Great Terror War*; *The Costs of War: International Law, the UN, and World Order after Iraq*; *Achieving Human Rights*; and *International Law and the Third World: Reshaping Justice*.

Norman G. Finkelstein currently writes and lectures. His books include *The Holocaust Industry: Reflections on the Exploitation of Jewish Suffering*; *Beyond Chutzpah: On the Misuse of Anti-Semitism and the Abuse of History*; *'This Time We Went Too Far': Truth and Consequences of the Gaza Invasion*; *Knowing Too Much: Why the American Jewish Romance with Israel Is Coming to an End*; and *What Gandhi Says: About Nonviolence, Resistance and Courage*.

Daniele Ganser is the director of the Swiss Institute for Peace and Energy Research (SIPER) in Basel, Switzerland. He teaches at Basel University and has been a senior researcher at the Center for Security Studies at ETH in Zurich. His book, *NATO's Secret Armies: Operation GLADIO and Terrorism in Western Europe*, has been translated into ten languages.

Greg Grandin is professor of history at New York University. His books include *Empire's Workshop: Latin America, the United States, and the Rise of the New Imperialism*; *The Last Colonial Massacre: Latin America in the Cold War*; and *The Blood of Guatemala: A History of Race and Nation*. His most recent book, *Fordlandia*, was shortlisted for the Pulitzer Prize, the National Book Award, and the National Book Critics Circle Award.

Edward S. Herman is professor emeritus of finance at the Wharton School of the University of Pennsylvania. His many authored and co-authored books include *Manufacturing Consent: The*

Political Economy of the Mass Media; *The 'Terrorism' Industry*; *The Global Media*; and *The Politics of Genocide*.

Ted Honderich is Grote professor emeritus of the philosophy of mind and logic, University College London, and visiting professor, University of Bath. His recent books include *After the Terror*; *Terrorism for Humanity: Inquiries in Political Philosophy*; and *Humanity, Terrorism, Terrorist War: Palestine, 9/11, Iraq, 7/7*.

Ismael Hossein-zadeh is professor emeritus of economics, Drake University, Des Moines, Iowa. He is the author of *Soviet Non-Capitalist Development: The Case of Nasser's Egypt*, and *The Political Economy of U.S. Militarism*, and a contributor to *Hopeless: Barack Obama and the Politics of Illusion*.

Richard Jackson is deputy director at the National Centre for Peace and Conflict Studies (NCPACS) at the University of Otago, New Zealand, and founding editor of the journal, *Critical Studies on Terrorism*. His publications include *Critical Terrorism Studies: A New Research Agenda*; *Terrorism: A Critical Introduction*; and *Contemporary Debates on Terrorism*.

Index